Microsoft®

Windows Vista

Introductory Concepts and Techniques

Gary B. Shelly

Thomas J. Cashman

Steven M. Freund

Raymond E. Enger

THOMSON
COURSE TECHNOLOGY™

COURSE TECHNOLOGY   25 THOMSON PLACE   BOSTON MA 02210

SHELLY
CASHMAN
SERIES®

Australia • Canada • Denmark • Japan • Mexico • New Zealand • Philippines • Puerto Rico • Singapore • South Africa • Spain • United Kingdom • United States

THOMSON

COURSE TECHNOLOGY ™

crosoft Windows Vista
ory Concepts and Techniques

Gary B. Shelly

Thomas J. Cashman

Steven M. Freund

Raymond E. Enger

Executive Editor
Alexandra Arnold

Senior Product Manager
Mali Jones

Associate Product Manager
Klenda Martinez

Editorial Assistant
Jon Farnham

Print Buyer
Julio Esperas

Content Project Manager
Matthew Hutchinson

Developmental Editor
Karen Stevens

Marketing Manager
Tristen Kendall

Marketing Coordinator
Julie Schuster

QA Manuscript Reviewers
**John Freitas, Serge Palladino,
Susan Whalen**

Art Director
Bruce Bond

Cover Design
Joel Sadagursky

Cover Photo
Jon Chomitz

Compositor
GEX Publishing Services

Printer
RRD Menasha

Microsoft®
Windows Vista
Introductory Concepts and Techniques

Contents

Appendices

Preface

The Shelly Cashman Series® offers the finest textbooks in computer education. We are proud of the fact that our Microsoft Windows 3.1, Microsoft Windows 95, Microsoft Windows 98, Microsoft Windows 2000, and Microsoft Windows XP books have been so well received by students and instructors. With each new edition of our Windows books, we have made significant improvements based on the software and comments made by instructors and students.

Microsoft Windows contains many changes in the user interface and feature set. Recognizing that the new features and functionality of Microsoft Windows Vista would impact the way that students are taught skills, the Shelly Cashman Series development team carefully reviewed our pedagogy and analyzed its effectiveness in teaching today's student. An extensive customer survey produced results confirming what the series is best known for: its step-by-step, screen-by-screen instructions, its project-oriented approach, and the quality of its content.

We learned, though, that students entering computer courses today are different than students taking these classes just a few years ago. Students today read less, but need to retain more. They need not only to be able to perform skills, but to retain those skills and know how to apply them to different settings. Today's students need to be continually engaged and challenged to retain what they're learning.

As a result, we've renewed our commitment to focusing on the user and how they learn best. This commitment is reflected in every change we've made to our Windows Vista books.

Objectives of This Textbook

Microsoft Windows Vista: Introductory Concepts and Techniques is intended for a course that includes an introduction to Windows Vista. No experience with a computer is assumed, and no mathematics beyond the high school freshman level is required. The objectives of this book are:

- To teach the fundamentals of Microsoft Windows Vista

- To expose students to practical examples of the computer as a useful tool

- To acquaint students with the proper procedures to manage and organize document storage options for coursework, professional purposes, and personal use

- To help students discover the underlying functionality of Windows Vista so they can become more productive

- To develop an exercise-oriented approach that allows learning by doing

The Shelly Cashman Approach

Features of the Shelly Cashman Series Microsoft Windows Vista books include:

- **Step-by-Step, Screen-by-Screen Instructions** Each of the tasks required to complete a project is clearly identified throughout the chapter. Now, the step-by-step instructions provide a context beyond point-and-click. Each step explains why students are performing a task, or the result of performing a certain action. Found on the screens accompanying each step, call-outs give students the information they need to know when they need to know it. Now, we've used color to distinguish the content in the call-outs. The Explanatory call-outs (in black) summarize what is happening on the screen and the Navigational call-outs (in red) show students where to click.

- **Q&A** Found within many of the step-by-step sequences, Q&As raise the kinds of questions students may ask when working through a step sequence and provide answers about what they are doing, why they are doing it, and how that task might be approached differently.

- **Experimental Steps** These new steps, within our step-by-step instructions, encourage students to explore, experiment, and take advantage of the features of Windows Vista. These steps are not necessary to complete the projects, but are designed to increase the confidence with the software and build problem-solving skills.

- **Thoroughly Tested Instruction** Unparalleled quality is ensured because every screen in the book is produced by the author only after performing a step, and then each project must pass Course Technology's Quality Assurance program.

- **Other Ways Boxes** The Other Ways boxes displayed at the end of most of the step-by-step sequences specify the other ways to do the task completed in the steps. Thus, the steps and the Other Ways box make a comprehensive reference unit.

- **BTW** These marginal annotations provide background information, tips, and answers to common questions that complement the topics covered, adding depth and perspective to the learning process.

- **Integration of the World Wide Web** The World Wide Web is integrated into the Windows Vista learning experience by (1) BTW annotations that send students to Web sites for up-to-date information and alternative approaches to tasks; (2) the Learn It Online section at the end of each chapter, which has chapter reinforcement exercises, learning games, and other types of student activities.

- **End-of-Chapter Student Activities** Extensive student activities at the end of each chapter provide the student with plenty of opportunities to reinforce the materials learned in the chapter through hands-on assignments. Several new types of activities have been added that challenge the student in new ways to expand their knowledge, and to apply their new skills to a project with personal relevance.

Q&A Why does my desktop look different from the one in Figure 1–5?

The Windows Vista desktop is customizable and your work or school may have modified the desktop to meet their needs.

Other Ways

1. Right-click icon, click Open, click Empty Recycle Bin, click the Close button, click the Yes button
2. Double-click the Recycle bin icon, click Empty Recycle Bin, click the Close button, click the Yes button

---

BTW Vista Capable and Premium Ready

When buying a computer, you may run across ones that are labeled Vista Capable and Vista Premium Ready. A Vista Capable computer can run the Vista Basic experience, but may need to be upgraded to support the Aero experience. Vista Premium Ready means that the computer can run Aero, but some features still may require additional hardware.

Organization of This Textbook

Microsoft Windows Vista: Introductory Concepts and Techniques consists of three chapters on Microsoft Windows Vista, two appendices, and a Quick Reference Summary.

End-of-Chapter Student Activities

A notable strength of the Shelly Cashman Series Microsoft Windows Vista books is the extensive student activities at the end of each chapter. Well-structured student activities can

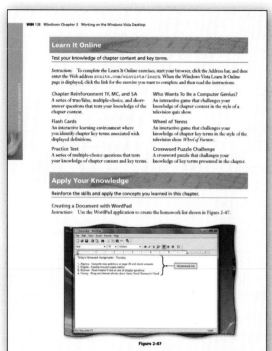

make the difference between students merely participating in a class and students retaining the information they learn. The activities in the Shelly Cashman Series Windows books include the following.

CHAPTER SUMMARY A concluding paragraph, followed by a listing of the tasks completed within a chapter together with the pages on which the step-by-step, screen-by-screen explanations appear.

LEARN IT ONLINE Every chapter features a Learn It Online section that is comprised of six exercises. These exercises include True/False, Multiple Choice, Short Answer, Flash Cards, Practice Test, and Learning Games.

APPLY YOUR KNOWLEDGE This exercise usually requires students to open and manipulate a file from the Data Files that parallels the activities learned in the chapter. To obtain a copy of the Data Files for Students, follow the instructions on the inside back cover of this text.

EXTEND YOUR KNOWLEDGE This exercise allows students to extend and expand on the skills learned within the chapter.

MAKE IT RIGHT This exercise requires students to analyze a document, identify errors and issues, and correct those errors and issues using skills learned in the chapter.

IN THE LAB Three all new in-depth assignments per chapter require students to utilize the chapter concepts and techniques to solve problems on a computer.

CASES AND PLACES Five unique real-world case-study situations, including Make It Personal, an open-ended project that relates to student's personal lives, and one small-group activity.

Instructor Resources CD-ROM

The Shelly Cashman Series is dedicated to providing you with all of the tools you need to make your class a success. Information about all supplementary materials is available through your Course Technology representative or by calling one of the following telephone numbers: Colleges, Universities, and Continuing Ed departments, 1-800-648-7450; High Schools, 1-800-824-5179; and Career Colleges, Business, Government, Library and Resellers, 1-800-648-7450.

The Instructor Resources CD-ROM for this textbook include both teaching and testing aids. The contents of each item on the Instructor Resources CD-ROM (ISBN 1-4239-1179-2) are described in the following text.

INSTRUCTOR'S MANUAL The Instructor's Manual consists of Microsoft Word files, which include chapter objectives, lecture notes, teaching tips, classroom activities, lab activities, quick quizzes, figures and boxed elements summarized in the chapters, and a glossary page. The new format of the Instructor's Manual will allow you to map through every chapter easily.

SYLLABUS Sample syllabi, which can be customized easily to a course, are included. The syllabi cover policies, class and lab assignments and exams, and procedural information.

FIGURE FILES Illustrations for every figure in the textbook are available in electronic form. Use this ancillary to present a slide show in lecture or to print transparencies for use in lecture with an overhead projector. If you have a personal computer and LCD device, this ancillary can be an effective tool for presenting lectures.

POWERPOINT PRESENTATIONS PowerPoint Presentations is a multimedia lecture presentation system that provides slides for each chapter. Presentations are based on chapter objectives. Use this presentation system to present well-organized lectures that are both interesting and knowledge based. PowerPoint Presentations provides consistent coverage at schools that use multiple lecturers.

SOLUTIONS TO EXERCISES Solutions are included for the end-of-chapter exercises, as well as the Chapter Reinforcement exercises.

TEST BANK & TEST ENGINE In the ExamView test bank, you will find our standard question types (40 multiple-choice, 25 true/false, 20 completion) and new objective-based question types (5 modified multiple-choice, 5 modified true/false and 10 matching). Critical Thinking questions are also included (3 essays and 2 cases with 2 questions each) totaling the test bank to 112 questions for every chapter with page number references, and when appropriate, figure references. A version of the test bank you can print also is included. The test bank comes with a copy of the test engine, ExamView, the ultimate tool for your objective-based testing needs. ExamView is a state-of-the-art test builder that is easy to use. ExamView enables you to create paper-, LAN-, or Web-based tests from test banks designed specifically for your Course Technology textbook. Utilize the ultra-efficient QuickTest Wizard to create tests in less than five minutes by taking advantage of Course Technology's question banks, or customize your own exams from scratch.

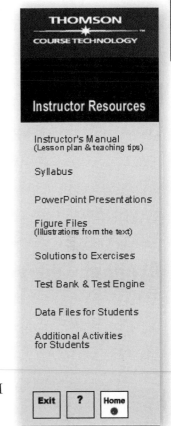

DATA FILES FOR STUDENTS All the files that are required by students to complete the exercises are included. You can distribute the files on the Instructor Resources CD-ROM to your students over a network, or you can have them follow the instructions on the inside back cover of this book to obtain a copy of the Data Files for Students.

ADDITIONAL ACTIVITIES FOR STUDENTS These additional activities consist of Chapter Reinforcement Exercises, which are true/false, multiple-choice, and short answer questions that help students gain confidence in the material learned.

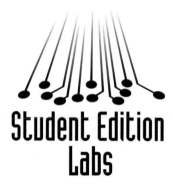

Assessment & Training Solutions

SAM 2007

SAM 2007 helps bridge the gap between the classroom and the real world by allowing students to train and test on important computer skills in an active, hands-on environment.

SAM 2007's easy-to-use system includes powerful interactive exams, training or projects on critical applications such as Word, Excel, Access, PowerPoint, Outlook, Windows, the Internet, and much more. SAM simulates the application environment, allowing students to demonstrate their knowledge and think through the skills by performing real-world tasks.

Designed to be used with the Shelly Cashman series, SAM 2007 includes built-in page references so students can print helpful study guides that match the Shelly Cashman series textbooks used in class. Powerful administrative options allow instructors to schedule exams and assignments, secure tests, and run reports with almost limitless flexibility.

Student Edition Labs

Our Web-based interactive labs help students master hundreds of computer concepts, including input and output devices, file management and desktop applications, computer ethics, virus protection, and much more. Featuring up-to-the-minute content, eye-popping graphics, and rich animation, the highly interactive Student Edition Labs offer students an alternative way to learn through dynamic observation, step-by-step practice, and challenging review questions.

Online Content

Blackboard is the leading distance learning solution provider and class-management platform today. Course Technology has partnered with Blackboard to bring you premium online content. Instructors: Content for use with *Microsoft Windows Vista: Introductory Concepts and Techniques* is available in a Blackboard Course Cartridge and may include topic reviews, case projects, review questions, test banks, practice tests, custom syllabi, and more.

Course Technology also has solutions for several other learning management systems. Please visit http://www.course.com today to see what's available for this title.

CourseCasts Learning on the Go. Always Available...Always Relevant.

Want to keep up with the latest technology trends relevant to you? Visit our site to find a library of podcasts, CourseCasts, featuring a "CourseCast of the Week," and download them to your portable media player at http://coursecasts.course.com.

Our fast-paced world is driven by technology. You know because you are an active participant — always on the go, always keeping up with technological trends, and always learning new ways to embrace technology to power your life.

Ken Baldauf, a faculty member of the Florida State University (FSU) Computer Science Department, is responsible for teaching technology classes to thousands of FSU students each year. He knows what you know; he knows what you want to learn. He is also an expert in the latest technology and will sort through and aggregate the most pertinent news and information so you can spend your time enjoying technology, rather than trying to figure it out.

Visit us at http://coursecasts.course.com to learn on the go!

CourseNotes

Course Technology's CourseNotes are six-panel quick reference cards that reinforce the most important and widely used features of a software application in a visual and user-friendly format. CourseNotes will serve as a great reference tool during and after the student completes the course. CourseNotes for Microsoft Office 2007, Word 2007, Excel 2007, Access 2007, PowerPoint 2007, Windows Vista, and more are available now!

To the Student . . .   Getting the Most Out of Your Book
Welcome to *Microsoft Windows Vista: Introductory Concepts and Techniques*. You can save yourself a lot of time and gain a better understanding of Microsoft Windows Vista if you spend a few minutes reviewing the figures and callouts in this section.

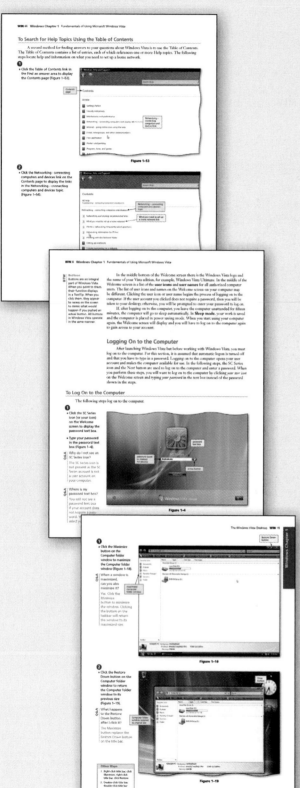

1 CONSISTENT STEP-BY-STEP, SCREEN-BY-SCREEN PRESENTATION
Chapter solutions are built using a step-by-step, screen-by-screen approach. This pedagogy allows you to build the solution on a computer as you read through the chapter. Generally, each step includes an explanation that indicates the result of the step.

2 MORE THAN JUST STEP-BY-STEP
BTW annotations in the margins of the book, Q&As in the steps, and substantive text in the paragraphs provide background information, tips, and answers to common questions that complement the topics covered, adding depth and perspective. When you finish with this book, you will be ready to use the Office programs to solve problems on your own. Experimental steps provide you with opportunities to step out on your own to try features of the programs, and pick up right where you left off in the chapter.

3 OTHER WAYS BOXES
Other Ways boxes that follow many of the step sequences explain the other ways to complete the task presented, such as using the mouse, Ribbon, shortcut menu, and keyboard.

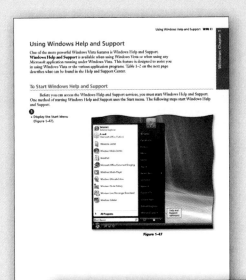

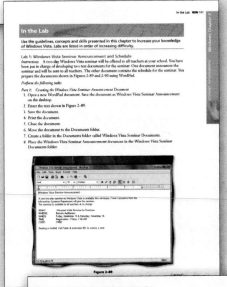

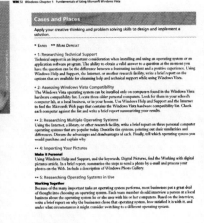

4 EMPHASIS ON GETTING HELP WHEN YOU NEED IT

Chapter 1 shows you how to use all the elements of Windows Vista Help. Being able to answer your own questions will increase your productivity and reduce your frustrations by minimizing the time it takes to learn how to complete a task.

5 REVIEW, REINFORCEMENT, AND EXTENSION

After you successfully step through a project in a chapter, a section titled Chapter Summary identifies the tasks with which you should be familiar. Terms you should know for test purposes are bold in the text. The SAM Training feature provides the opportunity for addional reinforcement on important skills covered in each chapter. The Learn It Online section at the end of each chapter offers reinforcement in the form of review questions, learning games, and practice tests. Also included are exercises that require you to extend your learning beyond the book.

6 LABORATORY EXERCISES

If you really want to learn how to use the programs, then you must design and implement solutions to problems on your own. Every chapter concludes with several carefully developed laboratory assignments that increase in complexity.

About Our New Cover Look

Learning styles of students have changed, but the Shelly Cashman Series' dedication to their success has remained steadfast for over 30 years. We are committed to continually updating our approach and content to reflect the way today's students learn and experience new technology.

This focus on the user is reflected in our bold new cover design, which features photographs of real students using the Shelly Cashman Series in their courses. Each book features a different user, reflecting the many ages, experiences, and backgrounds of all of the students learning with our books. When you use the Shelly Cashman Series, you can be assured that you are learning computer skills using the most effective courseware available.

We would like to thank the administration and faculty at the participating schools for their help in making our vision a reality. Most of all, we'd like to thank the wonderful students from all over the world who learn from our texts and now appear on our covers.

Microsoft Windows Vista

1 | Fundamentals of Using Microsoft Windows Vista

Objectives

You will have mastered the material in this chapter when you can:

- Describe Microsoft Windows Vista

- Explain operating system, server, workstation, and user interface

- Log on to the computer

- Identify the objects on the Microsoft Windows Vista desktop

- Display the Start menu

- Add gadgets to Windows Sidebar

- Identify the Computer and Documents windows

- Add and remove a desktop icon

- Open, minimize, maximize, restore, and close a Windows Vista window

- Move and size a window on the Windows Vista desktop

- Scroll in a window

- Launch an application program

- Switch between running application programs

- Use Windows Vista Help and Support

- Log off from the computer and turn off the computer

1 | Fundamentals of Using Microsoft Windows Vista

What is Microsoft Windows Vista?

An **operating system** is the set of computer instructions, called a computer program, that controls the allocation of computer hardware such as memory, disk devices, printers, and CD and DVD drives, and provides the capability for you to communicate with the computer. The most popular and widely used operating system is **Microsoft Windows**. **Microsoft Windows Vista**, the newest version of Microsoft Windows, allows you to easily communicate with and control your computer.

Windows Vista is commonly used on stand-alone computers, computer workstations, and portable computers. A **workstation** is a computer connected to a server. A **server** is a computer that controls access to the hardware and software on a network and provides a centralized storage area for programs, data, and information. Figure 1–1 illustrates a simple computer network consisting of a server, three workstations, and a laser printer connected to the server.

Windows Vista is easy to use and can be customized to fit individual needs. The operating system simplifies working with documents and applications, transferring data between documents, interacting with the different components of the computer, and using the computer to access information on the Internet or an intranet. The **Internet** is a worldwide group of connected computer networks that allows public access to information on thousands of subjects and gives users the ability to use this information, send messages, and obtain products and services.

This book demonstrates how to use Microsoft Windows Vista to control the computer and communicate with other computers both on a network and over the Internet. In Chapter 1, you will learn about Windows Vista and how to use the Windows Vista user interface.

Overview

As you read this chapter, you will learn how to use the Microsoft Windows Vista graphical user interface by performing these general tasks:

- Start Windows Vista and log on
- Open the Start menu, expand and close a menu
- Work with Windows Sidebar
- Launch an application
- Switch between applications
- Add and delete icons on the desktop
- Open, minimize, restore, move, size, scroll, and close a window
- Display folder contents
- Use the Help system to answer questions
- Log off and turn off the computer

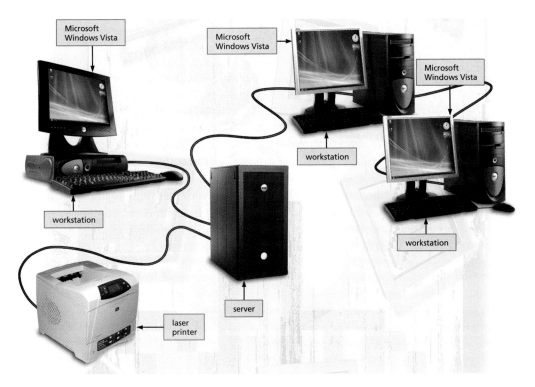

Figure 1–1

Plan
Ahead

Working with Microsoft Windows Vista

Working with an operating system requires a basic knowledge of how to start the operating system, log on and off the computer, and identify the objects on the Windows Vista desktop.

1. **Determine how you will be logging on to the computer.** Depending on the setup of the computer you are using, you may need an account and password. If it is a work or educational computer, you may be assigned an account.

2. **Establish which edition of Windows Vista is installed.** Since there are different editions of Windows Vista with different features, you should know which edition is installed on the computer you will be using.

3. **Determine the permissions you have on the computer you will be using.** Each user account can have different rights and permissions. Depending on which rights and permissions have been set for your account, you may or may not be able to perform certain operations.

4. **Determine if you have Internet access.** For some features of Windows Vista, such as help and support, there is a lot of material online that you may find useful. You will want to know if your computer has Internet access and if anything is required of you to use it.

Multiple Editions of Windows Vista

The Microsoft Windows Vista operating system is available in a variety of editions. The editions that you will most likely encounter are Windows Vista Starter, Windows Vista Home Basic, Windows Vista Home Premium, Windows Vista Business, Windows Vista Ultimate, and Windows Vista Enterprise. Because not all computers are the same or even used for the same functions, Microsoft provides these various editions so that each user can have the edition that best meets their needs. **Microsoft Windows Vista Ultimate Edition** is the most complete of all of the editions and has all of the power, security, mobility, and entertainment features. **Microsoft Windows Vista Home Premium Edition** contains many of the features of Microsoft Windows Vista Ultimate Edition, but is designed for entertainment and home use. The Home Premium Edition allows you to establish a network of computers in the home that share a single Internet connection, share a device such as a printer or a scanner, share files and folders, and play multi-computer games. The network can be created using Ethernet cable or telephone wire or can be wireless. These six editions are briefly described in Table 1–1. For more information about the new features of Windows Vista and the differences between the editions, see Appendix A.

Table 1–1 Windows Vista Editions	
Edition	**Description**
Windows Vista Starter Edition	This edition is made for countries that do not have developed technology markets. It only comes with the most basic features designed for beginning computer users. It is not available in the United States, the European Union, Australia, and Japan.
Windows Vista Home Basic Edition	This edition is easy to set up and maintain, provides security and parental controls, allows access to e-mail, simplifies searching for pictures and music, and allows the creation of simple documents. It is designed for individuals who have a home desktop or mobile PC.
Windows Vista Home Premium Edition	This edition is designed for individuals who have a home desktop or mobile PC that has the additional multimedia hardware necessary for the advanced Windows media software. It includes all of the features of the Home Basic Edition plus home networking capabilities and Windows Media Center. With Windows Media Center, the computer can be used to watch and record television, play video games, listen to music, and play and burn CDs and DVDs.
Windows Vista Business Edition	This edition is the first operating system designed specifically to meet the needs of small and mid-sized businesses. This edition includes features that make it easy to keep PCs up-to-date and running smoothly, as well as powerful ways to find, organize, and share information on the road or at the office. It is designed for the work or educational environment where there is a greater need for networking, and does not contain games or the Windows Media Center.
Windows Vista Ultimate Edition	This edition is the most complete edition of Windows Vista. It includes all of the features of the other editions plus advanced power, security, mobility and entertainment capabilities and features. For example, it includes support for Windows Tablet and Touch Technology, Windows SideShow, Windows Mobility Center, Windows DreamScene, and Windows BitLocker Drive Encryption (see Appendix A, for a full description of these features).
Windows Vista Enterprise Edition	This edition was designed to help global organizations and enterprises with complex IT infrastructures to lower IT costs, reduce risk, and stay connected. This edition only is available to volume license customers who have PCs covered by Microsoft Software Assurance. This edition is most similar to the Business edition but includes more sophisticated features such as Windows BitLocker Drive Encryption (see Appendix A, for a full description of this feature).

Microsoft Windows Vista

Microsoft Windows Vista (called **Windows Vista** for the rest of the book) is an operating system that performs the functions necessary for you to communicate with and use the computer. Windows Vista is available in 32-bit and 64-bit versions for all editions except Windows Vista Starter Edition.

Windows Vista is used to run **application programs**, which are programs that perform an application-related function such as word processing. Windows Vista includes several application programs, including Windows Internet Explorer, Windows Media Player, Windows Movie Maker, and Windows Mail. **Windows Internet Explorer**, or **Internet Explorer**, integrates the Windows Vista desktop and the Internet. Internet Explorer allows you to work with programs and files in a similar fashion, regardless of whether they are located on the computer, a local network, or the Internet. **Windows Media Player** lets you create and play CDs, watch DVDs, listen to radio stations all over the world, and search for and organize digital media files. **Windows Movie Maker** can transfer recorded audio and video from analog camcorders or digital video cameras to the computer, import existing audio and video files to use in the movies you make, and send finished movies by e-mail or post them on the World Wide Web. **Windows Mail** is an e-mail program that lets you exchange e-mail with friends and colleagues, trade ideas and information in a newsgroup, manage multiple mail and news accounts, and add stationery or a personal signature to messages; it also has junk e-mail filtering and protection against fraudulent messages. Windows Vista includes other applications, depending upon the edition you are using.

Windows Vista has a number of customizations that you can perform. Depending upon how you desire to use your computer, you can change the appearance of the desktop, Sidebar, Start menu, and more. As you proceed through this book, you will learn many ways to customize your experience. To use the application programs that can be run under Windows Vista, you need to understand the Windows Vista user interface.

BTW

Determining Edition Support
Before you upgrade an existing Windows system to Vista, you can determine which edition of Vista your computer will support by installing and running the Windows Vista Upgrade Advisor. To access the Windows Vista Upgrade Advisor, visit http://www.microsoft.com/windows, and then click, "Are you ready for Windows Vista?".

User Interfaces

A **user interface** is the combination of hardware and software that you use to communicate with and control the computer. Through the user interface, you are able to make selections on the computer, request information from the computer, and respond to messages displayed by the computer. Thus, a user interface provides the means for dialogue between you and the computer.

The computer software determines the messages you receive, how you should respond, and the actions that occur based on your responses. The goal of an effective user interface is to be **user-friendly**, which means that the software is easy to use by people with limited training. Research studies have indicated that the use of graphics plays an important role in helping users to interact effectively with a computer.

A **graphical user interface**, or **GUI** (pronounced gooey), is a user interface that displays graphics in addition to text when it communicates with the user. Windows Vista has two variations of GUIs: Windows Vista Basic experience and Windows Vista Aero experience. The Aero experience is not available in the Starter and Home Basic Editions.

BTW

Vista Capable and Premium Ready
When buying a computer, you may run across ones that are labeled Vista Capable and Vista Premium Ready. A Vista Capable computer can run the Vista Basic experience, but may need to be upgraded to support the Aero experience. Vista Premium Ready means that the computer can run Aero, but some features still may require additional hardware.

Aero Experience

Aero is a three-dimensional graphical user interface. To use Aero, your computer needs to have a compatible graphics adapter and an edition of Vista installed that supports Aero. The first thing you will notice about Aero is **Aero Glass,** which is a flashy translucent glass effect around the borders of the windows that allows you to partially see the items behind the windows. **Windows Flip** and **Windows Flip 3D**, another part of the Aero experience, make switching between your applications as visual and tactile as flipping through papers on your desk.

Aero provides a simple and entertaining interface for dealing with Windows Vista. Figure 1–2 shows examples of the Basic experience and the Aero experience. The figures in this book were created in the Aero experience.

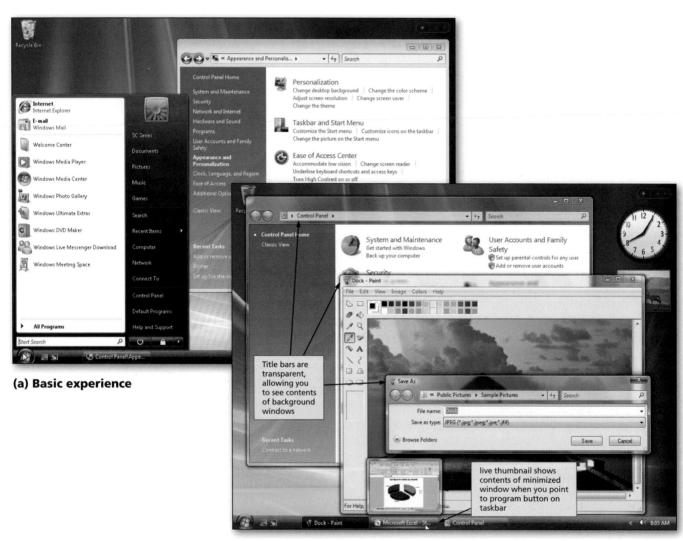

(a) Basic experience

(b) Aero experience

Figure 1–2

The Windows Vista graphical user interface was carefully designed to be easier to set up, simpler to learn, faster and more powerful, and better integrated with the Internet than previous versions of Microsoft Windows.

Launching Microsoft Windows Vista

When you turn on the computer, an introductory screen consisting of a progress bar and copyright messages (© Microsoft Corporation) is displayed. The progress bar animates continuously as the Windows Vista operating system loads. After a brief time, the Windows Vista logo appears. After the Vista logo appears, if your computer is set to start with **automatic logon**, you will be taken directly to your desktop without being asked to type a user name or password; otherwise, the Welcome screen displays (Figure 1–3).

The **Welcome screen** shows the user icons and names of every user on the computer. On the bottom left side of the Welcome screen, the **Ease of Access button** appears, which allows you to change accessibility options as long as you have permission to change them. On the bottom right side of the Welcome screen is the **Shut Down button**. Clicking the Shut Down button shuts down Windows Vista and the computer. To the right of the Shut Down button is the **Shut Down options arrow**, which provides access to a menu containing three commands, Restart, Sleep, and Shut Down. The **Restart command** closes open programs, shuts down Windows Vista, and then restarts the computer and Windows Vista. The **Sleep command** waits for Windows Vista to save your work and then turns off the fans and hard disk. To wake the computer from the Sleep state, press the Power button or lift the laptop cover, and then log on to the computer. The **Shut Down command** shuts down Windows Vista and turns off the computer.

BTW

User Icons
When a user account is created, an icon (picture) can be selected to identify the user. This user icon can be changed by using the Control Panel if you have the permission to change it. A school or work account may not allow you to change your user icon.

BTW

User Names and Passwords
A unique user name identifies each user. In the past, users often entered a variation of their name as their user name. For example, Nicki Kennedy might have chosen nickikennedy or nkennedy. Today, most Windows Vista users use their first and last name as the user name. A password is a combination of characters that allows you to access your account on the computer or your account on a network. Passwords should be kept confidential. For security purposes, schools and businesses may require you to change your password on a regular basis.

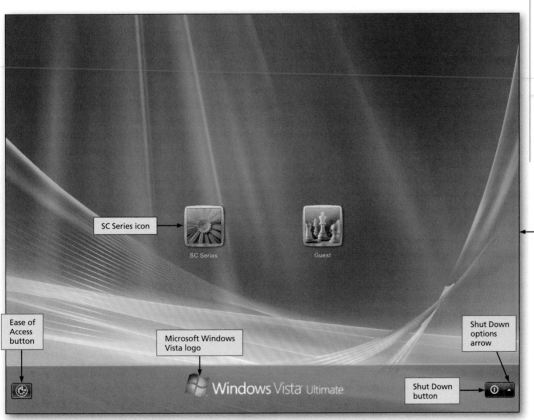

SC Series icon

SC Series

Guest

Welcome screen

Ease of Access button

Microsoft Windows Vista logo

Shut Down options arrow

Windows Vista Ultimate

Shut Down button

Figure 1–3

BTW

Buttons

Buttons are an integral part of Windows Vista. When you point to them, their function displays in a ToolTip. When you click them, they appear to recess on the screen to mimic what would happen if you pushed an actual button. All buttons in Windows Vista operate in the same manner.

In the middle bottom of the Welcome screen there is the Windows Vista logo and the name of your Vista edition, for example, Windows Vista Ultimate. In the middle of the Welcome screen is a list of the **user icons** and **user names** for all authorized computer users. The list of user icons and names on the Welcome screen on your computer may be different. Clicking the user icon or user name begins the process of logging on to the computer. If the user account you clicked does not require a password, then you will be taken to your desktop; otherwise, you will be prompted to enter your password to log on.

If, after logging on to the computer, you leave the computer unattended for fifteen minutes, the computer will go to sleep automatically. In **Sleep mode**, your work is saved and the computer is placed in power saving mode. When you start using your computer again, the Welcome screen will display and you will have to log on to the computer again to gain access to your account.

Logging On to the Computer

After launching Windows Vista but before working with Windows Vista, you must log on to the computer. For this section, it is assumed that automatic logon is turned off and that you have to type in a password. Logging on to the computer opens your user account and makes the computer available for use. In the following steps, the SC Series icon and the Next button are used to log on to the computer and enter a password. When you perform these steps, you will want to log on to the computer by clicking *your user icon* on the Welcome screen and typing *your password* in the text box instead of the password shown in the steps.

To Log On to the Computer

The following steps log on to the computer.

- Click the SC Series icon (or your icon) on the Welcome screen to display the password text box.

- Type your password in the password text box (Figure 1–4).

Q&A Why do I not see an SC Series icon?

The SC Series icon is not present as the SC Series account is not a user account on your computer.

Q&A Where is my password text box?

You will not see a password text box if your account does not require a password. You only have to select your user icon to log on.

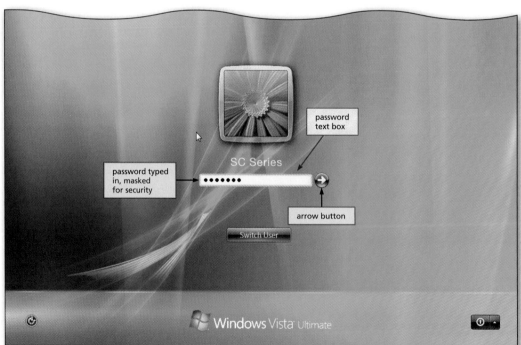

Figure 1–4

2

- Click the arrow button to log on to the computer to display the Welcome Center window and Windows Sidebar on the Windows Vista desktop (Figure 1–5).

Q&A Why does my desktop look different from the one in Figure 1–5?

The Windows Vista desktop is customizable and your work or school may have modified the desktop to meet their needs.

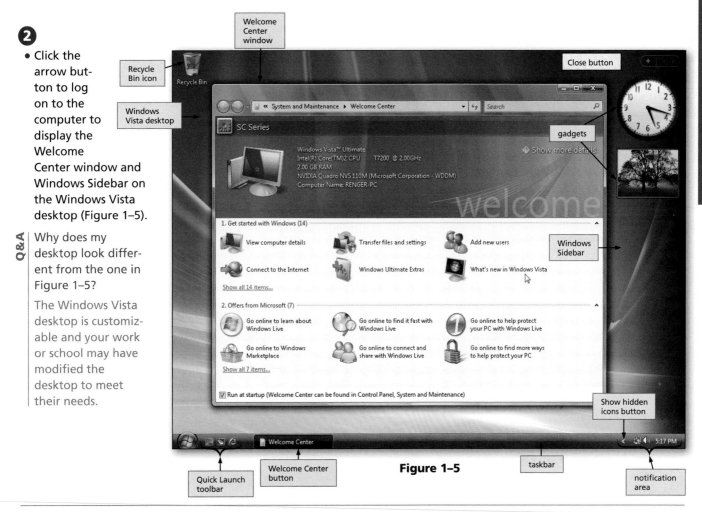

Figure 1–5

Although the Windows Vista desktop can easily be tailored to your needs, it does contain some standard elements. The items on the desktop in Figure 1–5 include the Recycle Bin icon and its name in the top-left corner of the desktop, the Welcome Center window in the center of the desktop, and the taskbar at the bottom of the desktop. The **Recycle Bin** allows you to discard unneeded objects. Your computer's desktop may contain more, fewer, or different icons, depending on how the desktop was modified.

The **taskbar** shown at the bottom of the screen in Figure 1–5 contains the Start button, Quick Launch toolbar, taskbar button area, and notification area. The **Start button** allows you to launch a program quickly, find or open a document, change the computer's settings, obtain Help, shut down the computer, and perform many more tasks. The **Quick Launch toolbar** contains icons for those applications you want to be able to access quickly. The **taskbar button area** contains buttons to indicate which windows are open on the desktop. The Welcome Center button is displayed in the taskbar button area.

The **notification area** contains the Show hidden icons button, notification icons, and the current time. The **Show hidden icons button** indicates that one or more inactive icon is hidden from view in the notification area. The **notification icons** provide quick access to utility programs that are currently running in the background on your computer. A program running in the background does not show up on the taskbar, but is still working. Icons may display temporarily in the notification area when providing status updates. For example, the printer icon is displayed when a document is sent to the printer and is removed when printing is complete. The notification area on your desktop may contain more, fewer, or different icons as the contents of the notification area can change.

BTW

The Notification Area
The Show hidden icons button displays on the left edge of the notification area if one or more inactive icon is hidden from view in the notification area. Clicking the Show hidden icons button displays the hidden icons in the notification area and replaces the Show hidden icons button with the Hide button. Moving the mouse pointer off the notification area removes, or hides, the inactive icons in the notification area and redisplays the Show hidden icons button.

Also on the Windows Vista desktop is the Windows Sidebar. The **Windows Sidebar** is a long, vertical strip on the right edge of the desktop that holds mini-programs called gadgets (Figure 1–5 on the previous page). A **gadget** is a mini-program that provides continuously updated information, such as current weather information, news updates, traffic information, and Internet radio streams. You can customize your Sidebar to hold the gadgets you choose.

The Welcome Center

The **Welcome Center** is displayed when the computer is used for the first time and allows you to complete a set of tasks to optimize the computer. The tasks may include adding user accounts, transferring files and settings from another computer, and connecting to the Internet. The Welcome Center can be turned off; therefore, you may not see it on your screen. It does not have to be displayed because you do not need to use it every time you want to complete a task in Windows Vista.

To Close the Welcome Center

The following step closes the Welcome Center window. If the Welcome Center window is not visible on your screen, you do not have to perform this step.

- Click the Close button on the Welcome Center window to close the Welcome Center (Figure 1–6).

Start button

Figure 1–6

The Windows Vista Desktop

The Windows Vista desktop and the objects on the desktop emulate a work area in an office. You may think of the Windows desktop as an electronic version of the top of your desk. You can place objects on the desktop, move the objects around on the desktop, look at them and then put them aside, and so on.

Opening the Start Menu

The **Start menu** allows you to easily access the most useful items on the computer. A **menu** is a list of related commands and the **commands** on a menu perform a specific action, such as searching for files or obtaining help. The Start menu contains commands that allow you to connect to and browse the Internet, launch an e-mail program, launch application programs, store and search for documents, folders, and programs, customize the computer, obtain help, and log off and turn off the computer.

To Display the Start Menu

The following steps display the Start menu.

- Click the Start button on the Windows Vista taskbar to display the Start menu (Figure 1–7).

Q&A

Why does my Start menu look different?

Depending upon your computer's configuration, the Start menu can look different. In a work or school environment, it may be customized for any number of reasons such as usage requirements or security issues.

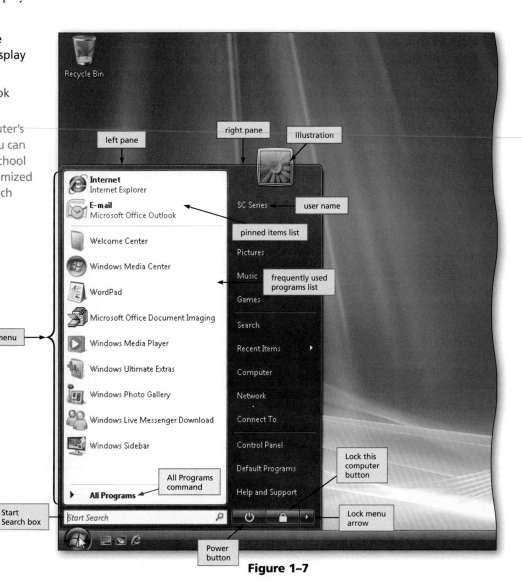

Figure 1–7

2

- Click the All Programs command on the Start menu to display the All Programs list (Figure 1–8).

Q&A Why does my All Programs list look different?

The applications installed on your computer may differ. Your All Programs list will show the applications that are installed on your computer.

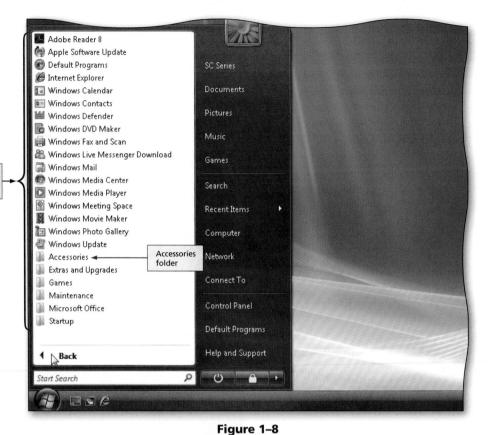

Figure 1–8

3

- Click the Accessories folder to display the Accessories list (Figure 1–9).

Q&A What are accessories?

Accessories are application programs that accomplish a variety of tasks commonly required on a computer. Most accessories are installed with the Vista operating system, including Calculator, Snipping Tool, Windows Mobility Center (if you have a portable computer), WordPad, etc. Your Accessories list may contain additional or fewer programs.

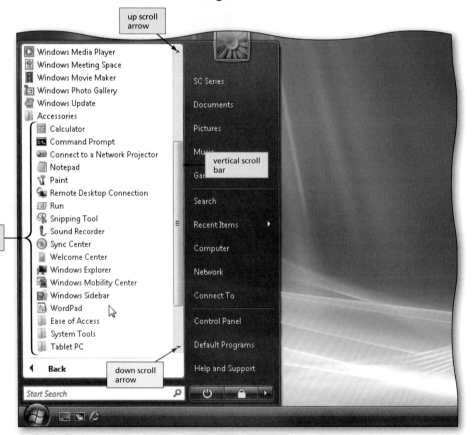

Figure 1–9

To Scroll Using Scroll Arrows, the Scroll Bar, and the Scroll Box

A **scroll bar** is a bar that is displayed when the contents of an area are not completely visible. A vertical scroll bar contains an **up scroll arrow**, a **down scroll arrow**, and a **scroll box** that enables you to view areas that currently are not visible. In Figure 1–9, a vertical scroll bar displays along the right side of the All Programs list. Scrolling can be accomplished in three ways: (1) click the scroll arrows; (2) click the scroll bar; and (3) drag the scroll box. You **drag** an object by pointing to an item, holding down the left mouse button, and moving the object to the desired location, and then release, or **drop**, the object by releasing the left mouse button. The following steps scroll the items in the All Programs list.

1

• Click the down scroll arrow on the vertical scroll bar to display additional folders at the bottom of the All Programs list (Figure 1–10). You may need to click more than once to get to the bottom of the All Programs list.

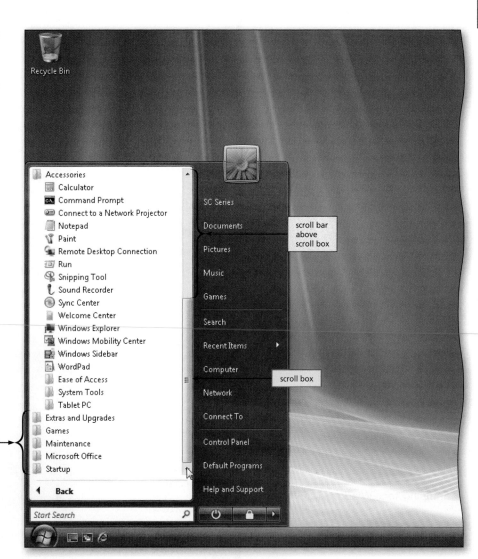

Figure 1–10

- Click the scroll bar above the scroll box to move the scroll box to the top of the All Programs list (Figure 1–11). You may need to click more than once to get to the top of the All Programs list.

Q&A

Why does it take more than one click to move the scroll box to the top of the scroll bar?

There may be more applications installed on your computer than on the one in the figure; in that case, you may have to click two or more times to move the scroll box to the top.

Figure 1–11

- Click the scroll box and drag down to the bottom of the scroll bar and display the bottom of the All Programs list (Figure 1–12).

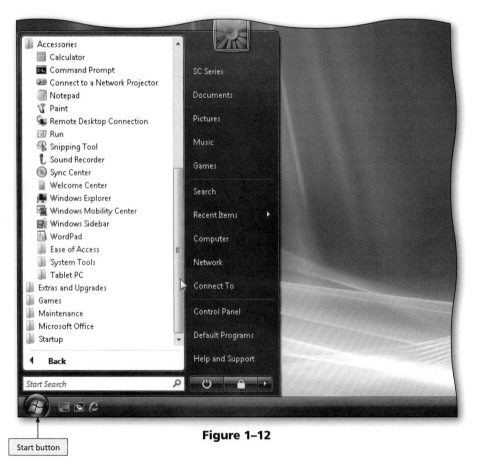

Figure 1–12

- Click the Start button to close the Start menu (Figure 1–13).

Figure 1–13

The Computer Folder

The **Computer folder** is accessible via the Start menu. When opened, the Computer folder opens in a **folder window**. The Computer folder is the place you can go to access hard disk drives, CD or DVD drives, removable media, and network locations that are connected to your computer. You also can access other devices such as external hard disks or digital cameras that you have connected to your system.

To Open the Computer Folder Window

The following steps open the Computer folder window.

- Click the Start button on the Windows Vista taskbar to open the Start menu (Figure 1–14).

Figure 1–14

2

• Click the Computer command on the right pane to open the Computer folder window (Figure 1–15).

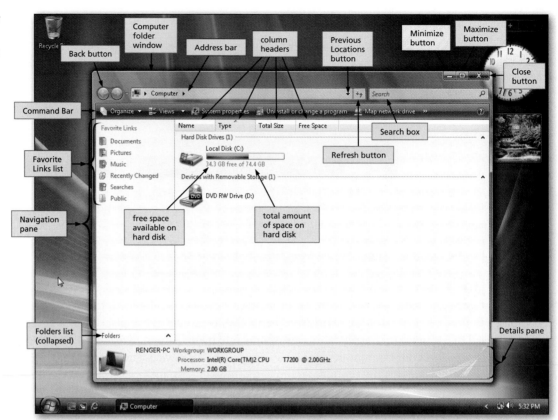

Figure 1–15

Other Ways

1. Click the Start button, right-click Computer, click Open
2. Press WINDOWS+E

Folder windows are the key tools for finding, viewing, and managing information on the computer. Folder windows have common design elements, as shown in Figure 1–15. The three buttons to the left of the **Address bar** allow you to navigate the contents of the right pane and view recent pages. On the right of the title bar are the Minimize button, the Maximize button, and the Close button, which can be used to reduce the window to the taskbar, increase the window to the full screen, or close the window.

The two right arrows in the Address bar allow you to revisit locations on the computer that you have visited using the Address bar. The **Previous Locations button** saves the locations you have visited and displays the locations using computer path names.

The **Refresh button** at the end of the Address bar refreshes the contents of the right pane of the Computer window. The **Search box** to the right of the Address bar contains the dimmed word, Search. You can type a term into the Search box for a list of files, folders, shortcuts, and programs containing that term within the location you are searching.

The **Command Bar** contains context-specific buttons used to accomplish various tasks on the computer related to organizing and managing the contents of the open window. Depending upon the selections you make in the Computer folder window, the Command Bar buttons will change to reflect the selections. For example, if you were to navigate to a DVD burner drive, the Command Bar would show the appropriate buttons for a DVD burner. The area below the Command Bar is separated into two panes; the left contains the Navigation pane and the right provides additional details organized into four columns. The **Navigation pane** on the left contains the Favorite Links section and the Folders list (shown as collapsed in Figure 1–15). The **Favorite Links list** contains your documents, pictures, music files, and more.

The four **column headers**, Name, Type, Total Size, and Free Space, that appear in the right pane allow you to sort and group the entries by each header category.

To Minimize and Redisplay a Window

Two buttons on the title bar of a window, the Minimize button and the Maximize button, allow you to control the way a window displays or does not display on the desktop. The following steps minimize and restore the Computer folder window.

- Click the Minimize button on the title bar of the Computer folder window to minimize the Computer folder window (Figure 1–16).

Q&A

What happens to the Computer folder window when I click the Minimize button?

The Computer folder window remains available, but is no longer an active window. It collapses down to a non-recessed, light gray button on the taskbar.

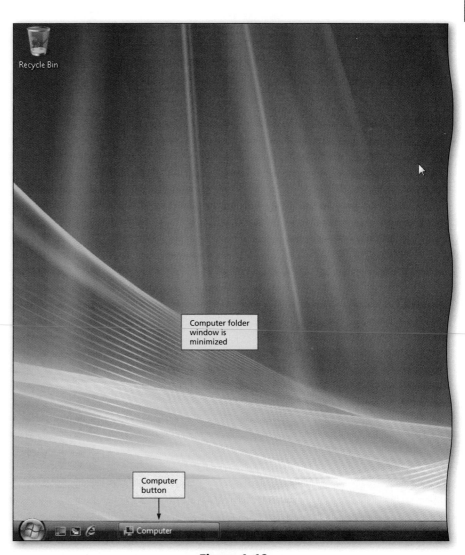

Computer folder window is minimized

Computer button

Figure 1–16

2

- Click the Computer button on the taskbar to display the Computer folder window (Figure 1–17).

Q&A

Why does the Computer button on the taskbar change?

The button changes to reflect the status of the Computer folder window. A black recessed button indicates that the Computer folder window is active on the screen. A light gray non-recessed button indicates that the Computer folder window is open but not active.

Figure 1–17

Q&A

Why do I see a picture when I click the Computer button?

Whenever you move your mouse over a button or click a button on the taskbar, a preview of the window will be displayed as part of the Aero experience.

Other Ways

1. Right-click title bar, click Minimize, in taskbar button area click taskbar button
2. Press WINDOWS+M, press WINDOWS+SHIFT+M

To Maximize and Restore a Window

Sometimes information is not completely visible in a window. One method of displaying the entire contents of a window is to enlarge the window using the **Maximize button**. The Maximize button increases the size of a window so it fills the entire screen, making it easier to see the contents of the window. When a window is maximized, the **Restore Down button** replaces the Maximize button on the title bar. Clicking the Restore Down button will return the window to the size it was before it was maximized. The following steps maximize and restore the Computer folder window.

1

- Click the Maximize button on the Computer folder window to maximize the Computer folder window (Figure 1–18).

Q&A When a window is maximized, can you also minimize it?

Yes. Click the Minimize button to minimize the window. Clicking the button on the taskbar will return the window to its maximized size.

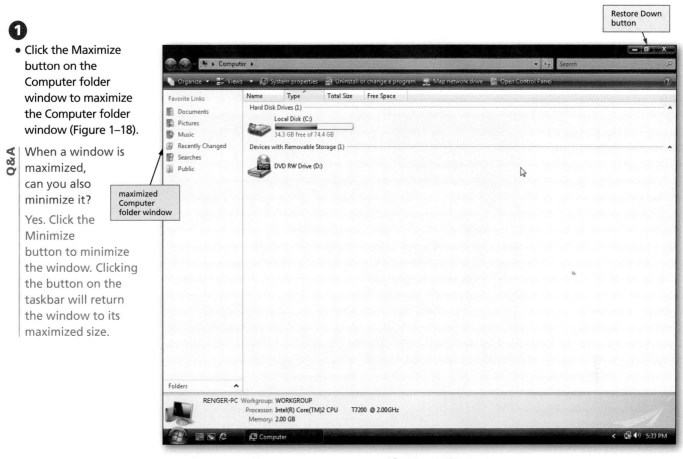

Figure 1–18

2

- Click the Restore Down button on the Computer folder window to return the Computer folder window to its previous size (Figure 1–19).

Q&A What happens to the Restore Down button after I click it?

The Maximize button replaces the Restore Down button on the title bar.

Other Ways

1. Right-click title bar, click Maximize, right-click title bar, click Restore
2. Double-click title bar, double-click title bar

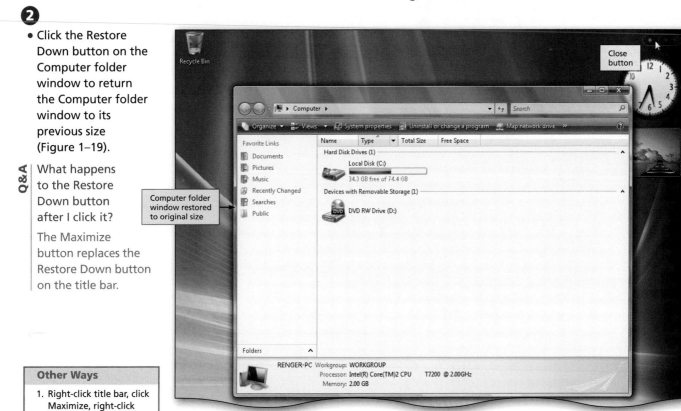

Figure 1–19

To Close a Window

The **Close button** on the title bar of a window closes the window and removes the taskbar button from the taskbar. To close the Computer folder window, complete the following step.

- Click the Close button on the title bar of the Computer folder window to close the Computer folder window (Figure 1–20).

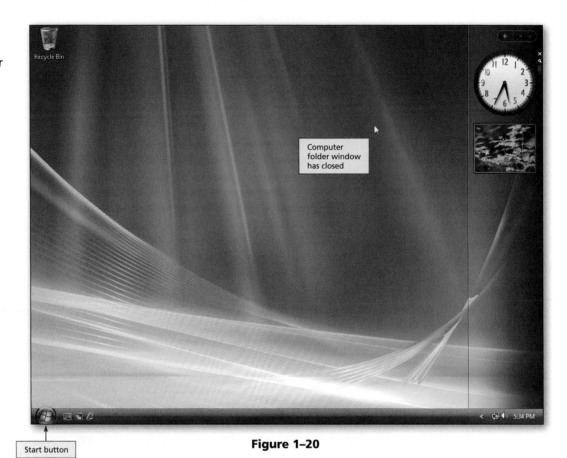

Figure 1–20

Other Ways
1. Right-click title bar, click Close
2. Press ALT+F4

To Add an Icon to the Desktop

Once you start doing a lot of work on your computer, you may want to add additional icons to the desktop. For example, you may want to add the Documents folder icon to the desktop for faster access. The **Documents folder window** is a central location for the storage and management of documents that Windows Vista has optimized for faster searching and organizing. The following steps add a shortcut to the Documents folder window to your desktop.

- Click the Start button to open the Start menu.

- Point to the Documents command on the right pane and then click the right mouse button (right-click).

- Point to the Send To command on the Documents shortcut menu to display the Send To submenu (Figure 1–21).

Q&A

What is a shortcut menu?

A shortcut menu appears when you right-click an object and contains commands specifically for use with that object.

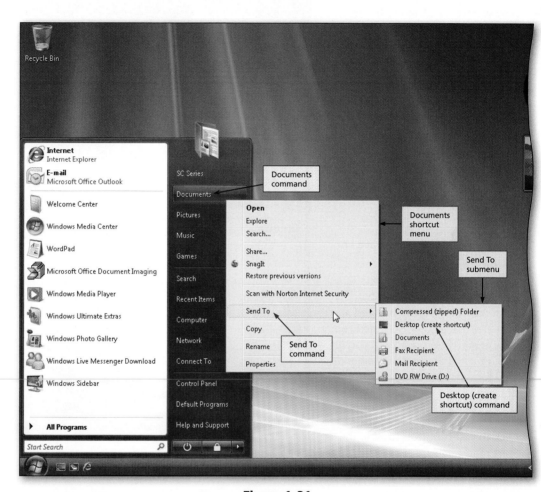

Figure 1–21

2

- Click the Desktop (create shortcut) command on the Send To submenu to place a shortcut to the Documents folder on the desktop (Figure 1–22).

Q&A Why would I want to use a shortcut menu?

Using shortcut menus can speed up your work and add flexibility to your interaction with the computer by making often used items available in multiple locations.

Q&A Why am I unable to add an item to my desktop?

Sometimes at work or in school labs users are not allowed to customize their desktop.

Q&A How many icons should I have on my desktop?

Icons can be added to your desktop by applications or by users; however, it is considered a best practice to keep your desktop as clutter free as possible. If you are not using an icon on the desktop, consider removing it from the desktop.

3

- Click the Start button to close the Start menu.

Figure 1–22

Other Ways

1. Right-click desktop, point to New, click Shortcut which opens the Create Shortcut Wizard, click Browse, click your user name, click Documents, Click OK button, click Next button, type shortcut name (or leave alone), click Finish

To Open a Window Using a Desktop Icon

The following step opens the Documents window using the shortcut you have just created on the desktop.

1

- Click the mouse button twice, in quick succession (double-click) on the Documents icon on the desktop to open the Documents folder window (Figure 1–23).

Q&A What does the Documents folder window allow me to do?

The Documents folder window is designed to provide a location for you to store your commonly used files. Many programs use this location by default when opening and closing files.

Q&A Why are the contents of my Documents folder different?

Because you have different documents and folders created on your computer, the contents of your Documents folder will be different than the one in Figure 1–23.

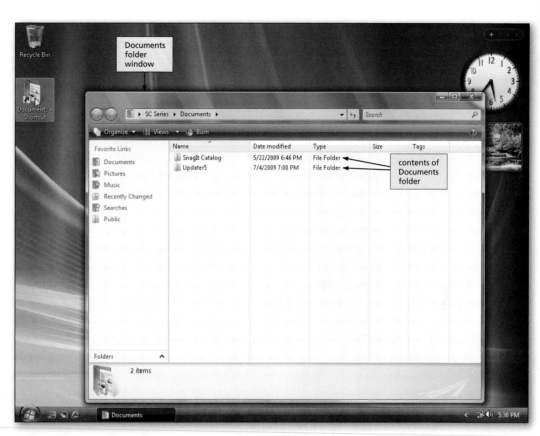

Figure 1–23

Other Ways

1. Right-click desktop icon, click Open on the shortcut menu

Double-Clicking Errors   While double-clicking an object, it is easy to click once instead of twice. When you click an object such as the Documents icon once, the icon becomes active and dimmed. To open the Documents folder window after clicking the Documents icon once, double-click the Documents icon as if you had not clicked the icon at all.

Another possible error occurs when the mouse moves after you click the first time and before you click the second time. In most cases when this occurs, the icon will appear dimmed as if you had clicked it just one time.

A third possible error is moving the mouse while you are pressing the mouse button. In this case, the icon might have moved on the screen because you inadvertently dragged it. To open the Documents folder window after dragging it accidentally, double-click the icon as if you had not clicked it at all.

To Move a Window by Dragging

You can move any open window to another location on the desktop by dragging the title bar of the window. The following step drags the Documents folder window to the center of the desktop.

1

- Drag the Documents folder window to the center of the screen, as shown in Figure 1–24.

Figure 1–24

Other Ways

1. Right-click title bar, click Move, drag window

To Expand the Folders List

In Figure 1–24, the Folders list in the Documents folder window is collapsed and an up arrow appears to the right of the Folders name. Clicking the up arrow or the Folders button expands the Folders list and reveals the contents of the Folders list. The following step expands the Folders list.

1

- Click the Folders button to expand the Folders list in the Navigation pane of the Documents folder window (Figure 1–25).

Q&A

What is shown in the Folders list?

The Folders list displays a hierarchical structure of files, folders, and drives on the computer.

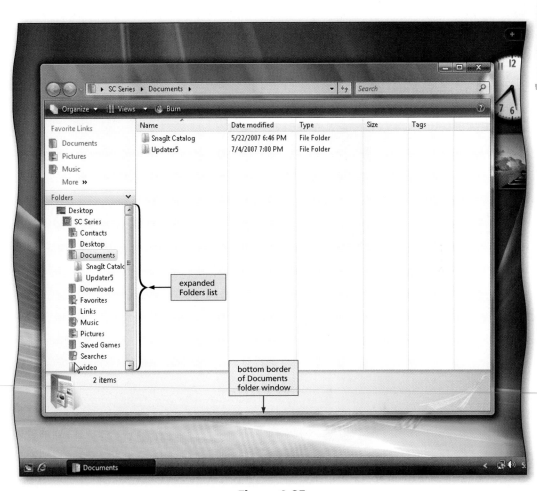

Figure 1–25

To Size a Window by Dragging

Sometimes information is not completely visible in a window. You learned how to use the Maximize button to increase the size of a window. Another method to change the size of the window is to drag the window borders. The following step changes the size of the Documents folder window.

1

- Point to the bottom border of the Documents folder window until the mouse pointer changes to a two-headed arrow.

- Drag the bottom border downward to display more of the Folders list (Figure 1–26).

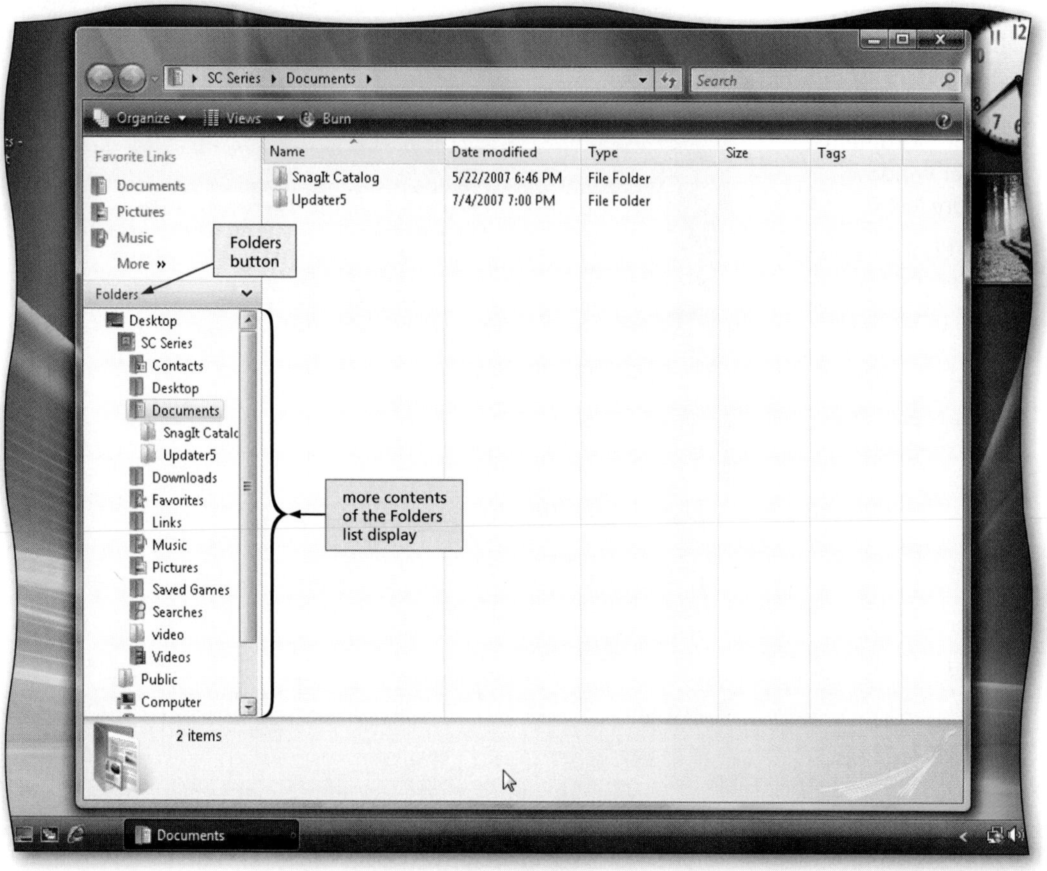

Q&A
Can I drag other sides besides the bottom border to enlarge or shrink the window?

Yes, you can drag the left, right, and top borders and any window corner to resize the window.

Q&A
Will Windows Vista remember the new size of the window after I close it?

Yes. Windows Vista remembers the size of the window when you close the window. When you reopen the window, it will display with the same size as when you closed it.

Figure 1–26

To Collapse the Folders List

The following step collapses the Folders list.

1

- Click the Folders button to collapse the Folders list (Figure 1–27).

Q&A

Should I keep the Folders list expanded or collapsed?

If you need to use the contents with the Folders list, it is handy to keep the list expanded. You can collapse the Folders list when the information is not needed.

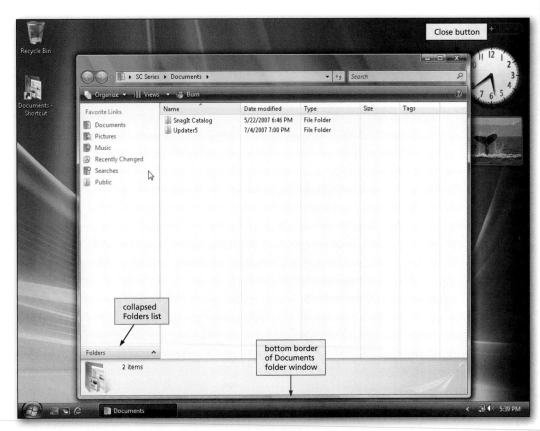

Figure 1–27

To Resize a Window

After moving and resizing a window, you may wish to return the window to its original size. To return the Documents folder window to approximately its original size, complete the following step.

1 Drag the bottom border of the Documents folder window up until the window is returned to approximately its original size.

To Close a Window

After you have completed work in a window, normally you would close it. To close the Documents folder window, complete the following step.

1 Click the Close button on the title bar of the Documents folder window to close the Documents folder window (Figure 1–28).

Figure 1–28

To Delete a Desktop Icon by Dragging

Although Windows Vista has many ways to delete desktop icons, one method of removing an icon from the desktop is to drag it to the Recycle Bin. The following steps delete the Documents icon by dragging the icon to the Recycle Bin.

- Point to the Documents - Shortcut icon on the desktop and press the left mouse button to select the icon (Figure 1–29). Do not release the left mouse button.

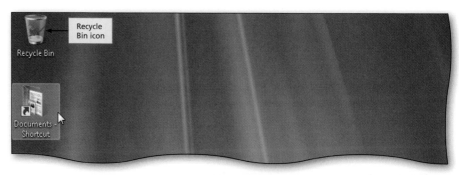

Figure 1–29

2

- Drag the Documents icon over the Recycle Bin icon on the desktop, and then release the left mouse button to place the shortcut in the Recycle Bin (Figure 1–30).

Experiment

- Double-click the Recycle Bin icon on the desktop to open a window containing the contents of the Recycle Bin. The Documents shortcut you have just deleted will display in this window. Close the Recycle Bin window.

Q&A

Why did my icon disappear?

Releasing the left mouse button moved the icon from the desktop to the Recycle Bin.

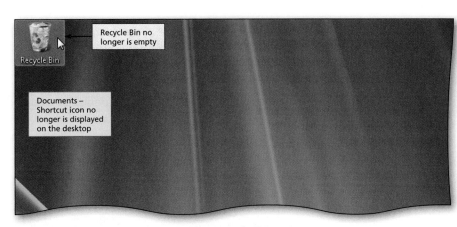

Figure 1–30

Other Ways

1. Right-click icon, click Delete, click Yes button
2. Right-click icon and hold, drag to Recycle Bin, release right mouse button, click Move Here

To Empty the Recycle Bin

The Recycle Bin prevents you from deleting files you actually might need. Up until the time you empty the Recycle Bin, you can recover deleted items from the Recycle Bin. The following steps empty the Recycle Bin. If you are not sure that you want to delete the files permanently in the Recycle Bin, read these steps without performing them.

1

- Right-click the Recycle Bin to show the shortcut menu (Figure 1–31).

2

- Click the Empty Recycle Bin command to permanently delete the contents of the Recycle Bin.

- Click the Yes button to confirm the operation.

Other Ways

1. Right-click icon, click Open, click Empty Recycle Bin, click the Close button, click the Yes button
2. Double-click the Recycle bin icon, click Empty Recycle Bin, click the Close button, click the Yes button

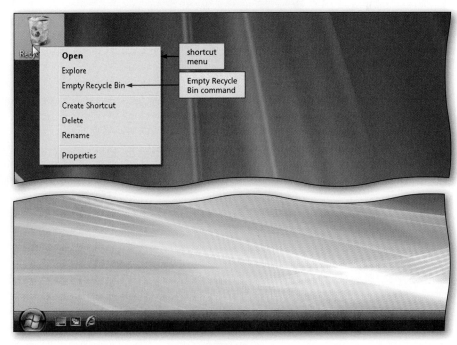

Figure 1–31

To Add a Gadget to the Windows Sidebar

The Windows Sidebar displays on the right side of the desktop and contains gadgets. Gadgets are mini-programs that display information and provide access to various useful tools. In Figure 1–13 on page WIN 15, the Windows Sidebar displays the clock and picture gadgets. The Windows Sidebar can be modified according to personal preference by adding or removing gadgets. Additional gadgets can be found in the **Gadget Gallery** or you can download gadgets from the Internet. Gadgets can include mini games, RSS feeds, and even online auction updates. In order to use gadgets, they first must be added to the Windows Sidebar. One method to add a gadget to the Windows Sidebar is to double-click the gadget in the Gadget Gallery. The following steps open the Gadget Gallery and add a gadget to the Windows Sidebar.

- Click the Add Gadgets button (see Figure 1-28 on page WIN 28) to open the Gadget Gallery on the desktop (Figure 1–32).

Q&A

Where can I find more gadgets?

You can download additional gadgets from `http:// vista.gallery. microsoft.com,` or search online to locate other gadget collections.

Figure 1–32

- Double-click the CPU Meter gadget in the Gadget Gallery to add the gadget to the top of the Windows Sidebar and display the performance measurements for your CPU (Figure 1–33).

- Click the Close button to close the Gadget Gallery.

Q&A Can I customize the Windows Sidebar?

Yes. You can select which gadgets you want to add or remove, add multiple instances of a particular gadget, and detach one or more gadgets from the Sidebar and place them on the desktop.

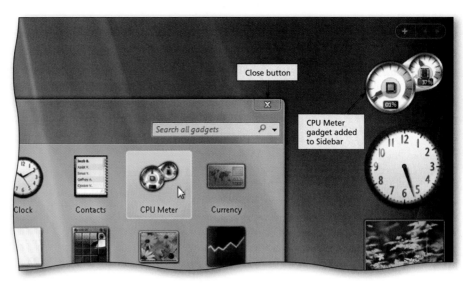

Figure 1–33

To Remove a Gadget from the Windows Sidebar

In addition to adding gadgets to the Windows Sidebar to customize your desktop, you might want to remove one or more gadgets from the Sidebar. The following steps remove a gadget from the Windows Sidebar.

- Point to the CPU Meter gadget to make the Close button visible (Figure 1–34).

- Click the Close button to remove the CPU Meter gadget from the Windows Sidebar.

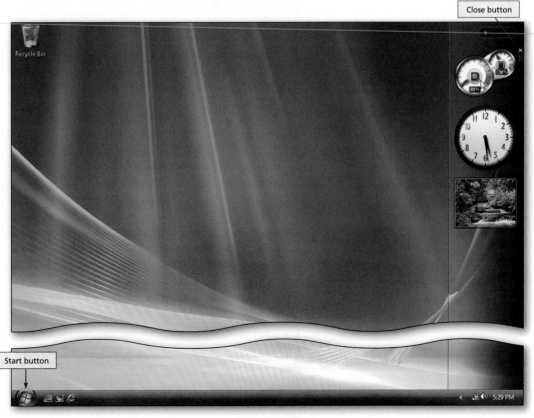

Figure 1–34

BTW

Application Programs
There are many application programs (Internet Explorer, Movie Maker, Media Player, and Windows Mail) that are installed as part of Windows Vista. Most application programs, however, such as Microsoft Office or Adobe® Photoshop®, must be purchased separately. Other application programs, like Mozilla Firefox or OpenOffice, are available for free.

Launching an Application Program

One of the basic tasks you can perform using Windows Vista is to launch an application program. A **program** is a set of computer instructions that carries out a task on the computer. An application program is a program designed to perform a specific user-oriented task. For example, a **word processing program** is an application program that allows you to create written documents; a **presentation graphics program** is an application program that allows you to create graphical presentations for display on a computer; and a **Web browser program** is an application program that allows you to explore the Internet and display Web pages.

The **default Web browser program** (Internet Explorer) appears in the pinned items list on the Start menu shown in Figure 1–7 on page WIN 11. Because the default **Web browser** is selected during the installation of the Windows Vista operating system, the default Web browser in the pinned items list on your computer may be different. In addition, you can easily select another Web browser as the default Web browser. Another frequently used Web browser is **Mozilla Firefox**.

To Start an Application Using the Start Menu

The most common activity performed on a computer is running an application program to accomplish tasks. You can start an application program by using the Start menu. The following steps open the Welcome Center using the Start menu.

- To display the Start menu, click the Start button.

- Display the Accessories list (Figure 1–35).

Figure 1–35

2

• Click the Welcome Center command to start the Welcome Center (Figure 1–36).

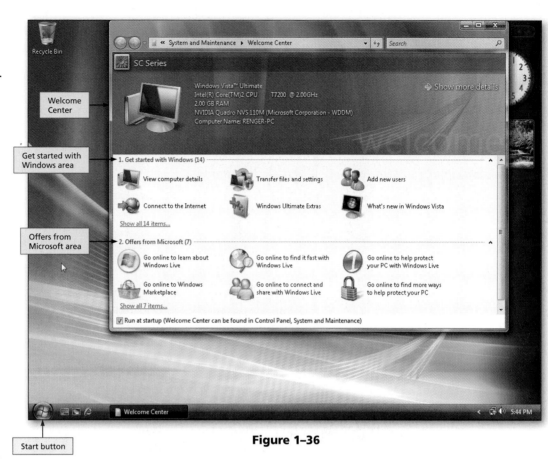

Figure 1–36

To Start an Application Using the Search Box

If you are unsure of where to find the application you wish to open in the Start menu, you can use the Start Search box to search for the application. **WordPad** is a popular application program available with Windows Vista that allows you to create, save, and print simple text documents. The steps on the following page search for the WordPad application using the Start Search box.

1

- Display the Start menu.

- Type wordpad in the Start Search box to have Windows Vista look for WordPad (Figure 1–37).

Q&A Why did different items display as I typed in the Start Search box?

As you type in the Start Search box, Windows Vista automatically tries to find items matching the text you enter.

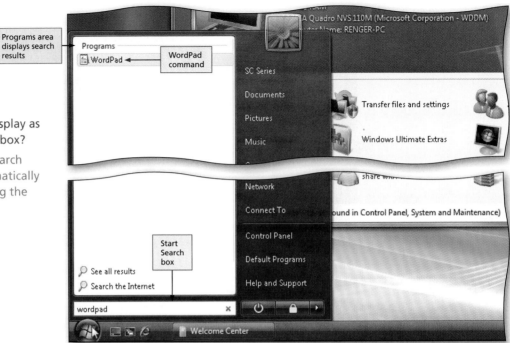

Figure 1–37

2

- Click the WordPad command in the Programs area to start WordPad (Figure 1–38).

Q&A Do I have to type the entire word before clicking the result?

No. As soon as you see the result you are looking for in the Programs area above the Start Search box, you can click it.

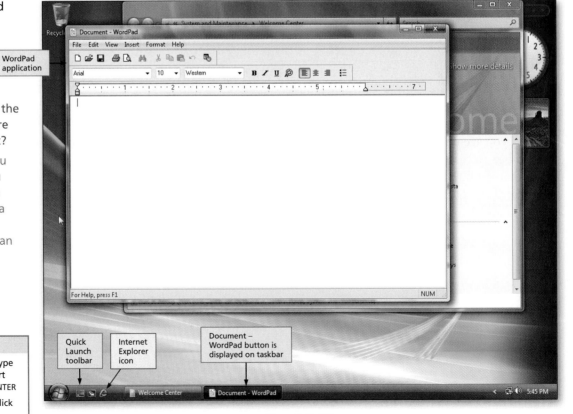

Figure 1–38

Other Ways

1. Open Start menu, type wordpad in the Start Search box, press ENTER

2. Open Start menu, click All Programs, open Accessories list, click WordPad

To Start an Application Using the Quick Launch Toolbar

Windows Vista allows users to access selected applications with one click of the mouse button via the Quick Launch toolbar. The following steps start the Internet Explorer application using the icon on the Quick Launch toolbar.

- Click the Internet Explorer icon on the Quick Launch toolbar to start Internet Explorer (Figure 1–39).

Q&A What if the Internet Explorer icon does not appear on my Quick Launch toolbar?

The Quick Launch toolbar is customizable, and yours may differ. Use one of the previous methods to open Internet Explorer instead.

Q&A Why does my Internet Explorer window look different?

Depending on your computer's setup, Internet Explorer may display a Web page other than the MSN.com Web page. For example, many school computer labs display their school's Web site when Internet Explorer first starts.

Figure 1–39

Other Ways

1. Open Start menu, click Internet Explorer
2. Press CTRL+ESC, press DOWN ARROW, press ENTER

To Switch Applications Using Windows Flip 3D

When you have multiple applications open simultaneously, invariably you will need to switch between them. Windows Flip 3D provides an easy and visual way to switch between the open applications on your computer. The steps on the following page switch from Internet Explorer to the WordPad application using Windows Flip 3D.

1

- Click the Switch Between Windows button on the Quick Launch toolbar to start Windows Flip 3D (Figure 1–40).

Q&A

Why does my Windows Flip not appear three-dimensional?

Your computer is set up to use the Basic experience, so you are seeing the basic Windows Flip which is not three-dimensional. Windows Flip 3D is part of the Aero experience.

Figure 1–40

2

- Press the TAB key repeatedly until the WordPad window appears at the front of the applications displayed in Windows Flip 3D (Figure 1–41).

Q&A

Do I have to use the TAB key?

You can also scroll the mouse wheel, if your mouse has one, until WordPad window is at the front.

Figure 1–41

3

- Click the WordPad window to exit Windows Flip 3D and make WordPad the active application (Figure 1–42).

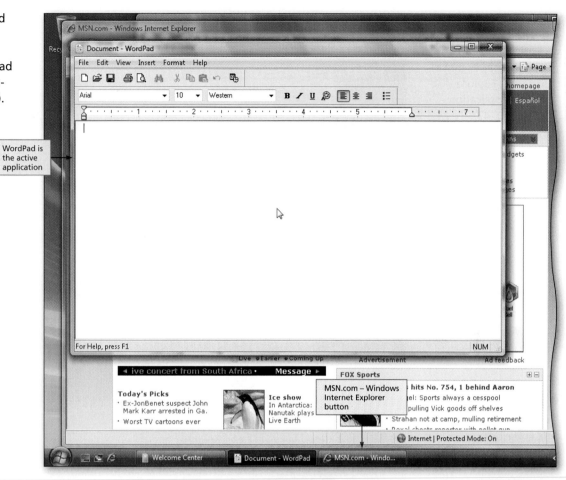

Figure 1–42

Other Ways

1. Press CTRL + WINDOWS + TAB, press TAB (or scroll the Mouse wheel, if you have one) until WordPad window is shown, click WordPad window

To Switch Applications Using the Taskbar

You also can switch applications using the taskbar. By clicking the button for the application, you make it the active application and bring the window to the front. The steps on the following page switch applications using the taskbar.

1

- Click the MSN.com - Windows Internet Explorer button on the taskbar to make Internet Explorer the active application (Figure 1–43).

Figure 1–43

2

- Click the Welcome Center button on the taskbar to make the Welcome Center the active window (Figure 1–44).

Figure 1–44

3

- Click the Document - WordPad button on the taskbar to make WordPad the active application (Figure 1–45).

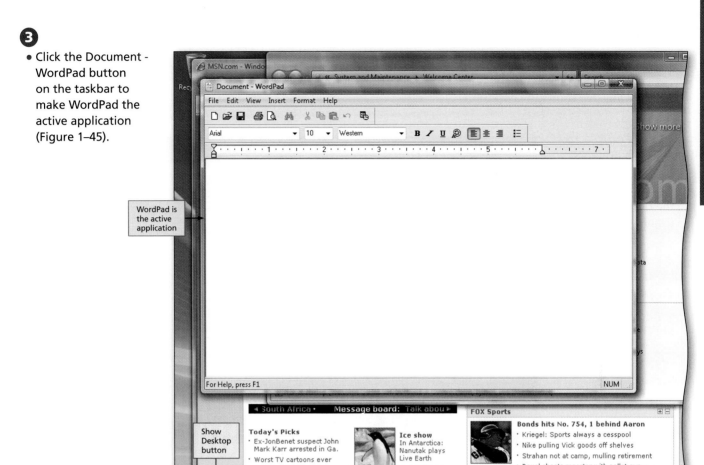

Figure 1–45

To Show the Desktop Using the Show Desktop Button

When you have several windows open at the same time and need to reveal the desktop without closing all of the open windows, you can use the Show Desktop button on the Quick Launch toolbar to show the desktop quickly. The following step shows the desktop.

- Click the Show desktop button on the Quick Launch toolbar to show the Desktop (Figure 1–46).

Q&A   Where did the Windows Sidebar go?

When you click the Show Desktop button, it shows the desktop without the Sidebar.

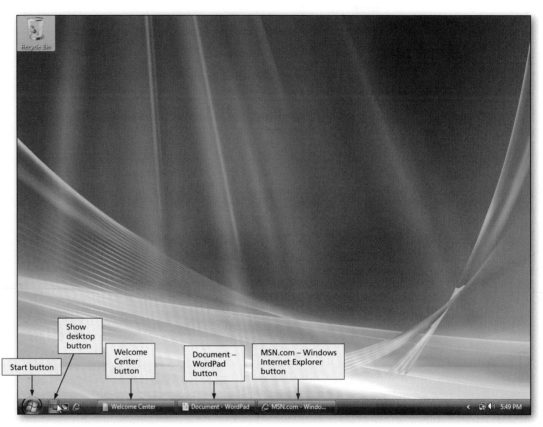

Figure 1–46

To Close Open Windows

After you are done viewing windows or using applications in Windows Vista, you should close them. The following steps close the open applications.

1 Click the Document - WordPad button on the taskbar to display the WordPad window. Click the Close button on the title bar of the WordPad window to close the WordPad window.

2 Click the MSN.com - Windows Internet Explorer button on the taskbar to display the Internet Explorer application. Click the Close button on the title bar of the Internet Explorer window to close the Internet Explorer window.

3 Display the Welcome Center and click the Close button on the title bar of the Welcome Center window to close the Welcome Center window.

Using Windows Help and Support

One of the more powerful Windows Vista features is Windows Help and Support. **Windows Help and Support** is available when using Windows Vista or when using any Microsoft application running under Windows Vista. This feature is designed to assist you in using Windows Vista or the various application programs. Table 1–2 on the next page describes what can be found in the Help and Support Center.

To Start Windows Help and Support

Before you can access the Windows Help and Support services, you must start Windows Help and Support. One method of starting Windows Help and Support uses the Start menu. The following steps start Windows Help and Support.

- Display the Start Menu (Figure 1–47).

Figure 1–47

2

- Click the Help and Support command to display the Windows Help and Support window (Figure 1–48).

- If necessary, click the Maximize button on the Windows Help and Support title bar to maximize the Windows Help and Support window.

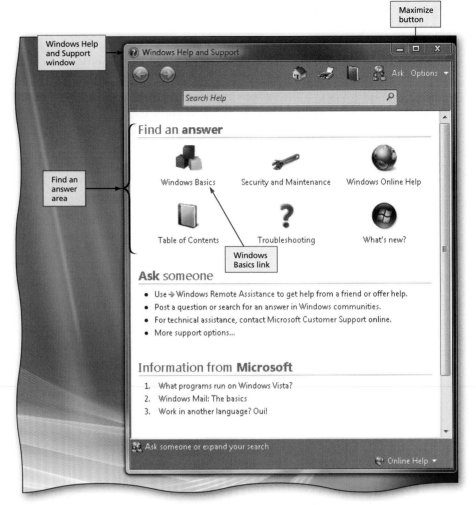

Figure 1–48

Other Ways

1. Press CTRL+ESC, press RIGHT ARROW, press UP ARROW, press ENTER
2. Press WINDOWS+F1

Table 1–2 Windows Help and Support Center Content Areas	
Area	**Function**
Find an answer	This area contains six Help topics: Windows Basics, Table of Contents, Security and Maintenance, Troubleshooting, Windows Online Help, and What's new?. Clicking a category displays a list of related subcategories and Help topics.
Ask someone	This area allows you to get help from a friend or offer help to others by using Windows Remote Assistance, post a question or search for an answer in Windows communities, and get technical assistance from Microsoft Customer Support online. Clicking the More support options link allows you to search the Knowledge Base, get in-depth technical information from Microsoft Website for IT professionals, and Windows Online Help and Support.
Information from Microsoft	This area contains links provided by Microsoft. These links are regularly updated if you are connected to the Internet.

To Browse for Help Topics in Windows Basics

After starting Windows Help and Support, your next step is to find Help topics that relate to your questions. Windows Help and Support organizes Help topics by headings and subheadings, as illustrated in Figure 1-49. The following steps use the 'Find an answer' area in the Windows Help and Support to locate a Help topic that describes how to use the Windows Help and Support.

1

- Click the Windows Basics link in the Find an answer area to display the Windows Basics: all topics page (Figure 1–49).

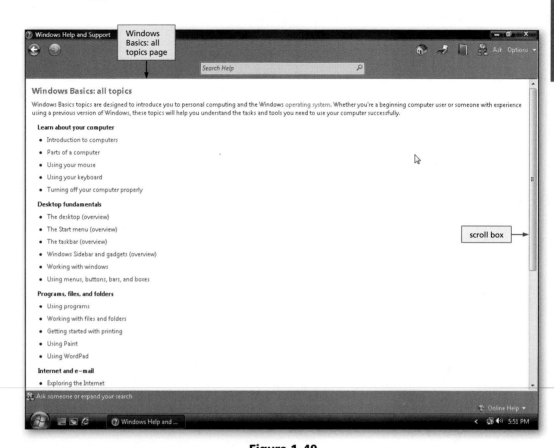

Figure 1–49

• Scroll down to view the Getting
  help link under the Help and
  support heading (Figure 1–50).

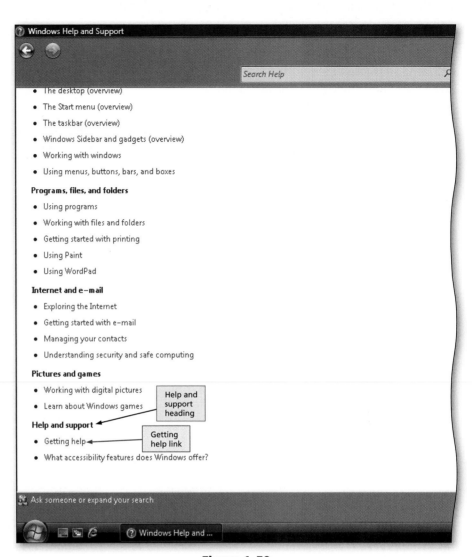

Figure 1–50

3

- Click the Getting help link to display the Getting help page (Figure 1–51).

- Read the information on the Getting help page.

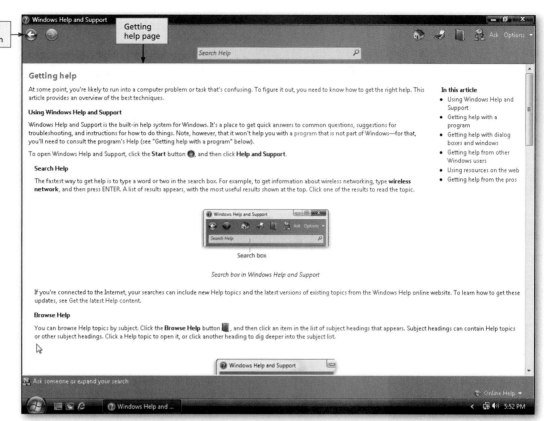

Figure 1–51

4

- Click the Back button on the Navigation toolbar two times to return to the page containing the Find an answer area (Figure 1–52).

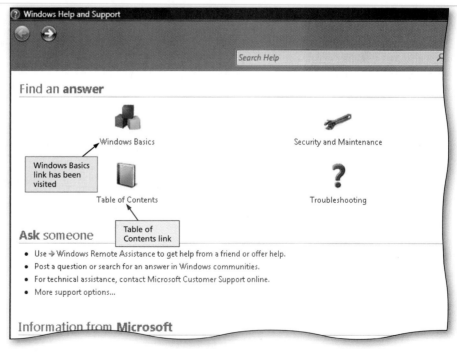

Figure 1–52

To Search for Help Topics Using the Table of Contents

A second method for finding answers to your questions about Windows Vista is to use the Table of Contents. The Table of Contents contains a list of entries, each of which references one or more Help topics. The following steps locate help and information on what you need to set up a home network.

- Click the Table of Contents link in the Find an answer area to display the Contents page (Figure 1–53).

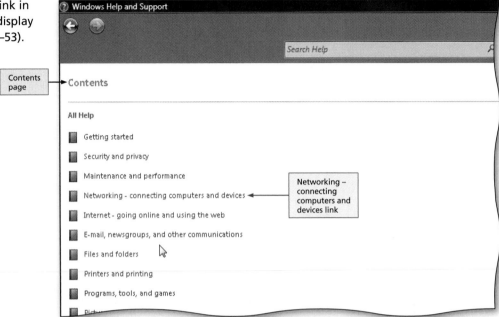

Figure 1–53

- Click the Networking - connecting computers and devices link on the Contents page to display the links in the Networking - connecting computers and devices topic (Figure 1–54).

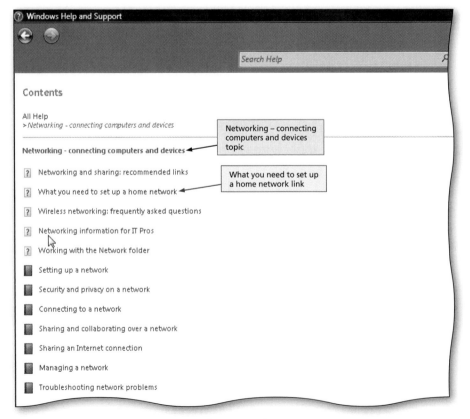

Figure 1–54

3

- Click the What you need to set up a home network link to show the What you need to set up a home network help page (Figure 1–55).

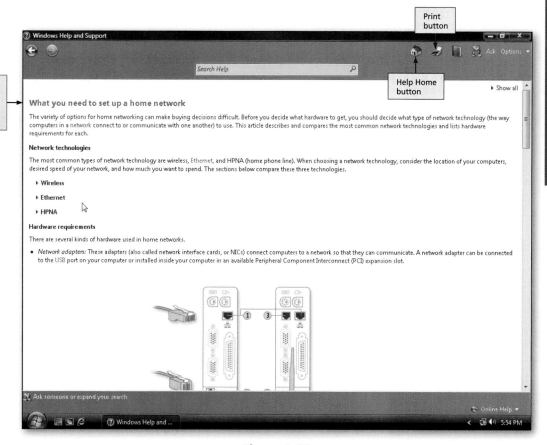

Figure 1–55

Other Ways

1. Press TAB until category or topic is highlighted, press ENTER, repeat for each category or topic

To Print a Help Topic

There are times when you might want to print a help topic so that you can have a printout for reference. The following steps show you how to print a Help topic. If you are unable to print from your computer (for example, you are in a school lab with no printer), read the following steps without actually performing them.

- Click the Print button on the Help toolbar to display the Print dialog box (Figure 1–56).

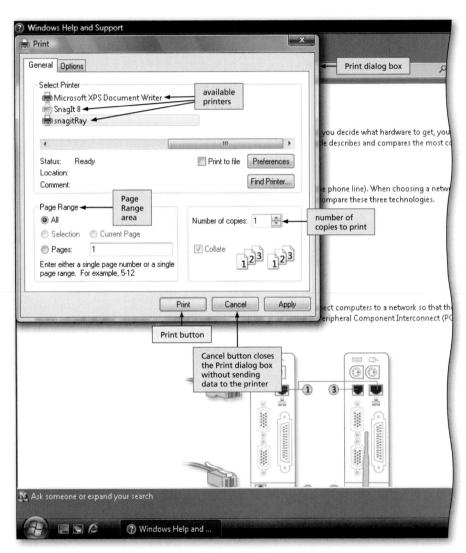

Figure 1–56

2

• Click the Print button in the Print dialog box to print the Help topic (Figure 1–57).

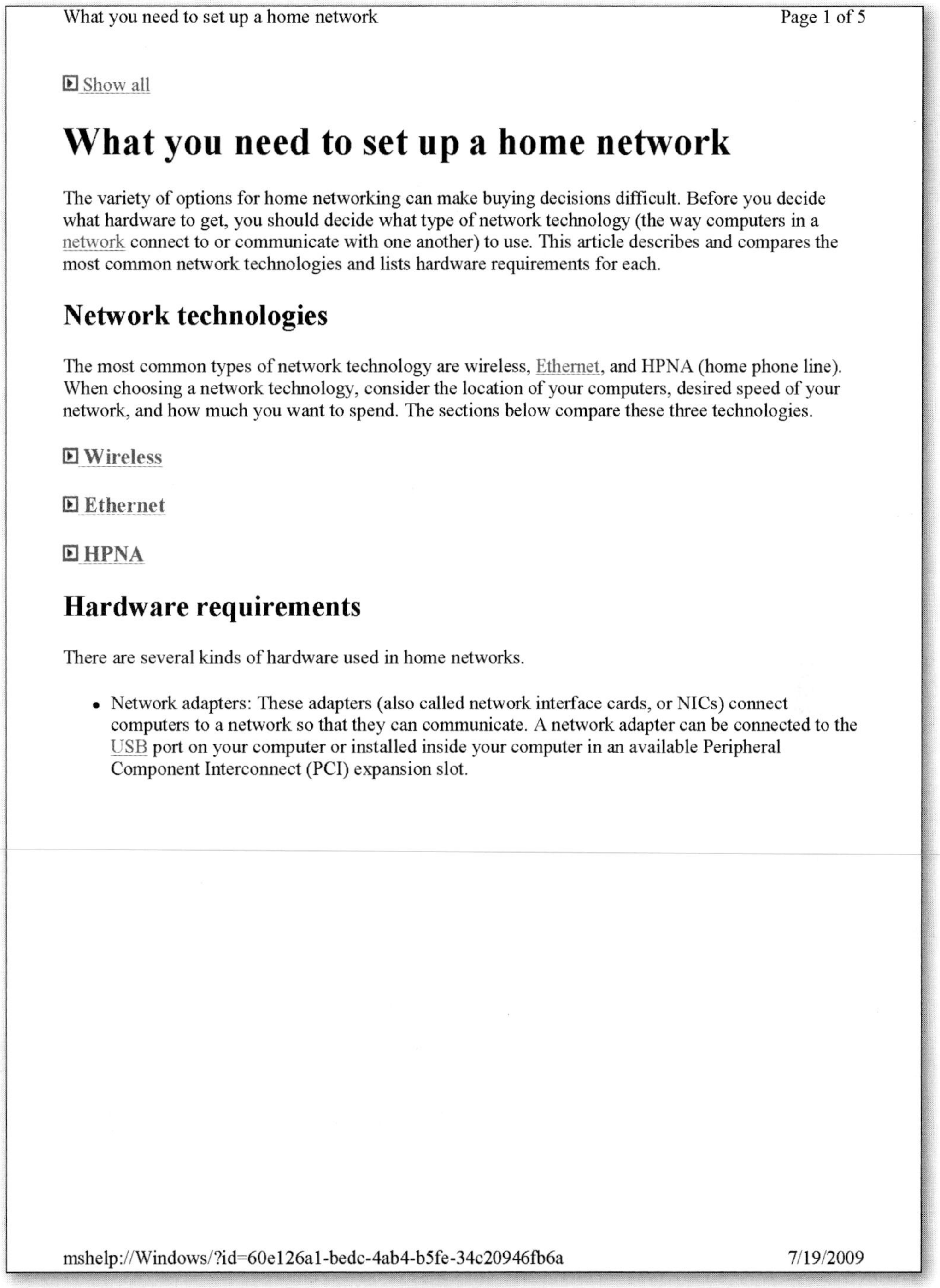

What you need to set up a home network   Page 1 of 5

▶ Show all

What you need to set up a home network

The variety of options for home networking can make buying decisions difficult. Before you decide what hardware to get, you should decide what type of network technology (the way computers in a network connect to or communicate with one another) to use. This article describes and compares the most common network technologies and lists hardware requirements for each.

Network technologies

The most common types of network technology are wireless, Ethernet, and HPNA (home phone line). When choosing a network technology, consider the location of your computers, desired speed of your network, and how much you want to spend. The sections below compare these three technologies.

▶ **Wireless**

▶ **Ethernet**

▶ **HPNA**

Hardware requirements

There are several kinds of hardware used in home networks.

• Network adapters: These adapters (also called network interface cards, or NICs) connect computers to a network so that they can communicate. A network adapter can be connected to the USB port on your computer or installed inside your computer in an available Peripheral Component Interconnect (PCI) expansion slot.

mshelp://Windows/?id=60e126a1-bedc-4ab4-b5fe-34c20946fb6a   7/19/2009

Figure 1–57

To Return to the Help Home Page

1 Click the Help and Support Home button on the Navigation toolbar to return to the page containing the Find an answer area (Figure 1–58).

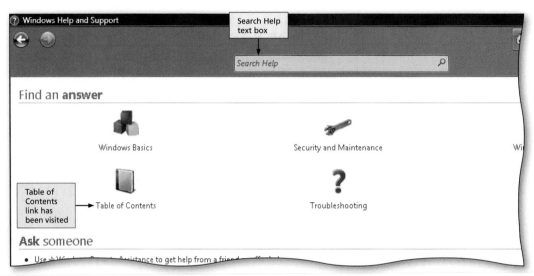

Figure 1–58

To Search Windows Help and Support

A third method for obtaining Help about Windows Vista is to use the Search Help text box in the Windows Help and Support window. The Search Help text box allows you to enter a keyword to display all Help topics containing the keyword. The following steps use the Search Help text box to locate information about computer viruses.

- Click the Search Help text box and type virus in the Search Help text box to provide a keyword for searching (Figure 1–59).

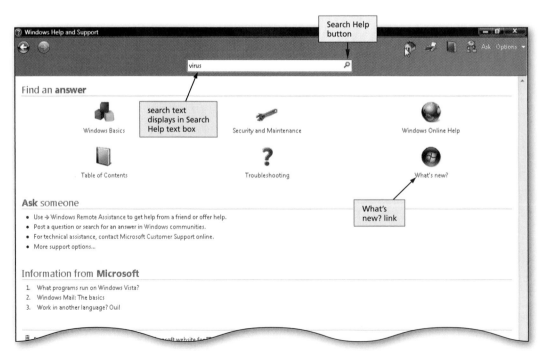

Figure 1–59

• Click the Search Help button to search for items matching virus (Figure 1–60).

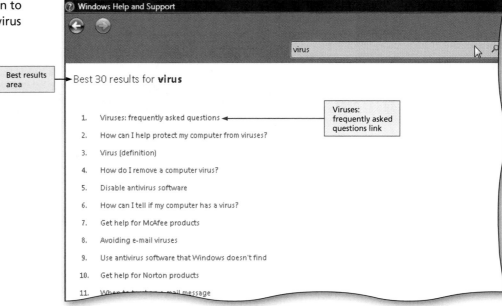

Figure 1–60

❸

• Click Viruses: frequently asked questions in the Best 30 results for viruses area to display the Viruses: frequently asked questions help page (Figure 1–61).

Figure 1–61

Other Ways

1. Press ALT+S, type keyword, press ENTER

When you search Help, the results of the search are sorted to produce the best matches for your keyword. When the computer is connected to the Internet, Windows Help and Support also searches the Microsoft Knowledge Base Web site for topics or articles that are relevant to the keyword you enter. The Best results area shows 30 results at a time. If there are more than 30 results for your keyword, a link will appear at the end of the Best 30 results list that lets you see more results. The total number of results will depend upon the search keywords.

To View a Windows Help and Support Demo

A fourth method for obtaining Help about Windows Vista is to view Windows Help and Support demos. The following steps, which display a demo about security, assume that you have Windows Media Player configured on your computer. If you have not yet configured Windows Media Player, please see your instructor.

- Click the Back button two times to return to the help home page containing the Find an answer area.

- Click the What's new link in the Find an answer area to display the What's new in Windows Vista Ultimate page (Figure 1–62).

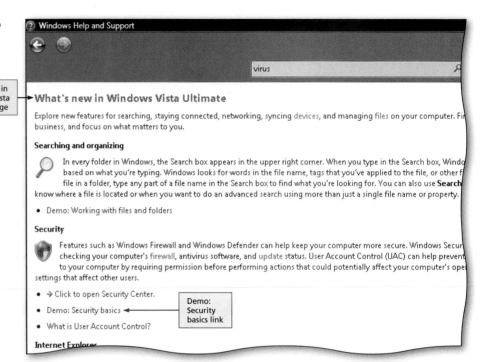

Figure 1–62

- Click the Demo: Security basics link to display the Demo: Security basics demo Help page (Figure 1–63).

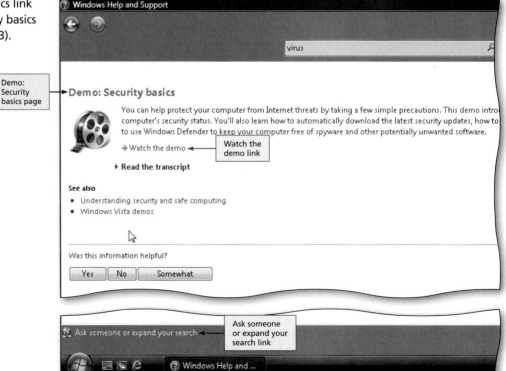

Figure 1–63

- Click the Watch the demo link to open the demo in Windows Media Player (Figure 1–64).

- Click the Close button on the title bar on the Windows Media Player window.

Figure 1–64

To Get More Help

If you do not find the results you are seeking, you can use Windows Help and Support to ask someone or find ways to expand your search. The following step opens the Ask someone or expand your search area.

- Click the Ask someone or expand your search link at the bottom of the Windows Help and Support window to open the Get customer support or other types of help page (Figure 1–65).

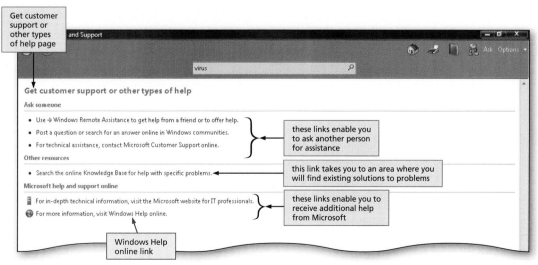

Figure 1–65

To Search Windows Help Online

Using Windows Help online allows you to search a broader range of content, get help from others, share a Help topic, or save a link to a Help topic for future reference by adding it to your favorites in Internet Explorer. The following steps open Internet Explorer to access Windows Help online.

1

- Click the Windows Help online link to open Internet Explorer and display the Windows Vista: Help and How-to Web page (Figure 1–66).

Q&A

Why am I unable to access Windows Help online?

You must have an active Internet connection to use Windows Help online.

Figure 1–66

2

- Click the Security link on the Windows Help and How-to Web page to display the Windows Vista Help: Security Web page (Figure 1–67).

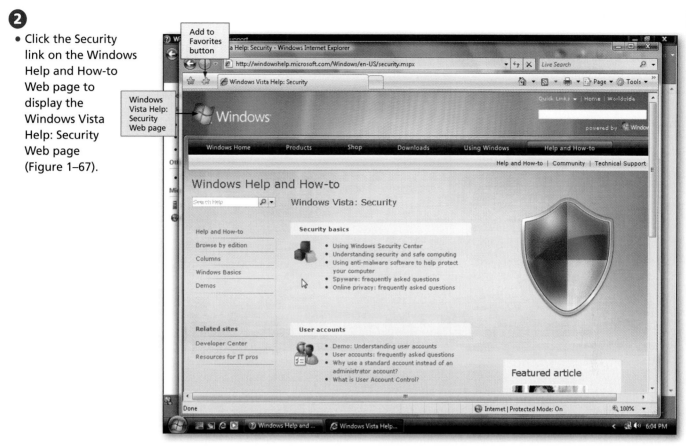

Figure 1–67

To Add a Page to Favorites

When you know you will want to return to a Windows Help page in the future, you can add it to your Favorites list in Internet Explorer. The following steps add the Windows Vista Help: Security page to your Favorites.

1

- Click the Add to Favorites button to display the Add to Favorites menu, and point to the Add to Favorites command (Figure 1-68).

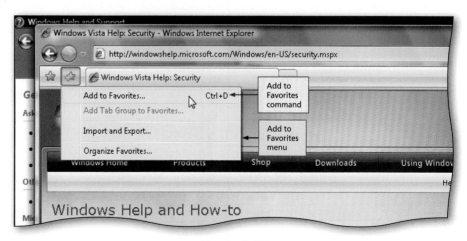

Figure 1–68

2

• Click the Add to Favorites command to display the Add a Favorite dialog box (Figure 1–69).

Figure 1–69

3

• Click the Add button to add the Windows Vista Help: Security page to your Favorites list (Figure 1–70).

Figure 1–70

4

- Click the Favorites Center button on the Internet Explorer toolbar to display the Explorer Bar.

- If necessary, click the Favorites button on the Explorer Bar to display the Favorites list (Figure 1–71).

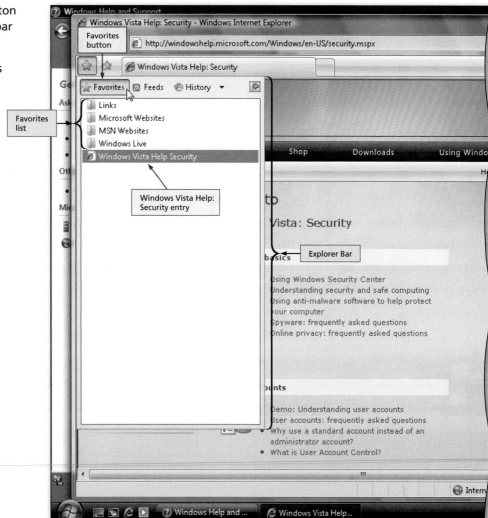

Figure 1–71

To Delete a Link from Favorites

When you are through referring to a Help topic stored in your Favorites, you may want to delete the link. The steps on the following page delete the security help page from your Favorites list.

1

- Right-click the Windows Vista Help: Security entry to display a shortcut menu (Figure 1–72).

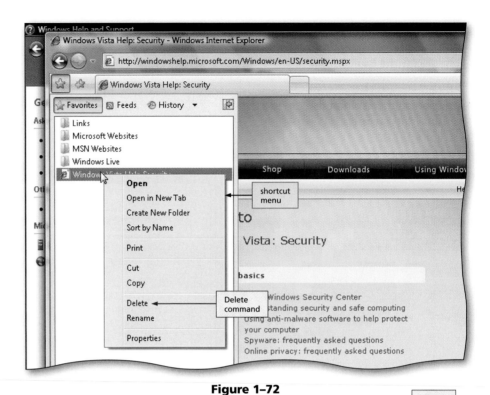

Figure 1–72

2

- Click the Delete command to close the shortcut menu and display the Delete File dialog box (Figure 1–73).

- Click the Yes button to delete the Windows Vista Help: Security Favorite from the Favorites list.

Q&A

Why does the dialog box ask me if I want to delete a file?

Internet Explorer and Windows Vista store your favorites as small text files in a special folder on your computer. When you add a favorite, you are creating a file. When you delete a favorite, you are deleting a file.

Figure 1–73

To Close Windows Internet Explorer and Windows Help and Support

1 Click the Close button on the title bar of the Windows Internet Explorer window.

2 Click the Close button on the title bar of the Windows Help and Support Center window.

Logging Off and Turning Off the Computer

After completing your work with Windows Vista, you should close your user account by logging off from the computer. In addition to logging off, there are several options available for ending your Windows Vista session. Table 1–3 describes the various options for ending your Windows Vista session.

Table 1–3 Options and Methods for Ending a Windows Vista Session	
Area	**Function**
Switch User	Click the Start button, point to the arrow next to the Lock button, and then click the Switch User command to keep your programs running in the background (but inaccessible until you log on again), and allow another user to log on.
Log Off	Click the Start button, point to the arrow next to the Lock button, and then click the Log Off command to close all your programs and close your user account. This method leaves the computer running so that another user can log on.
Lock	Click the Start button, and then click the Lock button to deny anyone except those who have authorized access to log on to the computer.
Restart	Click the Start button, point to the arrow next to the Lock button, and then click the Restart command to shut down and then restart the computer.
Sleep	Click the Start button, point to the arrow next to the Lock button, click the Sleep command, wait for Windows to save your work to memory and then power down your computer to a low-power state. This is useful if you are expecting to return to your computer in a short amount of time.
Hibernate	Click the Start button, point to the arrow next to the Lock button, click the Hibernate command, and then wait for Windows to save your work to the hard disk and power down your computer. This is useful if you are expecting to not use your computer for a few days.
Shut Down	Click the Start button, point to the arrow next to the Lock button, and then click the Shut Down command to close all your programs and turn off the computer.

To Log Off from the Computer

Logging off from the computer closes any open applications, gives you the opportunity to save any unsaved documents, ends the Windows Vista session, and makes the computer available for other users. A logging off message will display briefly as Windows Vista logs you off. When the process is finished, the Welcome screen will appear again. At this point, another user can log on to the computer. The steps on the following page log off from the computer. If you do not want to end your session on the computer, read the following steps but do not perform them.

● Display the Start menu
(Figure 1–74).

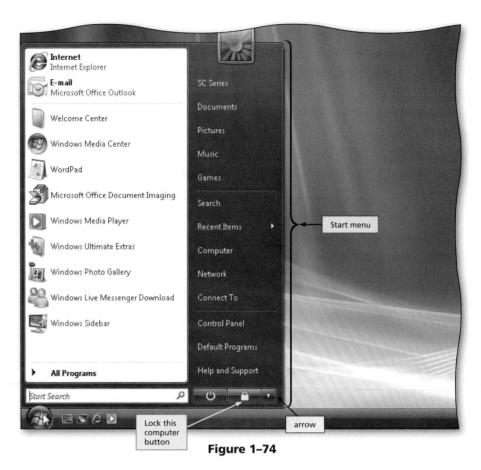

Figure 1–74

● Point to the arrow to the right
of the Lock button to display
the Shut Down options menu
(Figure 1–75).

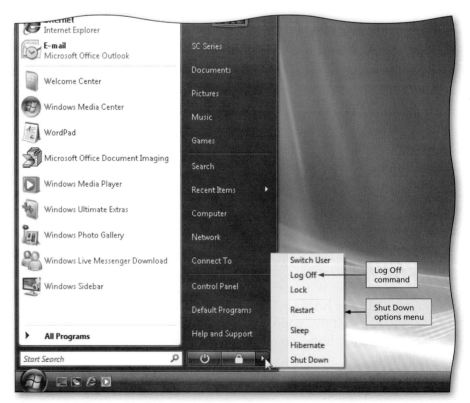

Figure 1–75

3

- Click the Log Off command, and then wait for Windows Vista to prompt you to save any unsaved data, if any, and log off (Figure 1–76).

Q&A

Why should I log off the computer?

Some Windows Vista users have turned off their computers without following the log off procedure only to find data they thought they had stored on disk was lost. Because of the way Windows Vista writes data on the hard disk, it is important you log off the computer so you do not lose your work. Logging off a computer is also a common security practice, preventing unauthorized users from tampering with the computer or your user account.

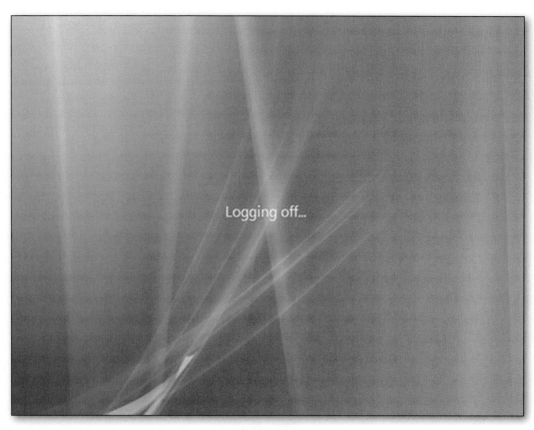

Logging off...

Figure 1–76

Other Ways
1. Press CTRL+ESC, press RIGHT ARROW, press RIGHT ARROW, press RIGHT ARROW, press L

To Turn Off the Computer

After logging off, you also may want to turn off the computer. Using the Shut down button on the Welcome screen to turn off the computer shuts down Windows Vista so that you can turn off the power to the computer. Many computers turn the power off automatically as part of shutting down. While Windows Vista is shutting down, a message shows stating 'Shutting down' along with an animated progress circle. When Windows Vista is done, the computer will shut off. You should not turn off your computer during this process, as you could lose data. The following step turns off the computer. However, if you do not want to turn off the computer, read the step without performing it.

- Click the Shut down button to turn off the computer (Figure 1–77).

Figure 1–77

Other Ways
1. Press ALT+F4, press DOWN ARROW, press OK

Chapter Summary

In this chapter you have learned how to work with the Microsoft Windows Vista graphical user interface. You launched Windows Vista, logged on to the computer, learned about the parts of the desktop, and added and removed a gadget from the Windows Sidebar. You opened, minimized, maximized, restored, and closed Windows Vista windows. You launched applications and used Windows Flip 3D to switch between them. Using Windows Help and Support, you located Help topics to learn more about Microsoft Windows Vista. You printed a Help topic, viewed a Help demo, and learned how to find Help topics online. You logged off from the computer using the Log Off command on the Start menu and then shut down Windows Vista using the Shut down button on the Welcome screen.

The following list includes all the new Windows Vista skills you have learned in this chapter.

1. Log On to the Computer (WIN 8)
2. Close the Welcome Center (WIN 10)
3. Display the Start Menu (WIN 11)
4. Scroll Using Scroll Arrows, the Scroll Bar, and the Scroll Box (WIN 13)
5. Open the Computer Folder Window (WIN 15)
6. Minimize and Redisplay a Window (WIN 17)
7. Maximize and Restore a Window (WIN 18)
8. Close a Window (WIN 20)
9. Add an Icon to the Desktop (WIN 21)
10. Open a Window Using a Desktop Icon (WIN 23)
11. Move a Window by Dragging (WIN 24)
12. Expand the Folders List (WIN 25)
13. Size a Window by Dragging (WIN 26)
14. Collapse the Folders List (WIN 27)
15. Delete a Desktop Icon by Dragging (WIN 28)
16. Empty the Recycle Bin (WIN 29)
17. Add a Gadget to the Windows Sidebar (WIN 30)
18. Remove a Gadget from the Windows Sidebar (WIN 31)
19. Start an Application Using the Start Menu (WIN 32)
20. Start an Application Using the Search Box (WIN 33)
21. Start an Application Using the Quick Launch Toolbar (WIN 35)
22. Switch Applications Using Windows Flip 3D (WIN 35)
23. Switch Applications Using the Taskbar (WIN 37)
24. Show the Desktop Using the Show Desktop Button (WIN 40)
25. Start Windows Help and Support (WIN 41)
26. Browse for Help Topics in Windows Basics (WIN 43)
27. Search for Help Topics Using the Table of Contents (WIN 46)
28. Print a Help Topic (WIN 48)
29. Search Windows Help and Support (WIN 50)
30. View a Windows Help and Support Demo (WIN 52)
31. Get More Help (WIN 53)
32. Search Windows Help Online (WIN 54)
33. Add a Page to Favorites (WIN 55)
34. Delete a Link from Favorites (WIN 57)
35. Log Off from the Computer (WIN 59)
36. Turn Off the Computer (WIN 62)

Learn It Online

Test your knowledge of chapter content and key terms.

Instructions: To complete the Learn It Online exercises, start your browser, click the Address bar, and then enter the Web address scsite.com/winvista/learn. When the Windows Vista Learn It Online page is displayed, click the link for the exercise you want to complete and then read the instructions.

Chapter Reinforcement TF, MC, and SA

A series of true/false, multiple-choice, and short answer questions that test your knowledge of the chapter content.

Flash Cards

An interactive learning environment where you identify chapter key terms associated with displayed definitions.

Practice Test

A series of multiple-choice questions that test your knowledge of chapter content and key terms.

Who Wants To Be a Computer Genius?

An interactive game that challenges your knowledge of chapter content in the style of television quiz show.

Wheel of Terms

An interactive game that challenges your knowledge of chapter key terms in the style of the television show *Wheel of Fortune*.

Crossword Puzzle Challenge

A crossword puzzle that challenges your knowledge of key terms presented in the chapter.

Apply Your Knowledge

Reinforce the skills and apply the concepts you learned in this chapter.

What's New in Windows Vista?

Instructions: Use Windows Help and Support to perform the following tasks.

Part 1: Launching Windows Help and Support

1. Click the Start button and then click Help and Support on the Start menu. If necessary, maximize the Windows Help and Support window.
2. Click the What's new? link in the Find an answer area in the Windows Help and Support window.

Part 2: Exploring Windows Vista Demos

1. In the Searching and organizing area, click the Demo: Working with files and folders link to display the Demo: Working with files and folders Web page (Figure 1–78), and then click the Watch the demo link. As you watch the demo, answer the questions below.

   a. The Start menu provides access to several folders. What are the three folders mentioned?

   _____

   b. How do you create a new folder?

   _____

   c. If you use a folder frequently, where should you put the folder?

   _____

Figure 1–78

2. Click the Back button below the Windows Help and Support title to return to the What's new in Windows Vista Ultimate heading.

Part 3:   What's New in Security?

1. In the Security area, click the Click to open Security Center link to open the Windows Security Center (Figure 1–79 on the next page). Answer the questions below.

   a.   What are the four security essentials shown in the Windows Security Center?

      _____

   b.   Close the Windows Security Center.

   c.   In the Security area, click the Demo: Security basics link and then click the Read the transcript link.

   d.   What is the quickest way to check your computer's security status and fix security problems?

      _____

   e.   What does a firewall do?

      _____

   f.   What does it mean when all the lights in the Security Center are green?

      _____

2. Click the Back button below the Windows Help and Support title to return to the What's new in Windows Vista Ultimate page.

Continued >

Apply Your Knowledge *continued*

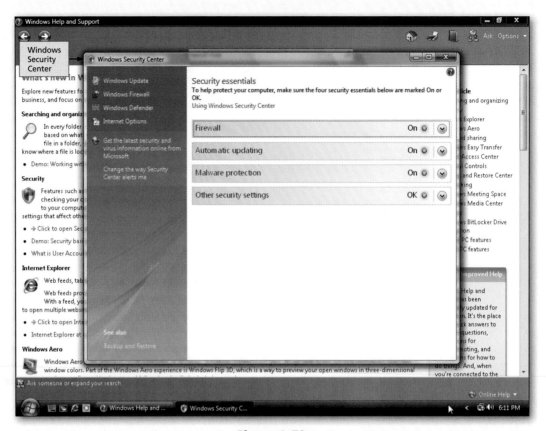

Figure 1–79

Part 4:   What's New in Parental Controls?

1. Scroll down to view the Parental Controls area.

   a.   In the Parental Controls area, click the What can I control with Parental Controls? link.

   b.   What can I do with Parental Controls?

        _____

        _____

   c.   After setting up Parental Controls, how can a parent keep a record of a child's computer activity?

        _____

2. Click the Back button below the Windows Help and Support title to view the topics in the Windows Help and Support window.

Part 5:   What's New in the Picture Area?

1. Scroll down the Windows Help and Support window to view the Pictures area.

   a.   In the Pictures area, click the Working with digital pictures link.

   b.   What are the two main ways to import pictures?

        _____

        _____

2. Click the Back button below the Windows Help and Support title to view the topics in the Windows Help and Support window.

Part 6: What's New in Mobile PC Features Area?

1. If necessary, scroll to view the Mobile PC features area, click the Using Windows Mobility Center link, and answer the following question.

   a. How do you open the Mobility Center?

   _____

   _____

2. Click the Close button in the Windows Help and Support window.

Extend Your Knowledge

Extend the skills you learned in this chapter and experiment with new skills. You may need to use Help to complete the assignment.

Using Windows Help and Support to Obtain Help

Instructions: Use Windows Help and Support to perform the following tasks.

1. Find Help about Windows keyboard shortcuts by typing keyboard shortcuts in the Search Help text box and then clicking the Search Help button (Figure 1–80). Click the first result listed.

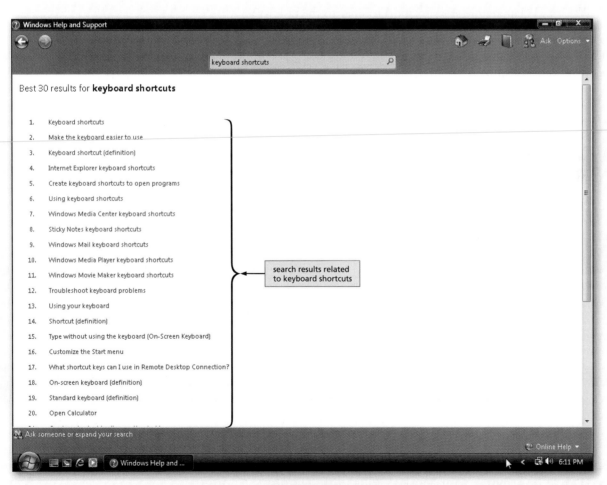

Figure 1–80

Continued >

Extend Your Knowledge *continued*

    a.   What general keyboard shortcut is used to display the Start menu?

    b.   What general keyboard shortcut is used to display the shortcut menu for an active window?

    c.   What general keyboard shortcut is used to view the properties for a selected item?

    d.   What dialog box keyboard shortcut is used to move backward through options?

    e.   What dialog box keyboard shortcut is used to display Help?

    f.   What Microsoft keyboard shortcut is used to display or hide the Start menu?

    g.   What Microsoft keyboard shortcut is used to open the Computer folder window?

2. Use the Help Table of Contents to answer the following questions.

    a.   How do you reduce computer screen flicker?

    b.   What dialog box do you use to change the appearance of the mouse pointer?

    c.   How do you minimize all windows?

    d.   What is a server?

3. Use the Search Help text box in Windows Help and Support to answer the following questions.

    a.   How can you reduce all open windows on the desktop to taskbar buttons?

    b.   How do you launch a program using the Run command?

    c.   What are the steps to add a toolbar to the taskbar?

    d.   What wizard do you use to remove unwanted desktop icons?

4. The tools to solve a problem while using Windows Vista are called **troubleshooters**. Use Windows Help and Support to find the list of troubleshooters, and answer the following questions.

    a.   What problems does the home networking troubleshooter allow you to resolve?

    b.   List five Windows Vista troubleshooters.

5. Use Windows Help and Support to obtain information about software licensing and product activation, and answer the following questions.

    a.   What is software piracy?

    b.   What are the five types of software piracy?

    c.   Why should I be concerned about software piracy?

    d.   What is a EULA (end user licensing agreement)?

    e.   Can you legally make a second copy of Windows Vista for use at home, work, or on a portable computer?

    f.   What is Windows Product Activation?

6. Close the Windows Help and Support window.

In the Lab

Use the guidelines, concepts and skills presented in this chapter to increase your knowledge of Windows Vista. Labs are listed in order of increasing difficulty.

Lab 1: Improving Your Mouse Skills with Windows Gadgets

Instructions: Perform the following steps to play a game using a gadget.

1. Click the Add Gadgets button on the Windows Sidebar. Double-click the Picture Puzzle to add it to the Sidebar. Close the Add Gadget window.

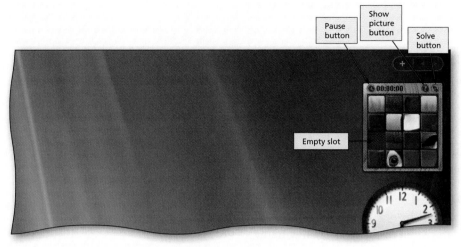

Figure 1–81

2. Click the Show picture button on the Picture Puzzle to see what the picture will look like once you solve the puzzle (Figure 1–81).

3. Play the Picture Puzzle game, by moving the puzzle tiles around by clicking on them when they are near the empty slot. Continue to rearrange the tiles until you have completed the picture (you can show the picture at any time to determine if you are close to the solution).

4. Click the Close button on the gadget to remove the gadget from the Sidebar.

In the Lab

Lab 2: Switching through Open Windows

Instructions: Perform the following steps to launch multiple programs using the Start menu and then use different methods to switch through the open windows.

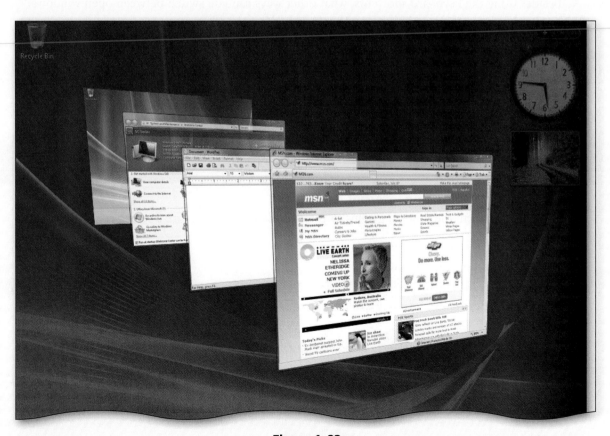

Figure 1–82

Continued >

In the Lab *continued*

Part 1: Launching the Welcome Center, WordPad, and Internet Explorer
1. Click the Start button, click the All Programs command, and then click the Internet Explorer command to launch Internet Explorer.
2. Click the Start button, click the All Programs command, click the Accessories folder, and then click the Welcome Center command to display the Welcome Center.
3. Click the Start button, click the All Programs command, click the Accessories folder, and then click WordPad to launch WordPad.

Part 2: Switching through the Windows
1. Press ALT+TAB to switch to the next open window.
2. Press WINDOWS+TAB to switch to the next open window.
3. Press CTRL+ALT+TAB to view the open applications. Press TAB. Click the WordPad window to switch to WordPad.
4. Press CTRL+WINDOWS+TAB to view the open applications. Press TAB. Click the Internet Explorer window to switch to Internet Explorer.

Part 3: Report your Findings
1. What is the difference between pressing ALT+TAB and pressing WINDOWS+TAB? _____
_____

2. What is the difference between pressing ALT+TAB and CTRL+ALT+TAB? _____
_____

3. What is your favorite method of switching between windows? _____
_____

4. Besides using the keyboard shortcuts, what other ways can you switch between open windows?

Part 4: Closing the open Windows
1. Close WordPad.
2. Close Internet Explorer.
3. Close the Welcome Center.

In the Lab

Lab 3: Launching and Using Internet Explorer

Instructions: Perform the following steps to Internet Explorer to explore a selection of Web sites.

Part 1: Launching the Internet Explorer Application
1. If necessary, connect to the Internet.
2. Click the Start button and then click Internet Explorer in the pinned items list on the Start menu. Maximize the Windows Internet Explorer window.

Part 2: Exploring Microsoft's Web Site
1. Click the URL in the Address bar to highlight the URL.
2. Type www.microsoft.com in the Address bar and then press the ENTER key.

3. Answer the following questions.

   a. What URL displays in the Address bar? _____

   _____

   b. What window title displays on the title bar? _____

   _____

4. If necessary, scroll the Web page to view the contents of the Web page. List five links shown on this Web page. _____

5. Click any link on the Web page. What link did you click? _____

   _____

6. Describe the Web page that displayed when you clicked the link? _____

   _____

7. If requested by your instructor, click the Print button to print the Web page.

Part 3: Exploring Disney's Web Site

1. Click the URL in the Address bar to highlight the URL.

2. Type `www.disney.com` in the Address bar and then press the ENTER key.

3. What title displays on the title bar? _____

   _____

4. Scroll the Web page to view the contents of the Web page. Do any graphic images display on the Web page? _____

5. Pointing to an image on a Web page and having the mouse pointer change to a hand indicates the image is a link. Does the Web page include an image that is a link? _____

   _____

   If so, describe the image. _____

   _____

6. Click the image to display another Web page. What window title displays on the title bar?

7. If requested by your instructor, click the Print button to print the Web page.

Part 4: Displaying Previously Displayed Web Pages

1. Click the Back button. What Web page displays? _____

2. Click the Back button twice. What Web page displays? _____

3. Click the Forward button. What Web page displays? _____

Part 5: Exploring the Shelly Cashman Series Web Site

1. Click the URL in the Address bar to highlight the URL.

2. Type `www.scsite.com` in the Address bar and then press the ENTER key.

3. Scroll the Web page to display the Operating Systems link, and then click the Operating Systems link.

4. Click the Microsoft Windows Vista link, and then click the title of your Windows Vista textbook.

5. Click any links that are of interest to you. Which link did you like the best? _____

   _____

6. Use the Back button or Forward button to display the Web site you like the best.

7. Click the Print button to print the Web page, if requested by your instructor.

8. Click the Close button on the Internet Explorer title bar to close Internet Explorer.

Cases and Places

Apply your creative thinking and problem solving skills to design and implement a solution.

● Easier   ●● More Difficult

● 1: Researching Technical Support

Technical support is an important consideration when installing and using an operating system or an application software program. The ability to obtain a valid answer to a question at the moment you have the question can be the difference between a frustrating incident and a positive experience. Using Windows Help and Support, the Internet, or another research facility, write a brief report on the options that are available for obtaining help and technical support while using Windows Vista.

● 2: Assessing Windows Vista Compatibility

The Windows Vista operating system can be installed only on computers found in the Windows Vista hardware compatibility list. Locate three older personal computers. Look for them in your school's computer lab, at a local business, or in your house. Use Windows Help and Support and the Internet to find the Microsoft Web page that contains the Windows Vista hardware compatibility list. Check each computer against the list and write a brief report summarizing your results.

●● 3: Researching Multiple Operating Systems

Using the Internet, a library, or other research facility, write a brief report on three personal computer operating systems that are popular today. Describe the systems, pointing out their similarities and differences. Discuss the advantages and disadvantages of each. Finally, tell which operating system you would purchase and explain why.

●● 4: Importing Your Pictures

Make it Personal

Using Windows Help and Support, and the keywords, Digital Pictures, find the Working with digital pictures article. In a brief report, summarize the steps to send a photo by e-mail and process your photos on the Web. Include a description of Windows Photo Gallery.

●● 5: Researching Operating Systems in Use

Working Together

Because of the many important tasks an operating system performs, most businesses put a great deal of thought into choosing an operating system. Each team member should interview a person at a local business about the operating system he or she uses with his or her computers. Based on the interview, write a brief report on why the businesses chose that operating system, how satisfied it is with it, and under what circumstances it might consider switching to a different operating system.

2 | Working on the Windows Vista Desktop

Objectives

You will have mastered the material in this chapter when you can:

- Create and save a document in the Documents folder

- Create, name, and save a text document directly in the Documents folder

- Change the view and arrange objects in groups in the Documents folder

- Create and name a folder in the Documents folder

- Move documents into a folder

- Add and remove a shortcut on the Start menu

- Open a document using a shortcut on the Start menu

- Create a shortcut on the desktop

- Open a folder using a desktop shortcut

- Open, modify, and print multiple documents in a folder

- Store files on a USB drive

- Delete multiple files and folders

- Work with the Recycle Bin

- Work with gadgets

- Close and show the Sidebar

2 | Working on the Windows Vista Desktop

Introduction

In Chapter 2, you will be learning about the Windows Vista desktop. With thousands of hardware devices and software products available for desktop and notebook computers, users need to manage these resources quickly and easily. One of Windows Vista's impressive features is the ease with which users can create and access documents and files on the desktop. You will organize the lives of two computer users by developing and updating their daily reminder lists. You will create folders, use shortcuts, open and modify multiple documents, and work with gadgets and the Windows Sidebar.

Mastering the desktop will help you to take advantage of user interface enhancements and innovations that make computing faster, easier, and more reliable, and that offer seamless integration with the Internet. Working on the Windows Vista desktop in this chapter, you will find out for yourself how these features can save time, reduce computer clutter, and ultimately help you work more efficiently.

Overview

As you read this chapter, you will learn how to work with Windows Vista to create the documents shown in Figure 2–1 and how to use the Windows Sidebar by performing these general tasks:

- Creating and editing a WordPad document
- Moving and renaming a file
- Creating and moving a folder
- Storing and retrieving documents from a USB drive
- Deleting and restoring shortcuts, files and folders using the Recycle Bin
- Customizing and rearranging gadgets
- Hiding and showing the Sidebar

Plan Ahead

Working on the Windows Vista Desktop
Working with the Windows Vista desktop requires a basic knowledge of how to use the desktop, insert a USB drive, access the Internet, and use a printer.

1. **Determine the permissions you have on the computer you will be using.** Each user account can have different rights and permissions. Depending on which rights and permissions have been set for your account, you may or may not be able to perform certain operations.

2. **Identify how to add a USB drive to your computer.** Depending on the setup of the computer you are using, there may be several ways to add a USB drive to your computer. You should know which USB ports you can use to add a USB drive to your computer.

3. **Determine how to access the Internet.** Many gadgets can be found online, free-of-charge. You will want to know if your computer has Internet access and how to access it

4. **Ascertain how to access a printer.** In order to print, you must know which printer you can use and where it is located.

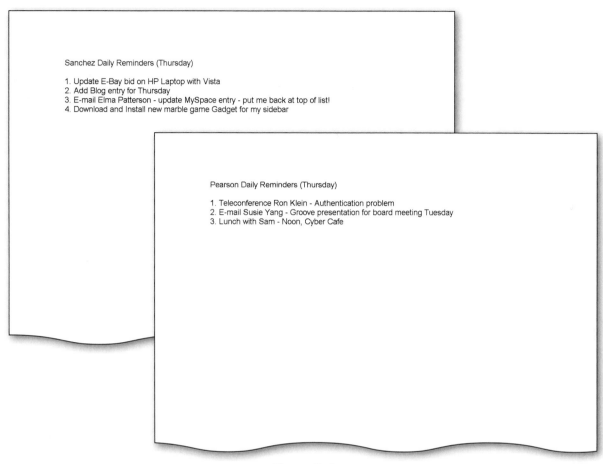

Sanchez Daily Reminders (Thursday)

1. Update E-Bay bid on HP Laptop with Vista
2. Add Blog entry for Thursday
3. E-mail Elma Patterson - update MySpace entry - put me back at top of list!
4. Download and Install new marble game Gadget for my sidebar

Pearson Daily Reminders (Thursday)

1. Teleconference Ron Klein - Authentication problem
2. E-mail Susie Yang - Groove presentation for board meeting Tuesday
3. Lunch with Sam - Noon, Cyber Cafe

Figure 2–1

Creating a Document in WordPad

As introduced in Chapter 1, a **program** is a set of computer instructions that carries out a task on the computer. An **application program** is a program that accomplishes specific tasks such as creating documents, browsing the web, or working with e-mail. For example, you create written documents with a **word processing program**, spreadsheets and charts with a **spreadsheet program**, and graphics presentations with a **presentation graphics program**. All of these applications display on your computer as you use them.

To help learn how to work with the Windows Vista desktop, you will create two daily reminders lists, one for Mr. Sanchez and one for Ms. Pearson. Because they will be reviewing their lists throughout the day, you will need to update the lists with new reminders as necessary. You decide to use **WordPad**, a popular word processing program available with Windows Vista, to create the daily reminders lists. The finished documents are shown in Figure 2–1.

You will first create the daily reminders document for Mr. Sanchez using WordPad, by launching the WordPad application program, typing the reminders, and then saving the document in the Documents folder. The **Documents folder** is created by Windows Vista as a central location for storing and managing documents and folders. In Windows terminology, this method of opening an application program and then creating a document is known as the **application-centric approach**.

To Launch a Program and Create a Document

The following steps launch WordPad and create a daily reminders document for Mr. Sanchez.

1

- Display the Start menu.

- Type wordpad in the Start Search box to prompt Windows Vista to search for the WordPad application.

- Press the ENTER key to launch the WordPad application and display the Document - WordPad window (Figure 2–2).

Q&A

Do I have to type the entire word before I press the ENTER key?

No. As soon as you see the result you are looking for at the top of the list in the Programs area above the Start Search box, you can press the ENTER key.

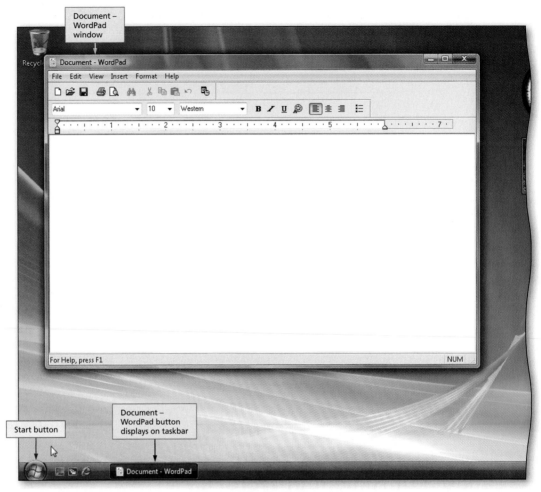

Figure 2–2

2

- **Type** Sanchez Daily Reminders (Thursday) **and then press the ENTER key two times.**

- **Type** 1. Update E-Bay bid on HP Laptop with Vista **and then press the ENTER key.**

- **Type** 2. Add Blog entry for Thursday **and then press the ENTER key.**

- **Type** 3. E-mail Elma Patterson - update MySpace entry - put me back at top of list! **and then press the ENTER key.**

- **Type** 4. Download and Install new marble game Gadget for my Sidebar **and then press the ENTER key (Figure 2–3).**

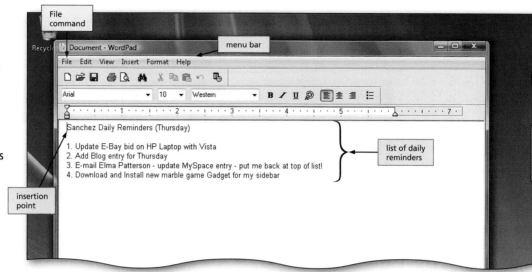

Figure 2–3

Other Ways

1. Open Start menu, type wordpad in the Start Search box, click WordPad

2. Open Start menu, click All Programs, click Accessories list, click WordPad

Saving Documents

When you create a document using a program such as WordPad, the document is stored in the main memory (RAM) of the computer. If you close the program without saving the document or if the computer accidentally loses electrical power, the document will be lost. To protect against the accidental loss of a document and to allow you to modify the document easily in the future, you should save your document. While you can save a file on the desktop, it is recommended that you save the document in a different location to keep the desktop free from clutter. For example, you can save files to the Documents folder or to a USB drive. A document saved to the Documents folder will be easier to find when searching.

When you save a document, you are creating a file. A **file** refers to a group of meaningful data that is identified by a name. For example, a WordPad document is a file; an Excel spreadsheet is a file; a picture made using Paint is a file; and a saved e-mail message is a file. When you create a file, you must assign a file name to the file. All files are identified by a **file name**. A file name should be descriptive of the saved file. Examples of file names are Sanchez Daily Reminders (Thursday), Office Supplies List, and Automobile Maintenance.

In order to associate a file with an application, Windows Vista assigns an extension to the file name of each document, which consists of a period followed by three, four, or five characters. Most documents created using the WordPad program are saved as rich text format documents with the .rtf extension, but they also can be saved as plain text with the .txt extension. A rich text format document allows for formatting of the text and insertion of graphics, which is not supported in plain text files.

Many computer users can tell at least one horror story of working on their computers for a long period of time and then losing all of their work because of a power failure or software problem. Consider this a warning: save often to protect your work.

BTW

File Names
A file name can contain up to 255 characters, including spaces. Any uppercase or lowercase character is valid when creating a file name, except a backslash (\), slash (/), colon (:), asterisk (*), question mark (?), quotation mark ("), less than symbol (<), greater than symbol (>), or vertical bar (|) as these symbols have special meaning for the operating system. Similarly, file names cannot be CON, AUX, COM1, COM2, COM3, COM4, LPT1, LPT2, LPT3, PRN, or NUL.

To Save a Document to the Documents Folder

The following steps save the document you created using WordPad to the Documents folder using the file name, Sanchez Reminders (Thursday).

- Click the File command on the menu bar to display the File menu (Figure 2–4).

Q&A

Why is there an ellipsis (…) following the Save As command?

The ellipsis (…) indicates that Windows Vista requires more information to carry out the command and will open a dialog box when you click the Save As command.

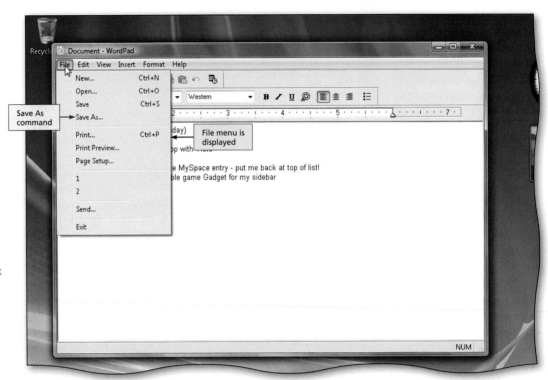

Figure 2–4

- Click the Save As command to display the Save As dialog box (Figure 2–5).

- Type Sanchez Daily Reminders (Thursday) in the File name text box.

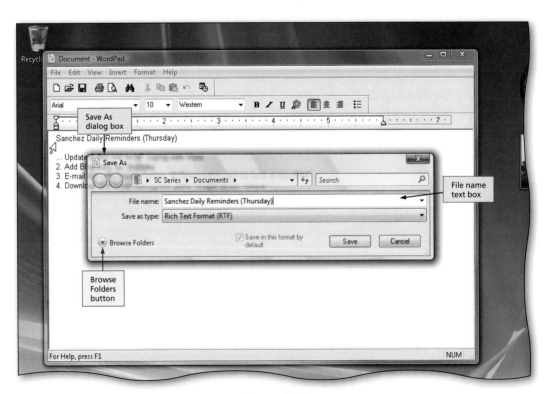

Figure 2–5

3
- Click the Browse Folders button to expand the folders list (Figure 2–6).

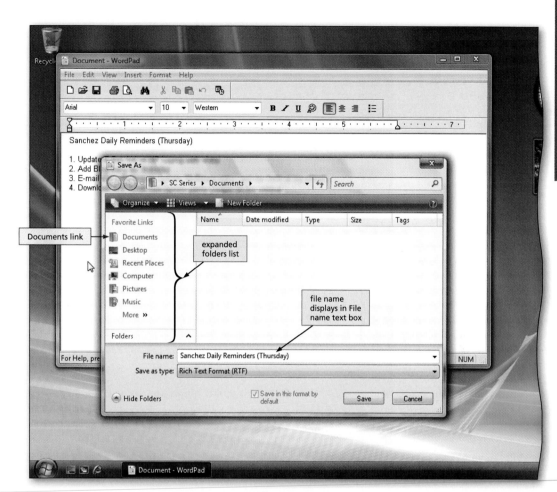

Figure 2–6

4
- Click the Documents link to select the Documents folder (Figure 2–7).

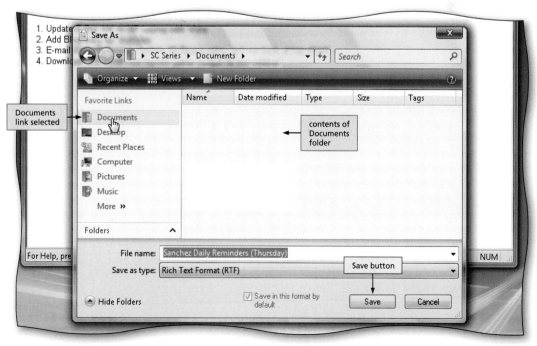

Figure 2–7

• Click the Save button to save the document and close the Save As dialog box (Figure 2–8).

Q&A

Why did the title bar of WordPad change?

Now that you have saved the document with a file name, the file name will display on the title bar and on the button on the taskbar. The file name on the button in the taskbar button area contains an ellipsis (…) to indicate the entire file name does not fit on the button. To display the entire button name along with a live preview, point to the button.

Will I have to use Save As every time to save?

Now that you have saved the document, you can use the Save command to save changes to the document without having to type a new name or select a new storage location. If you want to save the file with a different name or to a different location, you would use the Save As command. By changing the location using the Address bar, you can save a file on the hard disk of the computer or a USB drive.

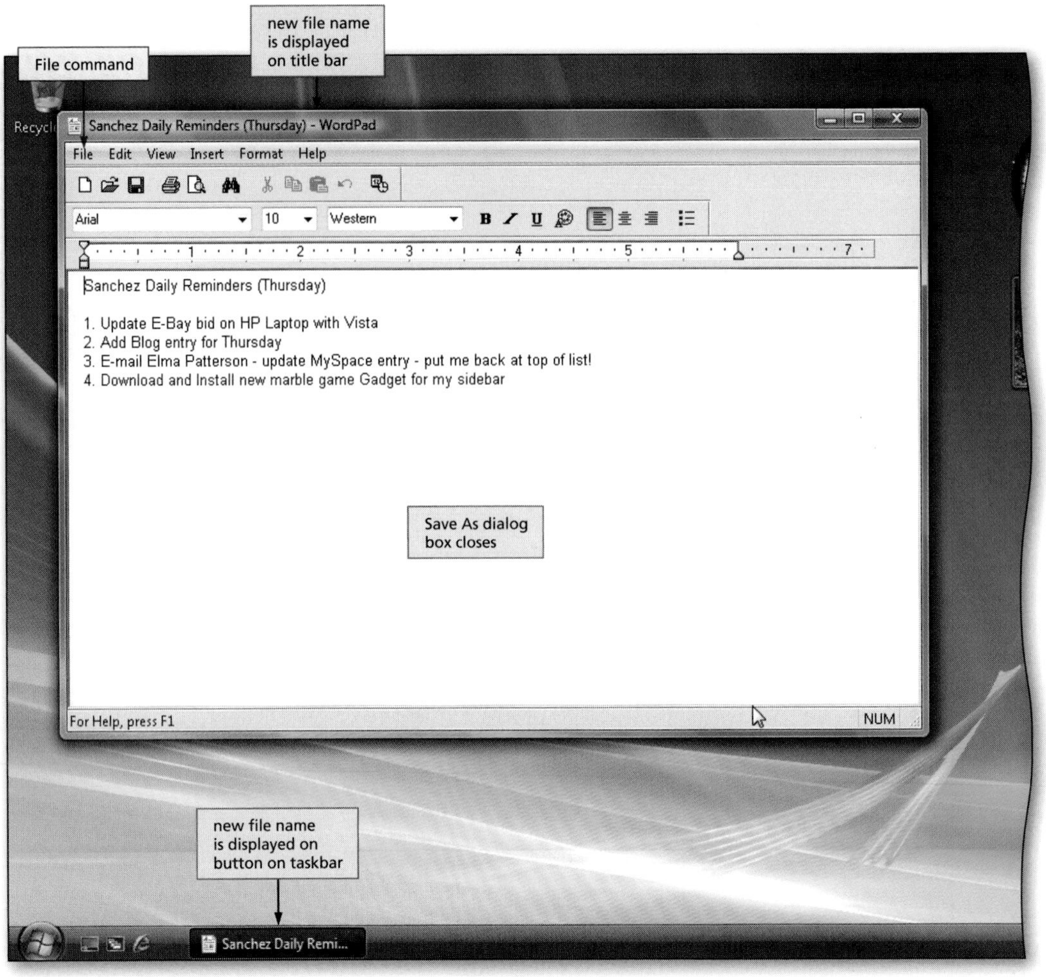

File command

new file name is displayed on title bar

Sanchez Daily Reminders (Thursday) - WordPad

File   Edit   View   Insert   Format   Help

Arial   10   Western   **B** *I* <u>U</u>

Sanchez Daily Reminders (Thursday)

1. Update E-Bay bid on HP Laptop with Vista
2. Add Blog entry for Thursday
3. E-mail Elma Patterson - update MySpace entry - put me back at top of list!
4. Download and Install new marble game Gadget for my sidebar

Save As dialog box closes

For Help, press F1   NUM

new file name is displayed on button on taskbar

Sanchez Daily Remi...

Figure 2–8

To Open the Print Dialog Box from an Application Program

Paper printouts are and will remain an important form of output for electronic documents. However, many sophisticated application programs are expanding their printing capabilities to include sending e-mail and posting documents to Web pages of the World Wide Web. One method of printing a document is to print it directly from an application program. The following steps open the Print dialog box in WordPad.

1

• Click the File command on the menu bar to display the File menu.

2

• Click the Print command to display the Print dialog box (Figure 2–9).

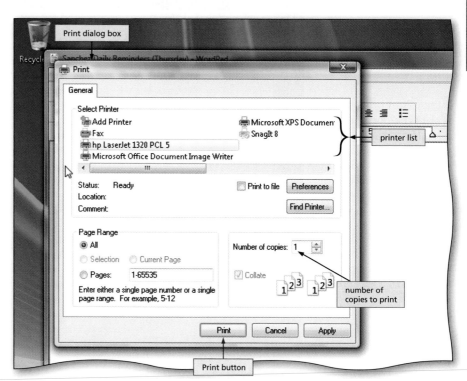

Figure 2–9

The highlighted printer icon in the Select Printer area indicates that, in this case, the hp LaserJet printer is ready to print the document. Windows Vista automatically installs additional print options: an Add Printer option, a fax option, and a Microsoft XPS Document Writer option. Add Printer instructs Windows Vista to locate and identify any printers attached to the computer. Fax can be used to select a Fax device for printing or for sending a fax. The Microsoft XPS Document Writer printer allows you to create XPS documents. XPS documents look the same in print as they do on the screen and can be shared electronically with anyone who has an XPS viewer. They can be identified by the .xps extension. If you have other printers installed (such as the SnagIt 8 in Figure 2–9), you will be able to see them in the list. The highlighted printer is the selected destination for your printouts.

BTW

Printing Options
The Page Range area contains four option buttons. The option buttons give you the choice of printing all pages of a document (All), selected parts of a document (Selection), current page (Current Page), or selected pages of a document (Pages). The selected All option button indicates all pages of a document will print.

To Print a Document

The following step prints the Sanchez Daily Reminders (Thursday) document.

- Ready the printer according to the printer's instructions.

- If necessary, click the appropriate printer to select your printer.

- Click Print button to print the document (Figure 2–10).

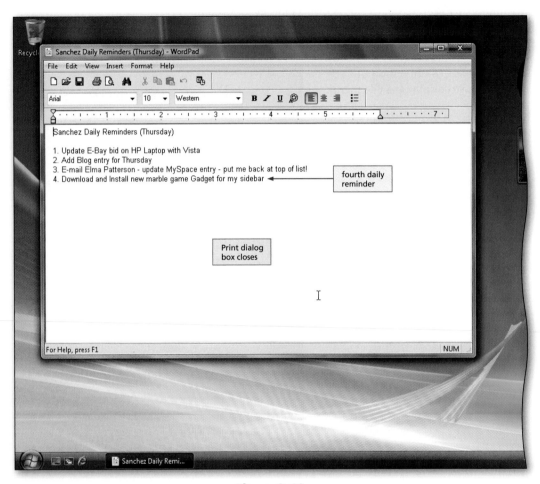

Figure 2–10

To Edit a Document

Undoubtedly, you will want to make changes to a document after you have created it and saved it. For any document, your edits can be as simple as correcting a spelling mistake or as complex as rewriting the entire document. The following step edits the Sanchez Daily Reminders (Thursday) document by adding a new reminder.

1

- Click directly after the fourth daily reminder and then press the ENTER key.

- Type 5. Register for next semester's classes and then press the ENTER key (Figure 2–11).

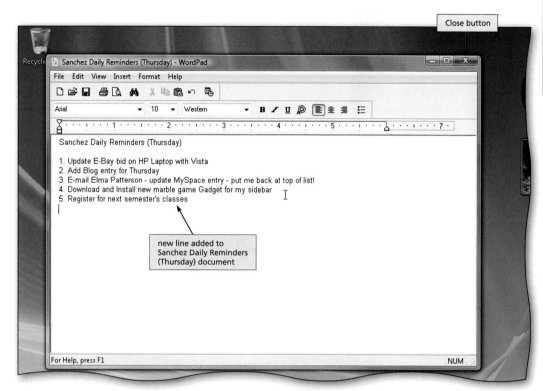

Figure 2–11

To Close and Save a Document

If you forget to save a document after you have edited it, a dialog box will display asking if you want to save your changes. This is how WordPad helps protect you from losing your work. If you choose to not save your changes, then all edits you made since the last time you saved will be lost. If you select cancel, your changes are not saved, but the document remains open and you can continue working. The following steps on the next page close and save the Sanchez Daily Reminders (Thursday) document.

- Click the Close
button on the title
bar to display the
WordPad dialog box
(Figure 2–12).

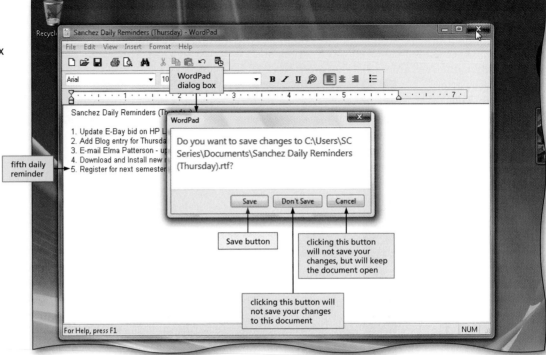

Figure 2–12

- Click the Save
button in the
WordPad dialog box
to save your changes
to the document
and close WordPad
(Figure 2–13).

Other Ways

1. On title bar double-click
   WordPad icon, click the
   Save button
2. On title bar click
   WordPad icon, click
   Close, click the Save
   button
3. On File menu click Exit,
   click the Save button
4. Press ALT+F, press X;
   or press ALT+F4, press
   ENTER

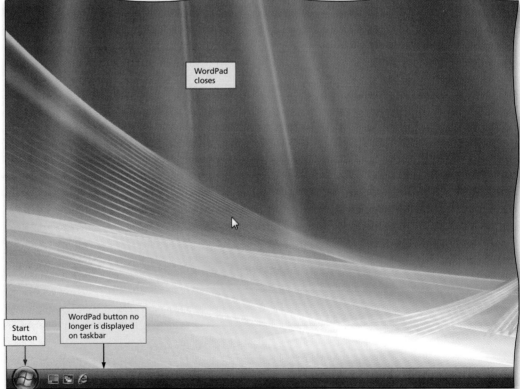

Figure 2–13

Creating a Document in the Documents Folder

After completing the reminders list for Mr. Sanchez, the next step is to create a similar list for Ms. Pearson. Opening an application program and then creating a document (application-centric approach) was the method used to create the first document. Although the same method could be used to create the document for Ms. Pearson, another method is to create the new document in the Documents folder without first starting an application program. Instead of launching a program to create and modify a document, you first create a blank document directly in the Documents folder and then use the WordPad program to enter data into the document. This method, called the **document-centric approach**, will be used to create the document that contains the reminders for Ms. Pearson.

To Open the Documents Folder

The following step opens the Documents folder.

1

- Display the Start menu.

- Click the Documents command to display the Documents folder window (Figure 2–14).

Figure 2–14

To Create a Blank Document in the Documents Folder

The phrase, creating a document in the Documents folder, may be confusing. The document you actually create contains no data; it is blank. You can think of it as placing a blank piece of paper with a name inside the Documents folder. The document has little value until you add text or other data to it. The following steps create a blank document in the Documents folder to contain the daily reminders for Ms. Pearson.

- Right-click an open area of the Documents folder to display the shortcut menu.

- Point to the New command on the shortcut menu to display the New submenu (Figure 2–15).

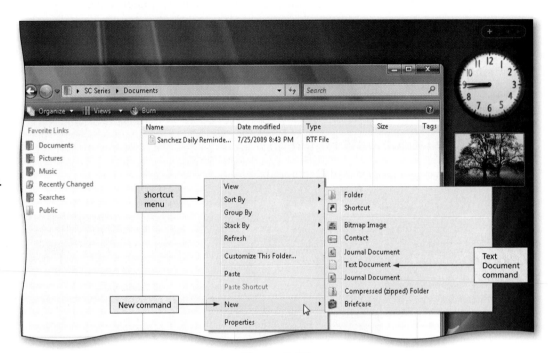

Figure 2–15

- Click the Text Document command to display an icon for a new text document in the Documents folder window (Figure 2–16).

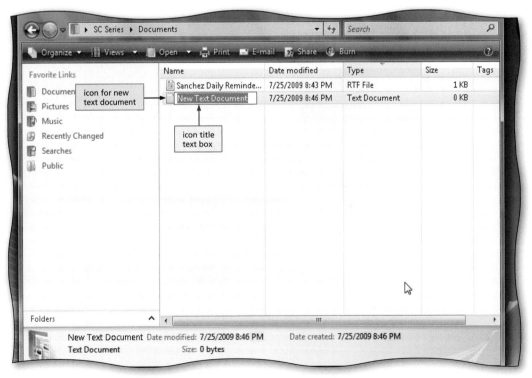

Figure 2–16

To Name a Document in the Documents Folder

After you create a blank document, you need to name the document so it is easily identifiable. In Figure 2–16, the default file name (New Text Document) is highlighted and the insertion point is blinking, indicating that you can enter a new file name. Until you name the document, the blank document will appear at the bottom of the list in the Documents folder. The following step assigns the file name, Pearson Daily Reminders (Thursday), to the blank document you just created.

- Type Pearson Daily Reminders (Thursday) in the icon title text box, and then press the ENTER key to assign a name to the new file and alphabetically sort the file in the Documents folder (Figure 2–17).

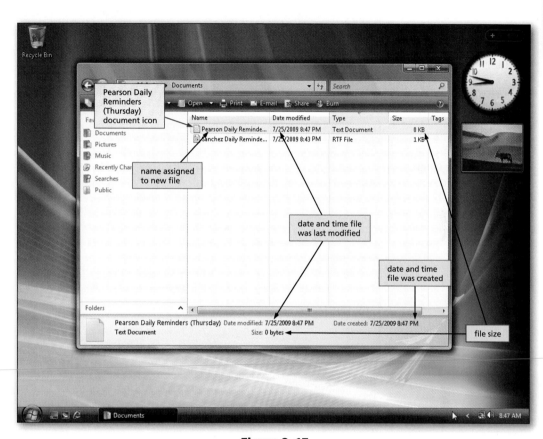

Figure 2–17

Other Ways

1. Right-click icon, on shortcut menu click Rename, type Pearson Daily Reminders (Thursday), press ENTER

2. Click icon to select icon, press F2, type Pearson Daily Reminders (Thursday), press ENTER

To Open a Document with WordPad

Although you have created the Pearson Daily Reminders (Thursday) document, the document contains no data. To enter data into the blank document, you must open the document. Because text files open with Notepad by default, you need to use the shortcut menu to open the file using WordPad. The following steps open a document with WordPad.

1

- Right-click the Pearson Daily Reminders (Thursday) document icon to display the shortcut menu.

- Point to the Open With command on the shortcut menu to display the Open With submenu (Figure 2–18).

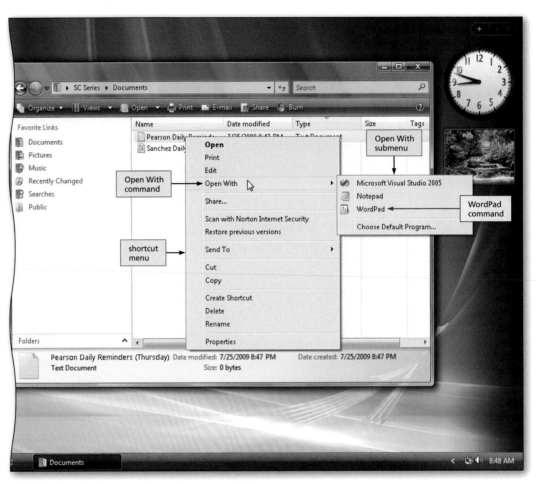

Figure 2–18

2

- Click the WordPad command on the Open With submenu to open the Pearson Daily Reminders (Thursday) document in WordPad (Figure 2–19).

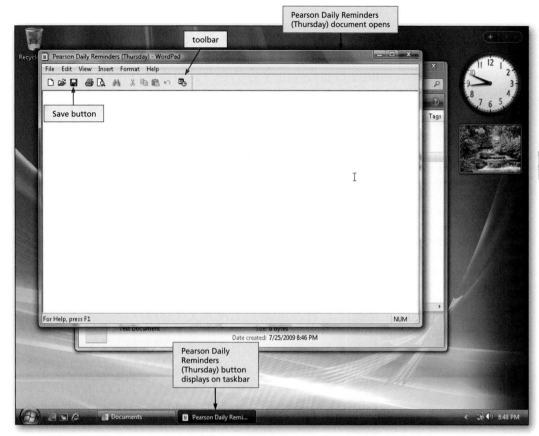

Figure 2–19

To Enter Data into a Blank Document

After the document is open, you can enter the required data by typing the text (the daily reminders) in the document. The following step enters the text in the Pearson Daily Reminders (Thursday) document.

1

- Type Pearson Daily Reminders (Thursday) and then press the ENTER key twice.

- Type 1. Teleconference Ron Klein – Authentication Problem and then press the ENTER key.

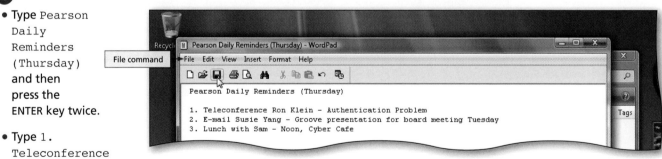

Figure 2–20

- Type 2. E-mail Susie Yang – Groove presentation for board meeting Tuesday and then press the ENTER key.

- Type 3. Lunch with Sam – Noon, Cyber Cafe and then press the ENTER key (Figure 2–20).

- Click the Save button on the toolbar to save the file.

To Save a Text Document in Rich Text Format (RTF)

Entering text into the Pearson Daily Reminders (Thursday) document modifies the document, which results in the need to save it. If you make many changes to a document, you should save the document as you work. When you created the blank text document Windows Vista assigned it the .txt extension, so you will need to use Save As to save it in Rich Text Format, which is WordPad's default format. Using the Rich Text Format will allow you to use all of WordPad's features, including formatting options. The following steps save the document in Rich Text Format.

- Click the File command on the menu bar to display the File menu.

- Click the Save As command to open the Save As dialog box.

- Click the Save as type list box arrow to display the Save as type list (Figure 2–21).

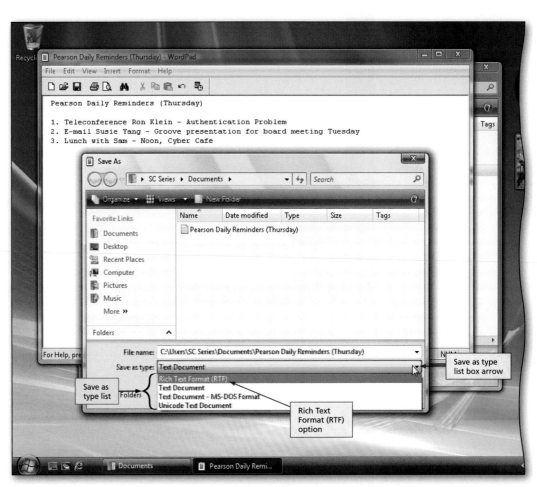

Figure 2–21

2

- Click the Rich Text Format (RTF) option to change the file type to .rtf.

- Type Pearson Daily Reminders (Thursday).rtf in the File name text box to change the file name (Figure 2–22).

- Click the Save button to save the document in Rich Text Format.

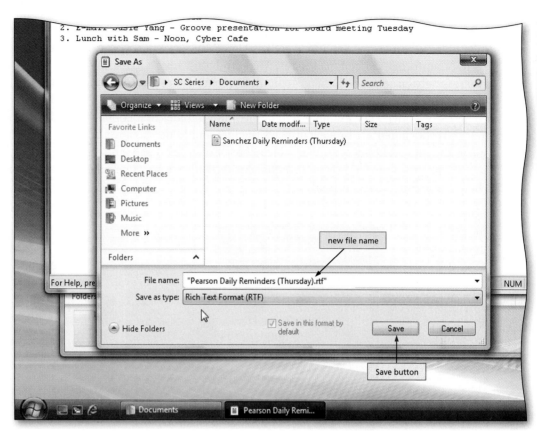

Figure 2–22

To Close the Document

You have saved your changes to Pearson Daily Reminders (Thursday), and now you can close the document.

 Click Exit on the File menu, to close the Document and exit WordPad.

Working with the Documents Folder

Once you create documents in the Documents folder, using either the application-centric or document-centric approach, you can continue to modify and save the documents, print the documents, or create a folder to contain the documents and move the documents to the folder. Having a single storage location for documents makes it easy to create a copy of the documents so that they are not accidentally lost or damaged.

BTW

The Documents Folder
Windows Vista creates a unique Documents folder for each computer user. When you have multiple users on a single computer, having a unique central storage area for each user makes it easier to back up important files and folders.

To Change the View to Small Icons

The default view in the Documents folder (shown in Figure 2–23) is the Details view. The Details view shows a list of file folders plus common columns such as Date Modified and Type. You can use the Views button to change your view to other formats. The Small Icons, Medium Icons, Large Icons, and Extra Large Icons formats display the icons in increasingly larger sizes. When Medium, Large, or Extra Large Icon formats are selected, Windows Vista provides a Live Preview option. With Live Preview, the icons display images that more closely reflect the actual contents of the files or folders. For example, a folder icon for a folder that contains text documents would show sample pages from those documents. List view displays the files and folders as a list of names without any extra details. Tiles view displays the files and folders as tiles, which consist of an icon and icon description. With all of these views, the default arrangement for the icons is to be alphabetical by file name. The following steps change the view from the Details view to the Small Icons format.

- Click the More options arrow button next to the Views button on the toolbar of the Documents folder window to display the Views menu (Figure 2–23).

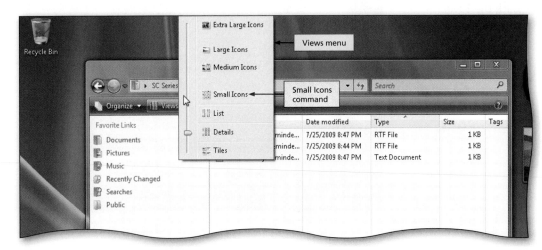

Figure 2–23

- Click the Small Icons command to display the files and folders as Small Icons (Figure 2–24).

Experiment

- Select each of the options from the Views menu to see the various ways that Windows can display folder contents. After you have finished, be sure to select the Small Icons command from the Views menu.

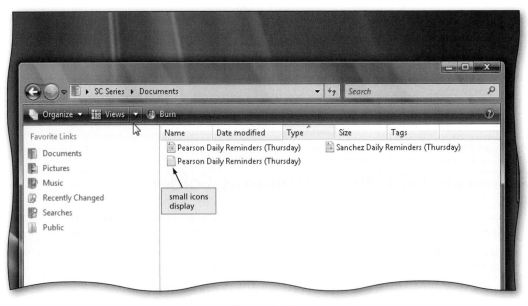

Figure 2–24

Other Ways

1. Right-click open space in the Documents folder, point to View, click Small Icons

To Arrange the Items in a Folder in Groups by Type

There are other methods of arranging the icons in the Documents folder. One practical arrangement is to display the icons in groups based upon file type. This arrangement places files of the same type (File Folder, Text Documents, Microsoft Word, Microsoft Excel, and so on) in separate groups. When a window contains many files and folders, this layout makes it faster and easier to find a particular file or folder. The following steps group the icons in the Documents folder by file type.

- Right-click the open space below the list of files and folders in the Documents folder to display the shortcut menu.

- Point to the Group By command to display the Group By submenu (Figure 2–25).

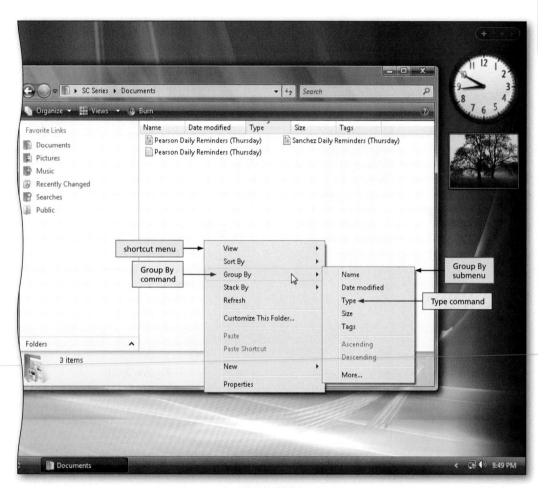

Figure 2–25

2

- Click the Type command to display the files and folders grouped by type (Figure 2–26).

Q&A

Can I group the files and folders in other ways?

You can group the files by any of the options on the Group By submenu. This includes Name, Date modified, Size, and Tags. To remove the groupings, select (None) on the Group By submenu.

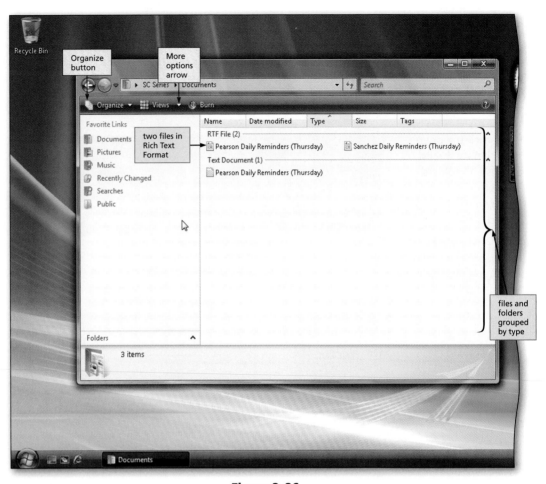

Figure 2–26

Other Ways

1. Press ALT + V, press P, press T, press ENTER

To Change to Medium Icons Format

Because Small Icons format is not the best view when creating folders, you will change the view to Medium Icons.

1 Click the More options arrow button next to the Views button on the toolbar and then click the Medium Icons command to change to Medium Icons format.

To Create and Name a Folder in the Documents Folder

Windows Vista allows you to place one or more documents into a folder in much the same manner as you might take a document written on a piece of paper and place it in a file folder. You want to keep the Sanchez and Pearson documents together so you can find and reference them easily from among other text documents stored in the Documents folder. In order to keep multiple documents together in one place, you first must create a folder in which to store them. The following steps create and name a folder titled Daily Reminders in the Documents folder to store the Sanchez Daily Reminders (Thursday) and Pearson Daily Reminders (Thursday) documents.

1

• Click the Organize button on the Documents folder toolbar to display the Organize menu (Figure 2–27).

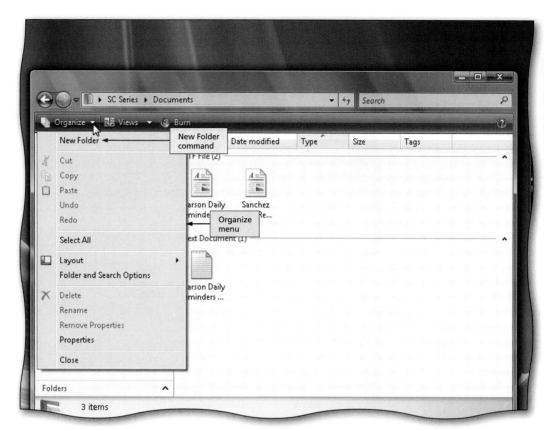

Figure 2–27

2

• Click the New Folder command on the Organize menu to create a new folder (Figure 2–28).

Figure 2–28

3

• Type Daily
Reminders in the
icon title text box
and then press the
ENTER key to name
the folder and sort
the folder in the
Documents folder
(Figure 2–29).

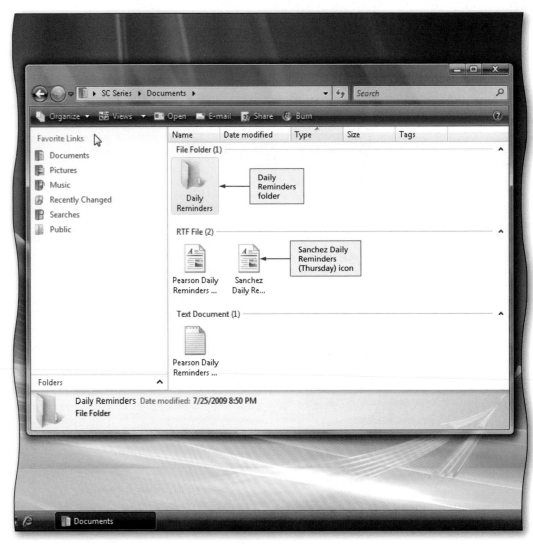

Figure 2–29

To Move a Document into a Folder

The ability to organize documents and files within folders allows you to keep the Documents folder organized when using Windows Vista. After you create a folder in the Documents folder, the next step is to move documents into the folder. The following steps move the Pearson Daily Reminders (Thursday) and the Sanchez Daily Reminders (Thursday) documents into the Daily Reminders folder.

1

- Right-click and drag (also known as right-drag) the Sanchez Daily Reminders (Thursday) icon onto the Daily Reminders folder icon to display the shortcut menu (Figure 2–30).

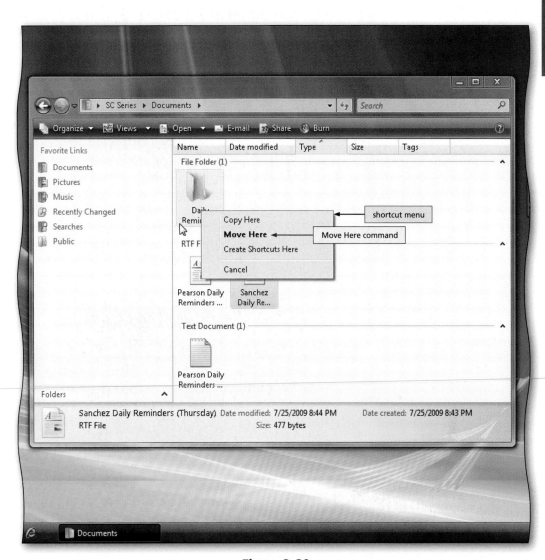

Figure 2–30

2

• Click the Move Here command on the shortcut menu to move the Sanchez Daily Reminders (Thursday) file to the Daily Reminders folder (Figure 2–31).

Q&A What are the other options in the shortcut menu?

When you right-drag, a short-cut menu opens and lists the available options. In this case, the options are Copy Here, Move Here, Create Shortcuts Here, and Cancel. Selecting Copy Here would create a copy of the Sanchez document in the Daily Reminders Folder, Create Shortcuts here would put a link to the Sanchez document (not the file or a copy of the file) in the Daily Reminders Folder and Cancel would end the right-drag process. The options in the shortcut menu may change, depending on the type of file and where you are dragging it.

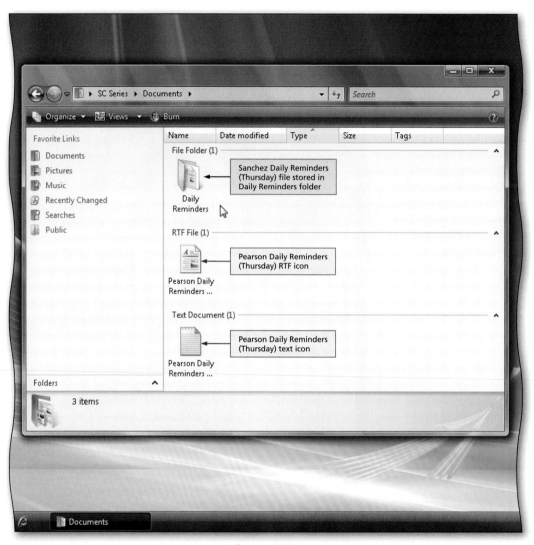

Figure 2–31

3

• Right-drag the Pearson Daily Reminders (Thursday) RTF icon onto the Daily Reminders icon to move it to the Daily Reminders Folder.

• Right-drag the Pearson Daily Reminders (Thursday) text icon onto the Daily Reminders icon to move it to the Daily Reminders Folder (Figure 2–32).

Q&A What happened to the Rich Text Format and Text Document groups?

Because the documents have been moved to Daily Reminders, the groups were no longer needed. Only if there were other RTF and text documents in the Documents folder would the groupings remain.

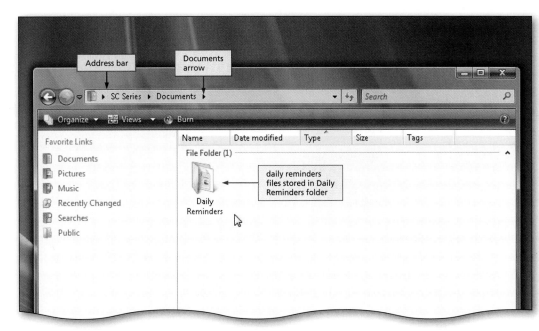

Figure 2–32

Other Ways	
1. Drag document icon onto folder icon	2. Right-click document icon, click Cut, right-click folder icon, click Paste

To Change Location Using the Address Bar

If you would like to navigate to the folder to see if your files are there, there are several ways to do this. The easiest way in Windows Vista is to use the Address bar. The **Address bar** appears at the top of the Documents folder window and displays your current location as a series of links separated by arrows. By clicking on the arrows, you change your location. The Forward and Back buttons can be used to navigate through the locations you have visited just like the forward and back buttons in a Web browser. The following steps change your location to the Daily Reminders folder.

• Click the Documents arrow on the Address bar to display a location menu that contains a list of folders in the Documents folder (Figure 2–33).

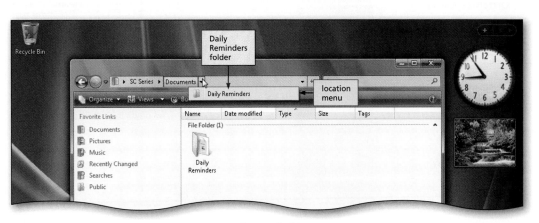

Figure 2–33

- Click the Daily Reminders folder on the location menu to move to the Daily Reminders folder (Figure 2–34).

Q&A Why did the view change to Details view?

When you changed to the Medium Icons view, the change only affected the Documents folder itself, not any subfolders. Once you opened the Daily Reminders folder, the view reverted to Details view, which is the default view for folders in the Documents folder.

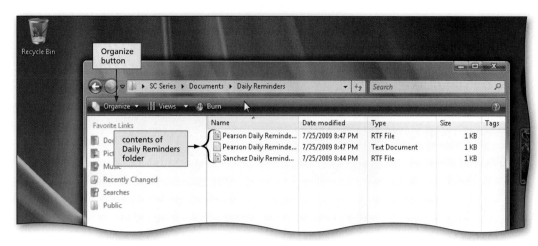

Figure 2–34

To Display and Use the Preview Pane

Now that you are in the Daily Reminders folder, you can add a Preview Pane to the layout, which will provide you with an even better Live Preview of your documents. When you select a document, the **Preview Pane** displays a live view of the document to the right of the list of files in the folder window. The following steps add the Preview Pane to the layout of the Daily Reminders folder and then show a Live Preview of the Sanchez document.

- Click the Organize button on the toolbar to display the Organize menu.

- Point to the Layout command on the Organize menu to display the Layout submenu (Figure 2–35).

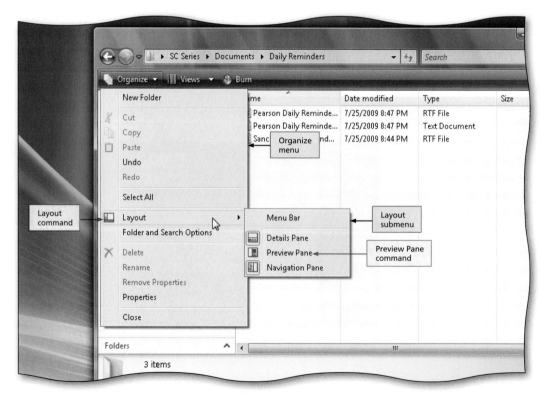

Figure 2–35

2

- Click the Preview Pane command to display the Preview Pane (Figure 2–36).

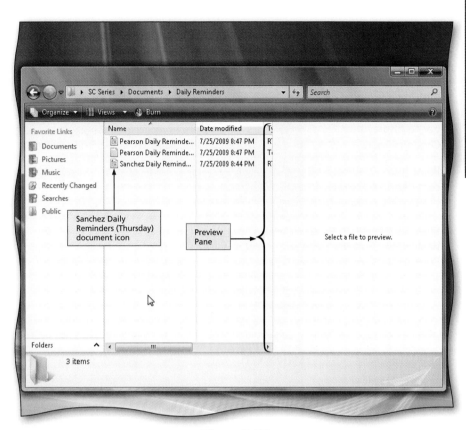

Figure 2–36

3

- Click Sanchez Daily Reminders (Thursday) document icon to display a preview of the document in the Preview Pane (Figure 2–37).

 Why did the menu bar change?

Depending upon what items are selected in the folder window, the menu bar options will change to reflect the options available to you.

Experiment

- Select different documents to see their preview in the Preview Pane.

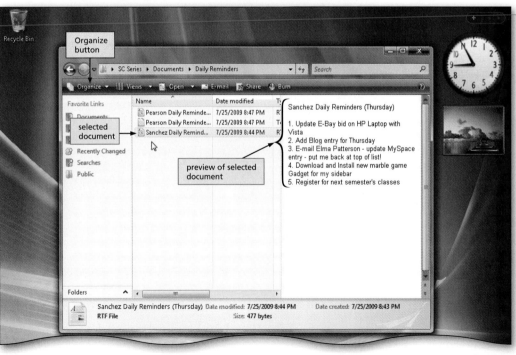

Figure 2–37

To Close the Preview Pane

After verifying that your files are in the Daily Reminders folder, you can close the Preview Pane and then use the Address bar to return to the Documents folder. The following step closes the Preview Pane.

1

- Click the Organize button on the toolbar to display the Organize menu.

- Point to the Layout command to display the Layout submenu.

- Click Preview Pane to close the Preview Pane (Figure 2–38).

Figure 2–38

To Change Location Using the Back Button on the Address Bar

Besides clicking the arrows in the Address bar, you also can change locations by using the Back and Forward buttons. Using the Back button will allow you to return to a location that you have already visited. The following step changes your location to the Documents folder.

- Click the Back button on the Address bar to return to the Documents folder (Figure 2–39).

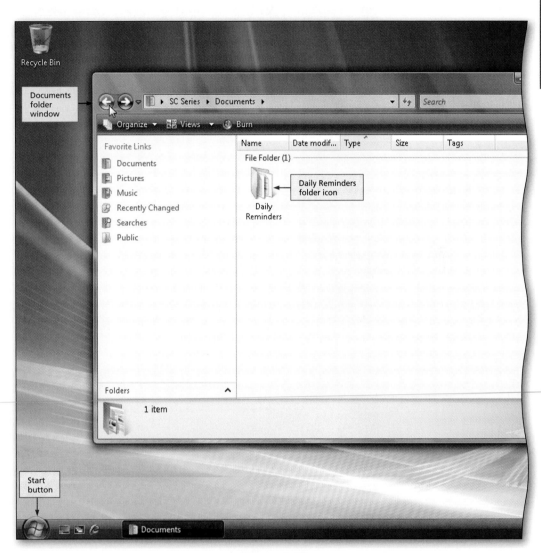

Figure 2–39

Creating Folder Shortcuts

One way to customize Windows Vista is to use shortcuts to launch application programs and open files or folders. A **shortcut** is a link to any object on the computer or on a network, such as a program, file, folder, Web page, printer, or another computer. Placing a shortcut to a folder on the Start menu or on the desktop can make it easier to locate and open the folder.

A shortcut icon is not the actual document or application. You do not actually place the folder on the menu; instead you place a shortcut icon that links to the folder on the menu. When you delete a shortcut, you delete the shortcut icon but do not delete the actual document or application. They remain on the hard disk.

To Add a Shortcut on the Start Menu

The following steps place the Daily Reminders folder shortcut on the Start menu.

1

- Drag the Daily Reminders folder icon onto the Start button to begin to add the icon to the Start menu. Do not release the left mouse button (Figure 2–40).

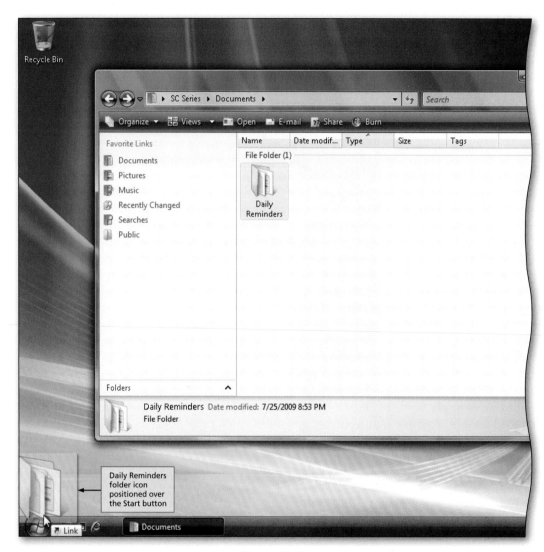

Figure 2–40

2

- Release the left mouse button to add the Daily Reminders icon to the Start menu (Figure 2–41).

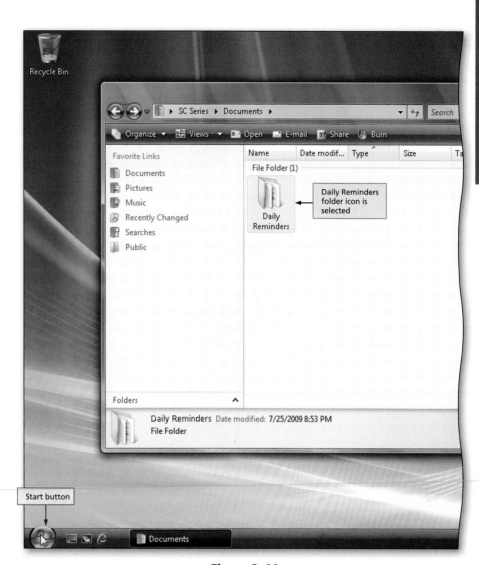

Figure 2–41

3

- Display the Start menu to see the Daily Reminders icon pinned to the Start menu (Figure 2–42).

Q&A

Can I add other shortcuts to the Start menu?

In addition to placing a folder shortcut on the Start menu, you also can place a shortcut to other objects (programs, files, USB drives, Web pages, printers, or other computers) on the Start menu in a similar manner. First display the object's icon on the desktop and then drag the icon onto the Start button.

Figure 2–42

Other Ways

1. Right-drag folder icon onto Start button

To Open a Folder Using a Shortcut on the Start Menu

After placing a shortcut to the Daily Reminders folder on the Start menu, you can open the Daily Reminders folder by clicking the Start button and then clicking the Daily Reminders command. The following step opens the Daily Reminders folder from the Start menu.

- Display the Start Menu.

- Click Daily Reminders to open the Daily Reminders folder (Figure 2–43).

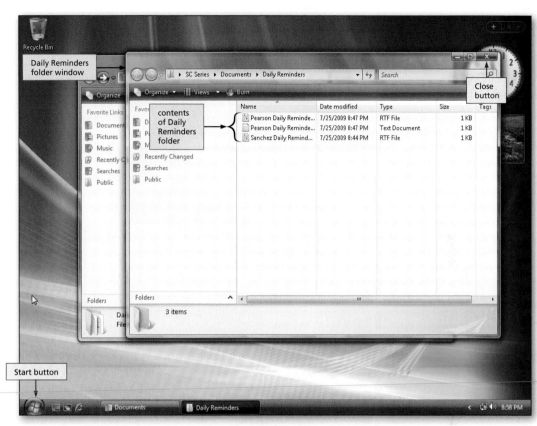

Figure 2–43

To Close the Daily Reminders Folder Window

After verifying that the folder opened correctly, you can close the window. The following step closes the Daily Reminders folder window.

1 Click the Close button on the title bar of the Daily Reminders folder window.

BTW

Deleting Shortcuts
When you delete a shortcut, you remove only the shortcut and its reference to the file or folder. The file or folder itself is stored elsewhere on the hard disk and is not removed.

To Remove a Shortcut from the Start Menu

The capability of adding shortcuts to and removing them from the Start menu provides great flexibility when customizing Windows Vista. Just as you can add shortcuts to the Start menu, you also can remove them. The following steps remove the Daily Reminders shortcut from the Start menu.

- Display the Start menu.

- Right-click the Daily Reminders command on the Start menu to display the shortcut menu (Figure 2–44).

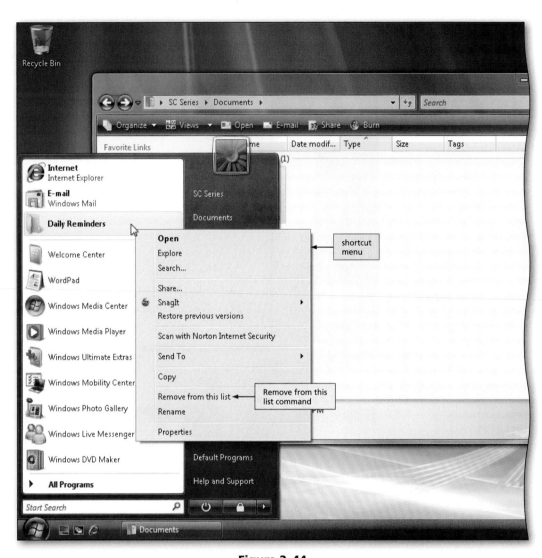

Figure 2–44

2

- Click Remove from this list command to remove the Daily Reminders shortcut from the Start menu (Figure 2–45).

- Close the Start menu.

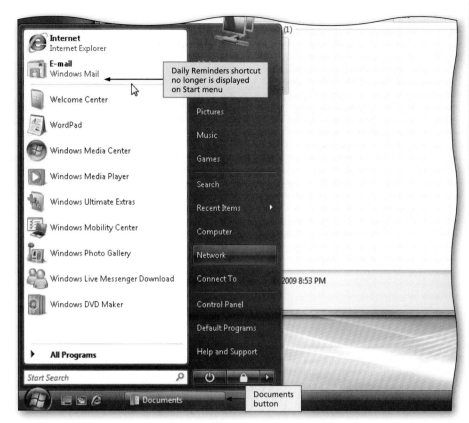

Figure 2–45

To Create a Shortcut on the Desktop

You also can create shortcuts directly on the desktop. Windows Vista recommends that only shortcuts be placed on the desktop rather than actual folders and files. This is to maximize the efficiency of file and folder searching, which will be covered in a later chapter. The following steps create a shortcut for the Daily Reminders folder on the desktop.

- If necessary, click the Documents button on the taskbar to make it the active window.

- Right-click the Daily Reminders folder to display the shortcut menu.

- Point to the Send To command to display the Send To submenu (Figure 2–46).

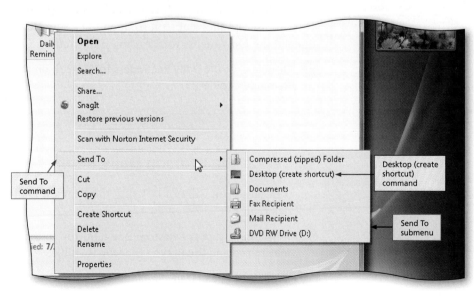

Figure 2–46

2

• Click the Desktop (create shortcut) command to create a shortcut on the desktop.

• Close the Documents folder (Figure 2–47).

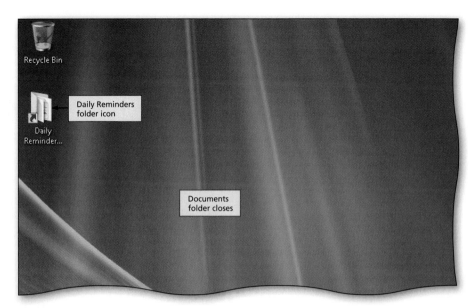

Figure 2–47

BTW

Opening Windows
In addition to clicking the taskbar button of an inactive window to make that window the active window, you may click any open area of the window. For example, many people click the title bar of a window to activate the window.

Opening and Modifying Documents within a Folder

When editing a document, you can open the document directly instead of first opening the application program and then opening the document. Does this feel more natural? Research has indicated that people feel comfortable working with documents directly instead of dealing with application programs and then documents.

You have received new information to add to Mr. Sanchez's daily reminders. An Internet meeting with the sales department in the western United States has been scheduled for 3:00 p.m. and the sales department must be notified of the meeting. To add these new items to the Daily Reminders document, you first must open the Daily Reminders folder that contains the document.

To Open a Folder Using a Shortcut on the Desktop

Because you have created a shortcut on the desktop for the Daily Reminders folder, you can use the shortcut icon to open the Daily Reminders folder the same way you opened the Documents folder using a shortcut in Chapter 1.

1 Double-click the Daily Reminders folder icon on the desktop to open the Daily Reminders folder.

To Delete the Pearson Daily Reminders (Thursday) Text File

Because you will not be using the Pearson Daily Reminders (Thursday) text file, you will delete it.

1 If necessary, click the Restore Down button so that the Daily Reminders folder is not maximized and the Recycle Bin icon is visible.

2 Drag the Pearson Daily Reminders (Thursday) text icon to the Recycle Bin to delete it.

To Open and Modify a Document in a Folder

Now you need to edit the remaining documents in the Daily Reminders folder. The following steps open the Sanchez Daily Reminders (Thursday) document and add new text about the Internet meeting.

- Open the Sanchez Daily Reminders (Thursday) document in WordPad.

- Press the DOWN ARROW key seven times to move the insertion point to the end of the document.

- Type 6. Notify Sales – NetMeeting at 3:00 p.m. and then press the ENTER key to modify the Sanchez Daily Reminders (Thursday) document (Figure 2–48).

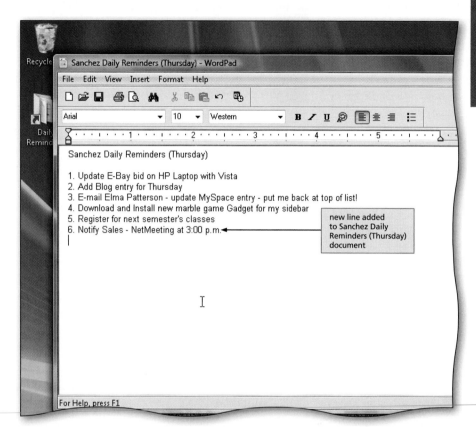

Figure 2–48

To Open and Modify Multiple Documents

Windows Vista allows you to have more than one document and application program open at the same time so you can work on multiple documents. The concept of multiple programs running at the same time is called **multitasking**. To illustrate how you can work with multiple windows open at the same time, you will now edit the Pearson Daily Reminders (Thursday) document to include a reminder to talk to Dan about Carol's birthday party. You will not have to close the Sanchez Daily Reminders (Thursday) document. The following steps open the Pearson Daily Reminders (Thursday) document and add the new reminder.

- Open the Pearson Daily Reminders (Thursday) document in WordPad.

Q&A

Why does the font look different in the two documents?

Since the Pearson Daily Reminders (Thursday) document was created as a text file, its font will appear different than that of the Sanchez Daily Reminders (Thursday) document. Remember, Rich Text Format documents allow for more formatting than plain text files.

2

- Press the DOWN ARROW key five times to move the insertion point to the end of the document in the WordPad window.

- Type 4. Call Dan – Birthday party for Carol and then press the ENTER key (Figure 2–49).

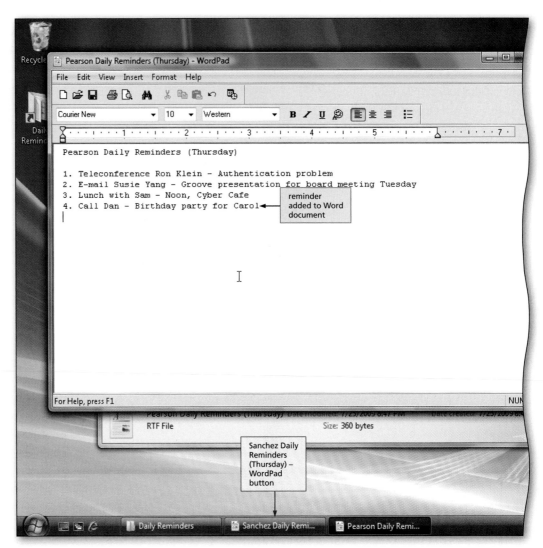

Figure 2–49

To Open an Inactive Window

After you have modified the Pearson Daily Reminders (Thursday) document, you receive information that a dinner meeting with Art Perez has been scheduled for Mr. Sanchez for 7:00 p.m. at The Crab House. You are directed to add this entry to Mr. Sanchez's reminders. To do this, you must make the Sanchez Daily Reminders (Thursday) - WordPad the active window. The following steps make the Sanchez Daily Reminders (Thursday) – WordPad window active and enter the new reminder.

1

- Click the Sanchez Daily Reminders (Thursday) - WordPad button on the taskbar to switch windows.

2

- When the window opens, type 7.
  Dinner with Art Perez –
  7:00 p.m., The Crab
  House and then press the ENTER
  key to update the document
  (Figure 2–50).

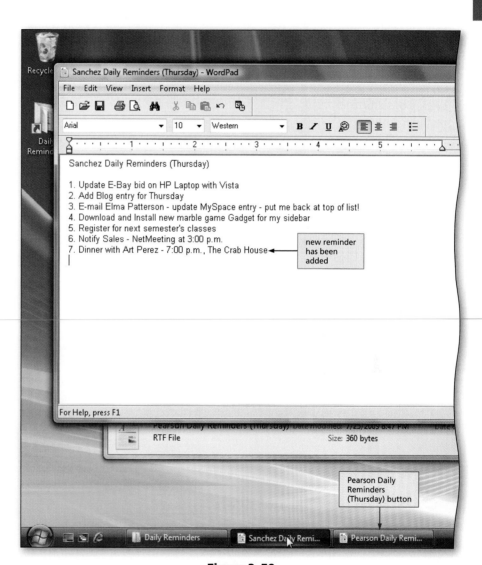

Figure 2–50

To Close Multiple Open Windows and Save Changes from the Taskbar

When you have finished working with multiple windows, close them. If the windows are open on the desktop, you can click the Close button on the title bar of each open window to close them. Regardless of whether the windows are open on the desktop or the windows are minimized using the Show the Desktop command, you also can close the windows using the buttons on the taskbar. The following steps close the Sanchez Daily Reminders (Thursday) - WordPad and Pearson Daily Reminders (Thursday) - WordPad windows from the taskbar.

- Right-click the
  Pearson Daily
  Reminders
  (Thursday) -
  WordPad button
  on the taskbar to
  display the shortcut
  menu (Figure 2–51).

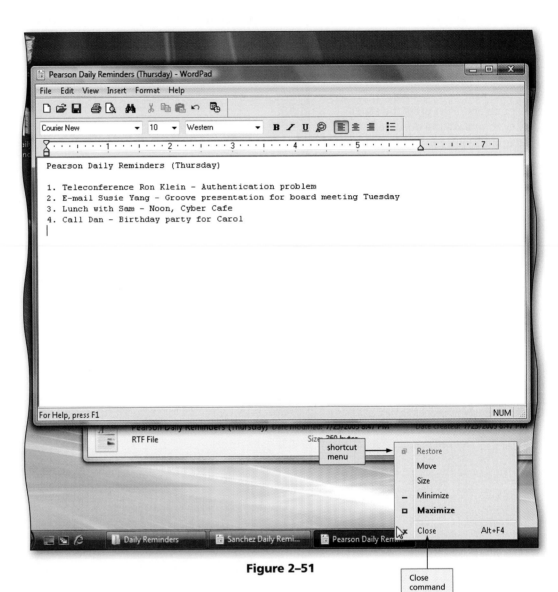

Figure 2–51

• Click the Close command to display the WordPad dialog box (Figure 2–52).

• Click the Save button in the WordPad dialog box to save the changes and close the document.

• Close and save the Sanchez Daily Reminders (Thursday) document.

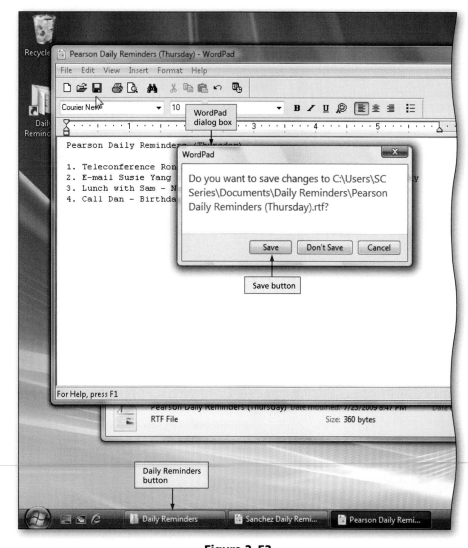

Figure 2–52

Other Ways

1. Click taskbar button, on File menu click Save, click Close button

2. Click taskbar button, on title bar click Close button, click Save button

3. Click taskbar button, on File menu click Exit, click Save button

To Print Multiple Documents from within a Folder

After you modify and save documents on the desktop, you may want to print them so you have an updated hard copy of the documents. Earlier in this chapter, you used the Print command on the File menu to print an open document. You also can print multiple documents from within a folder without actually opening the documents.

Before you can print them, you must select both of them. There are a couple of different ways to select multiple items. You can select the first item, then while holding down the CTRL key, you can select the other items, or you can select the first item, then while holding down the SHIFT key, you can select the other items. The first method works when the items you want to select are not together whereas the second method (using the SHIFT key) only works if all of the items are adjacent. The following steps on the next page print both the Sanchez Daily Reminders (Thursday) and the Pearson Daily Reminders (Thursday) documents from the Daily Reminders folder.

- Click the Daily Reminders button on the taskbar to make it the active window.

- Click the Pearson Daily Reminders (Thursday) icon in the Daily Reminders folder to select the icon.

- Press and hold the SHIFT key, click the Sanchez Daily Reminders (Thursday) icon, and then release the SHIFT key to select both items in the Daily Reminders folder (Figure 2–53).

- Click the Print button on the toolbar to print the two files.

3

- Click the Close button in the Daily Reminders window to close the Daily Reminders window.

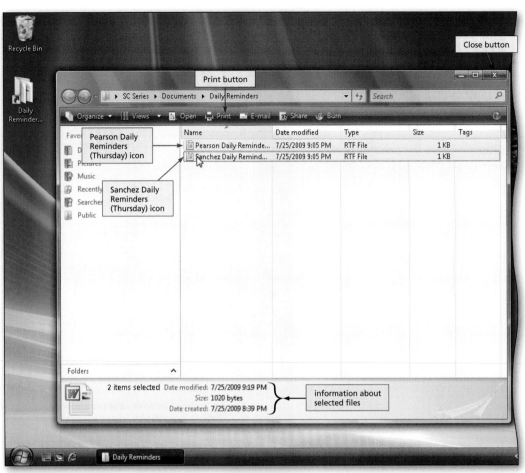

Figure 2–53

Other Ways

1. Select document icons, right-click, click Print
2. Press ALT+F, press P

BTW

Backups
Copying a file or folder to a USB drive is one way to create a backup, but often backing up files is a much more elaborate process. Most backup systems use tape or portable hard disks that contain hundreds of megabytes (millions of characters) and even gigabytes (billions of characters).

Copying a Folder onto a USB Drive

A shortcut on the desktop is useful when you frequently use one or more documents within the folder. It is a good policy to make a copy of a folder and the documents within the folder so if the folder or its contents are accidentally lost or damaged, you do not lose your work. This is referred to as making a **backup** of the files and folders. Another reason to make copies of files and folders is so that you can take the files and folders from one computer to another, for instance if you need to take a file or folder from a work computer to your home computer. A USB drive is a handy device for physically moving copies of files and folders from one computer to another.

To Copy a Folder onto a USB Drive

You want to be able to use the files you have created on another computer. To do so, you will need to copy the files to your USB drive. The following steps copy the Daily Reminders folder on to a USB drive.

1

- Insert a USB drive into an open USB port to display the AutoPlay menu (Figure 2–54).

Q&A Why does my USB drive have a different letter?

Depending on how many devices you have connected to your computer, your USB drive might have been assigned a different letter such as F or G.

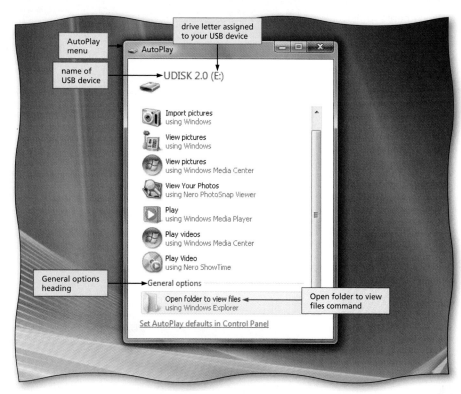

Figure 2–54

2

- Under the General options heading, click the Open folder to view files command to open a folder window (Figure 2–55).

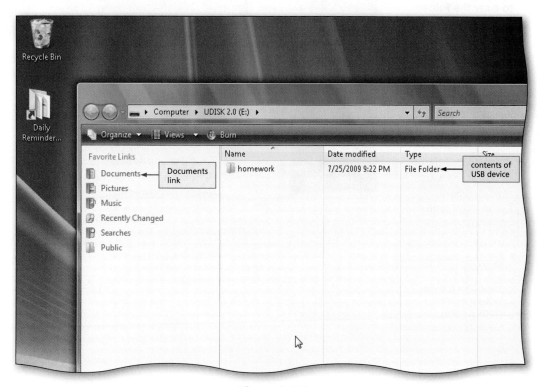

Figure 2–55

- Click the Documents link in the left pane to display the contents of the Documents folder.

- Right-click the Daily Reminders folder to display the shortcut menu.

- Point to the Send To command to display the Send To submenu. (Figure 2–56)

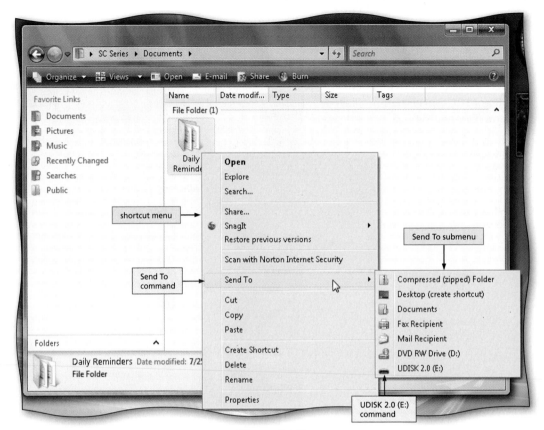

Figure 2–56

- Click UDISK 2.0 (E:) to copy the folder to the USB drive (Figure 2–57).

Q&A Can I back up the entire Documents folder?

Yes. It is important to regularly back up the entire contents of your Documents folder. To back up the Documents folder, display the Start menu, right-click the Documents command, click Send To on the shortcut menu, and then click the location of the backup drive.

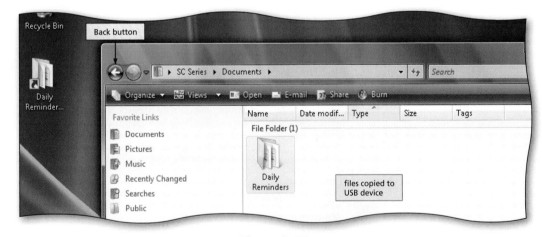

Figure 2–57

Other Ways

1. Press ALT + F, point to Send To, click UDISK 2.0 (E:)

To Open a Folder Stored on a USB Drive

After copying a folder onto a USB drive, in order to verify that the folder has been copied properly, you can open the folder from the USB drive and view its contents. The following steps open a folder stored on a USB drive.

- Click the Back button on the Address bar of the Documents folder to return to the USB drive window (Figure 2–58).

- Double-click the Daily Reminders icon to open the folder and verify the files are in the Daily Reminders folder.

❸

- Close the Daily Reminders folder.

- Close the USB drive window.

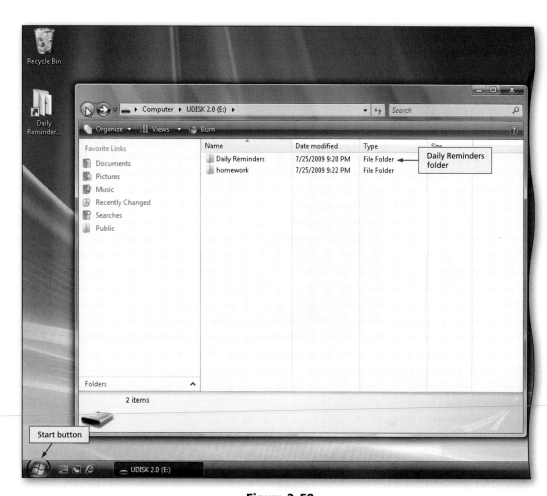

Figure 2–58

To Safely Remove a USB Drive

If you wish to open one of the documents in the folder stored on the USB drive you can use one of the methods covered earlier in this chapter to open and edit the file. After you are finished, you should safely remove the USB drive.

• Display the Start menu and then click the Computer command to open the Computer folder window (Figure 2–59).

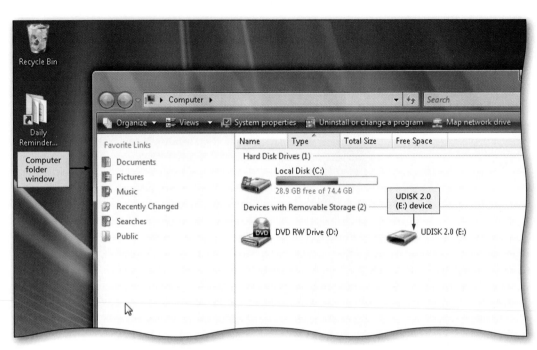

Figure 2–59

• Right-click the UDISK 2.0 (E:) device to display the shortcut menu (Figure 2–60).

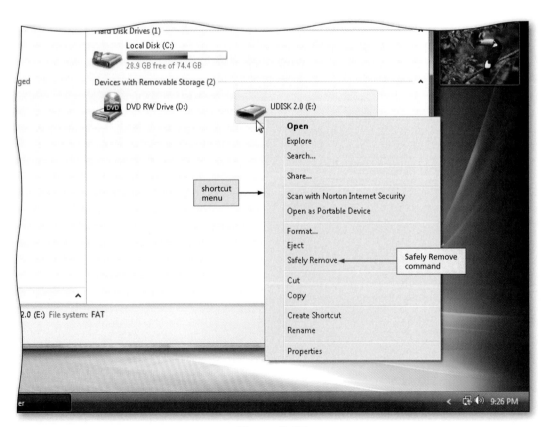

Figure 2–60

3

- Click the Safely Remove command on the shortcut menu to have Windows close the USB drive and display the Safe to Remove Hardware message in the Notification area (Figure 2–61).

- Remove the USB drive from the USB port.

- Close the Computer folder.

Q&A

Why do I need to safely remove the USB drive?

Even though you may not have anything open on the USB drive, Windows Vista still may be accessing it in the background. Safely removing the USB drive tells Windows Vista to stop communicating with the device. If you were to remove it while Windows Vista was still accessing it, you could lose your data stored on it.

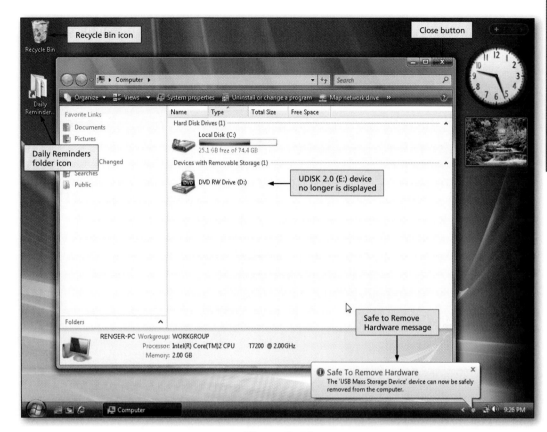

Figure 2–61

The Recycle Bin

Occasionally you will want to delete files and folders from the Documents folder. Windows Vista offers three different techniques to perform this operation: (1) drag the object to the Recycle Bin; (2) right-drag the object to the Recycle Bin; and (3) right-click the object and then click Delete on the shortcut menu.

It is important to realize what you are doing when you delete a file or folder. When you delete a shortcut from the desktop, you only delete the shortcut icon and its reference to the file or folder. The file or folder itself is stored elsewhere on the hard disk and is not deleted. When you delete the icon for a file or folder (not a shortcut), the actual file or folder is deleted. A shortcut icon includes an arrow to indicate that it is a shortcut, while a folder would not have the arrow as part of its icon.

When you delete a file or folder, Windows Vista places these items in the **Recycle Bin**, which is an area on the hard disk that contains all the items you have deleted. When the Recycle Bin becomes full, empty it. Up until the time you empty the Recycle Bin, you can recover deleted files and application programs. Even though you have this safety net, you should be careful whenever you delete anything from your computer.

To Delete a Shortcut from the Desktop

The following step removes a shortcut from the desktop.

1 Drag the Daily Reminders - Shortcut icon onto the Recycle Bin icon on the desktop to move the shortcut to the Recycle Bin.

To Restore an Item from the Recycle Bin

At some point you will discover that you accidentally deleted a shortcut, file, or folder that you did not wish to delete. As long as you have not emptied the Recycle Bin, you can restore them. The following steps restore the Daily Reminders - Shortcut icon to the desktop.

1

- Open the Recycle Bin.

- Click the Daily Reminders - Shortcut icon to select it (Figure 2–62).

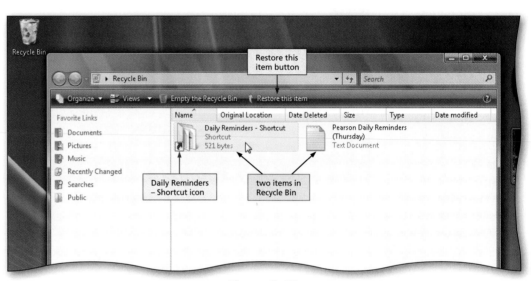

Figure 2–62

2

- Click the Restore this item button to put the Daily Reminders - Shortcut icon back on the desktop (Figure 2–63).

- Close the Recycle Bin window.

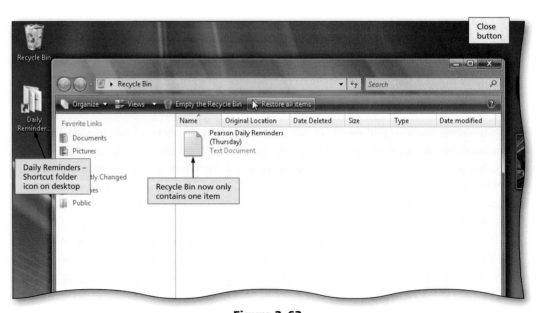

Figure 2–63

To Delete a Shortcut from the Desktop

Now you should delete the Daily Reminders shortcut icon again so that you can leave the desktop how you found it.

1 Drag the Daily Reminders - Shortcut icon onto the Recycle Bin icon on the desktop.

To Delete Multiple Files from a Folder

You can delete several files at one time. The following steps delete both the Sanchez Daily Reminders (Thursday) and the Pearson Daily Reminders (Thursday) documents.

1

- Open the Documents folder.

- Open the Daily Reminders folder.

- Click the Sanchez Daily Reminders (Thursday) document to select it.

- Press and hold the CTRL key, click the Pearson Daily Reminders (Thursday) document.

- Right-click the documents to display the shortcut menu (Figure 2–64).

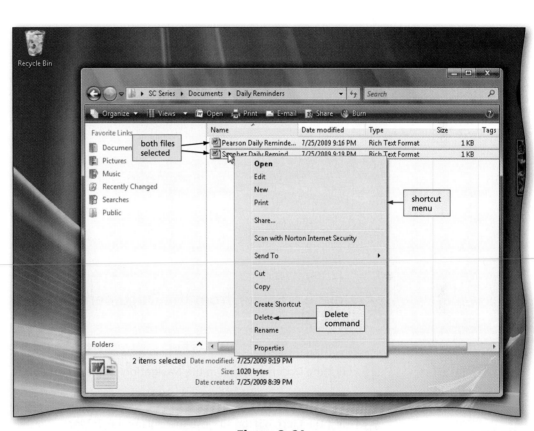

Figure 2–64

2

- Click the Delete command to display the Delete Multiple Items dialog box (Figure 2–65).

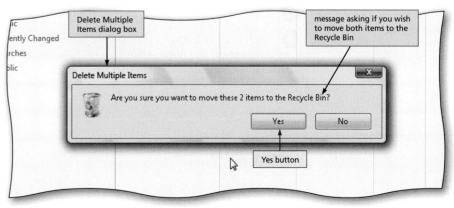

Figure 2–65

● Click the Yes button to move the files to the Recycle Bin (Figure 2–66).

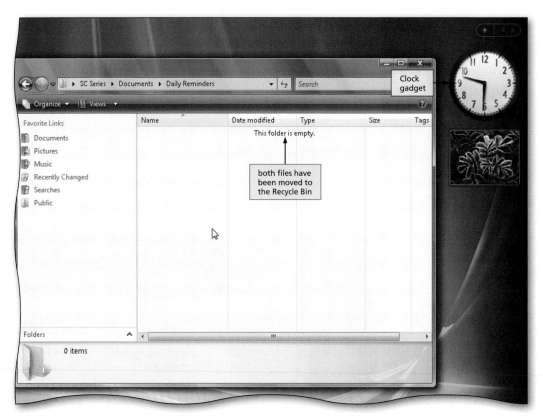

Figure 2–66

To Delete a Folder from the Documents Folder and Empty the Recycle Bin

You also can delete folders from the Documents folder using the same method.

1 Click the Documents link in the Navigation pane.

2 Delete the Daily Reminders folder.

3 Click the Close button to close the Documents folder.

4 Right-click the Recycle Bin to show the shortcut menu.

5 Click the Empty Recycle Bin command.

6 Click the Yes button in the Delete Multiple Files dialog box to permanently delete the contents of the Recycle Bin.

The Windows Sidebar

The Windows Sidebar is a vertical bar that is displayed on the side of your desktop. It is designed to contain mini-programs called gadgets. Through the use of these gadgets, the Windows Sidebar can display useful tools and information. In addition to the gadgets that come with Windows Vista, many developers are building their own gadgets. You can find new gadgets online at the Windows Vista Sidebar Web site, where they are organized into categories including games, multimedia, security, and safety, among others. Be careful if you choose to download a gadget. Not all gadgets have been created by Microsoft directly; therefore, you should verify any gadgets you download as coming from a trusted source.

To Customize the Clock Gadget

As you have learned in Chapter 1, you can add gadgets to the Windows Sidebar. You also can customize the existing gadgets. Depending on the gadget, you will have different options available to you for customizing the gadget. You decide to experiment with the Clock gadget as you would like to see a different clock design, and you would like to add your name to it. The following steps customize and personalize the Clock gadget.

1

- Right-click the Clock gadget on the Sidebar to display the shortcut menu (Figure 2–67).

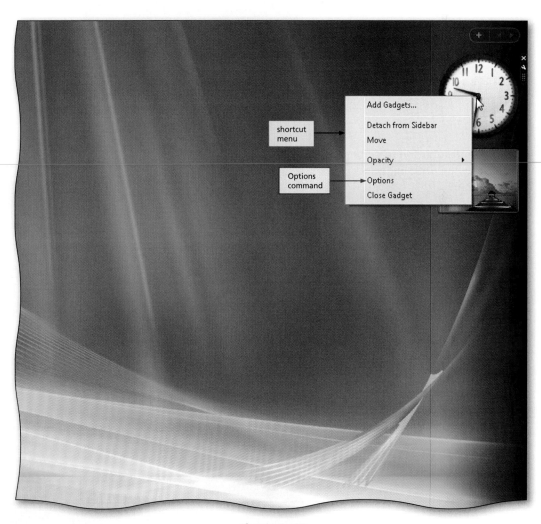

Figure 2–67

2

• Click the Options command to display the Clock dialog box (Figure 2–68).

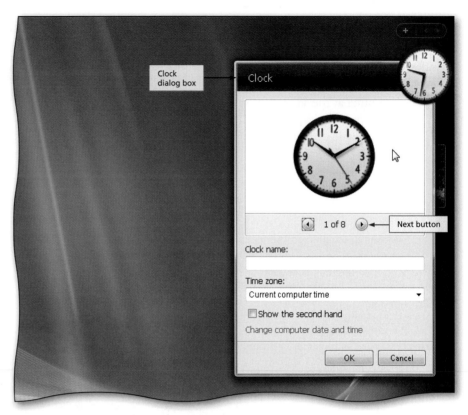

Figure 2–68

3

• Click the Next button three times to display the neon light clock (Figure 2–69).

Figure 2–69

4

- Click the Clock name text box to select it.

- Type Steve's (or your own name) in the Clock name text box (Figure 2–70).

Figure 2–70

5

- Click the OK button to apply your changes and close the Clock dialog box (Figure 2–71).

Q&A Do all gadgets have the same options?

Every gadget has different options. For example, the Calendar gadget can be customized to show a week or a month, not just the current day.

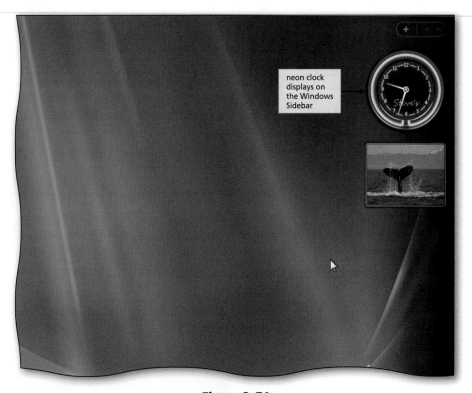

Figure 2–71

To Undo the Changes to the Clock Gadget

Although you like the new look for the Clock gadget, you decide that the original style was easier to read. You therefore want to undo the changes you have made. The following steps undo the changes to the Clock gadget.

1
- Right-click the Clock gadget and then click the Options command on the shortcut menu (Figure 2–72).

Figure 2–72

2
- Click the Next button five times to display the original clock.

- Delete the text from the Clock name text box (Figure 2–73).

- Click the OK button to apply your changes and close the Clock dialog box.

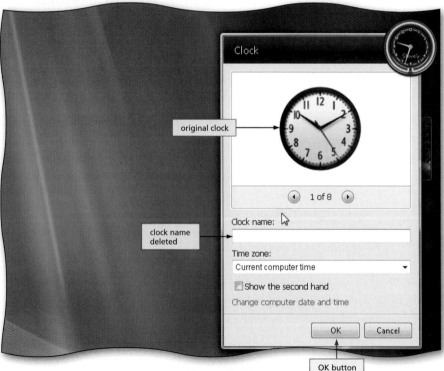

Figure 2–73

To Rearrange Gadgets on the Sidebar

Besides customizing the gadgets, you also can rearrange the gadgets on the Sidebar. Rearranging gadgets is as simple as dragging them to the location where you want. You decide to see how the gadgets would look in another arrangement. The following steps rearrange the gadgets on the Sidebar.

- Point to the Clock gadget to show the Move button (Figure 2–74).

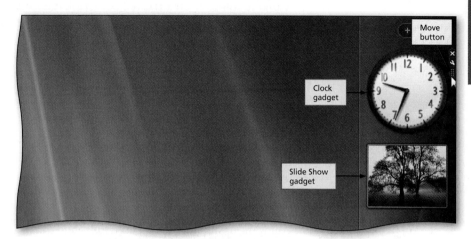

Figure 2–74

- Click the Move button and drag the Clock gadget below the Slide Show gadget to reposition it on the Sidebar (Figure 2–75).

Figure 2–75

- Point to the Slide Show gadget to show the Move button.

- Click the Move button and drag the Slide Show gadget below the Clock gadget to put the gadgets back in their original order (Figure 2–76).

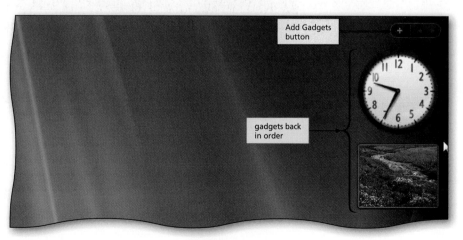

Figure 2–76

Finding More Gadgets

Besides the gadgets that come pre-installed with Windows Vista, you also can find gadgets online that offer news, sports updates, entertainment, or other useful tools and information. Once you find a gadget online that you are interested in, you can download and install it on your computer. Before downloading and installing a gadget, first make sure that it comes from a trusted source. A **trusted source** is a source that has been verified to be trustworthy either by you, by a trusted friend, or by a trusted organization such as Microsoft. Trusted sources are not known to offer gadgets that contain offensive content or malicious code that could possibly damage your computer or do any other type of harm. If you download from a trusted source, you can feel secure about what you are installing on your computer. If the developer of the gadget you want to download is not a trusted source, you should not download and install the gadget.

To Search for Gadgets Online

Now you decide to go online and browse for new gadgets, although you are not going to download and install any new gadgets at this time. You just want to become familiar with what types of gadgets are available. In fact, since you have been so busy, you want to find some gadgets to provide quick relief from work, without being too distracting or time-consuming. The following steps search for gadgets online.

- Click the Add Gadgets button to display the Gadget Gallery (Figure 2–77).

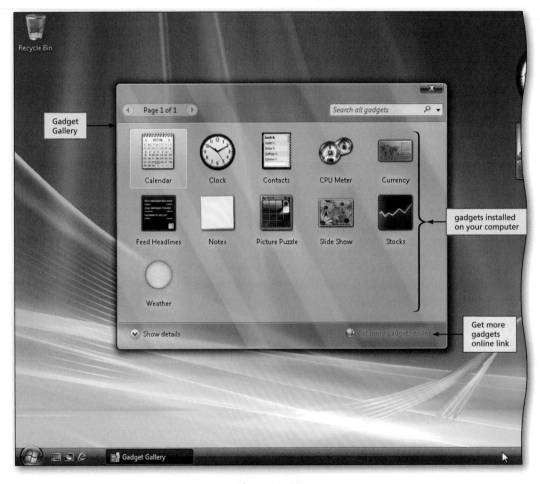

Figure 2–77

2

- Click the Get more gadgets online link to open Windows Internet Explorer and display the Personalize Windows Vista Sidebar Web page (Figure 2–78).

Q&A Why do I see different gadgets on my computer?

The Windows Vista Sidebar Web site is frequently updated. Each time you search for gadgets online, different gadgets may appear.

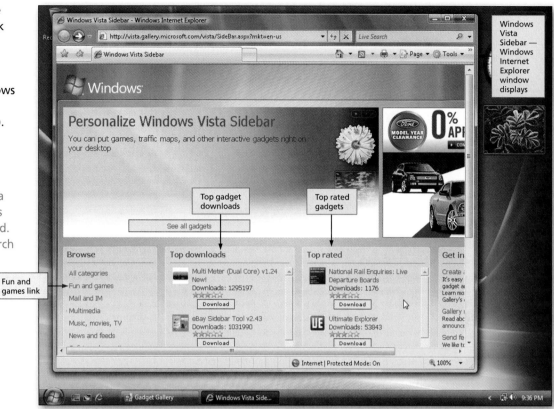

Figure 2–78

3

- Click the Fun and games link to display the gadgets in this category (Figure 2–79).

Experiment

- Try some of the other links to see what gadgets developers are creating. Take a look at the Safety and security gadgets as well as the Multimedia gadgets.

Figure 2–79

To Close the Internet Explorer and Gadget Gallery Windows

After having reviewed some of the gadgets available online, you decide to close Internet Explorer. You do not want to download gadgets yet; you want to wait until you have verified that the gadgets you want are from trusted sources. The following steps close Internet Explorer and the Gadget Gallery windows.

1 Click the Close button of the Windows Internet Explorer to close the window.

2 Click the Close button in the Gadget Gallery to close the window.

To Place a Gadget on the Desktop

Gadgets, when displayed in the Sidebar, are limited as to where they can appear. Windows Vista allows you to move a gadget from the Sidebar to other locations on the desktop. When you move a gadget off of the Sidebar, it often will change in appearance to reflect the fact that it is no longer constrained to fitting within the Sidebar. This does not mean that you can enlarge it to whatever size you want; some gadgets only expand a little when moved off of the Sidebar. You decide to see what the Slide Show gadget would look like when it is placed on the desktop, and whether you will have a better view of the pictures it displays. The following steps place the Slide Show gadget on the desktop.

- Right-click the Slide Show gadget to display the shortcut menu (Figure 2–80).

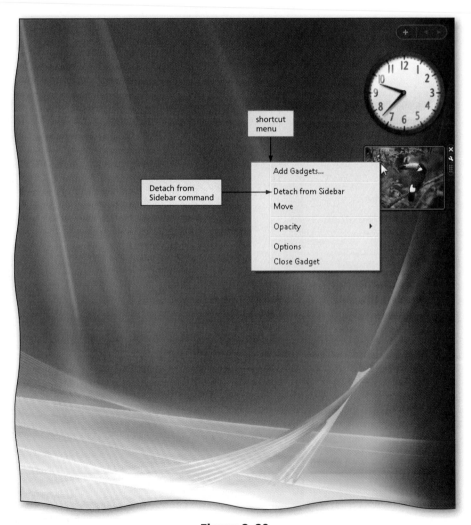

Figure 2–80

- Click Detach from Sidebar to place the Slide Show gadget on the desktop.

- Drag the Slide Show gadget to the center of the desktop (Figure 2–81).

Figure 2–81

To Remove a Gadget from the Desktop

After having placed the Slide Show gadget on the desktop, you decide to put it back on the Sidebar so that you have more of your desktop available. The following steps place the Slide Show gadget back on the Sidebar.

- Right-click the Slide Show gadget to display the shortcut menu (Figure 2–82).

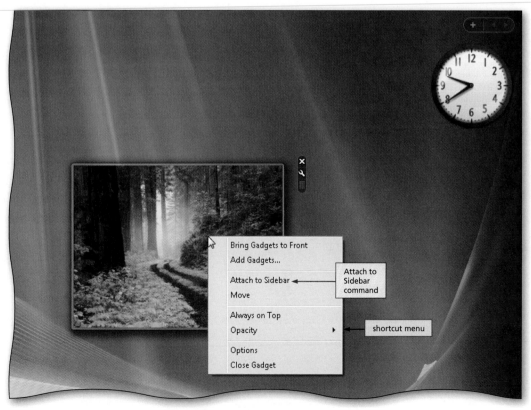

Figure 2–82

2

- Click the Attach to Sidebar command to place the Slide Show gadget back on the Sidebar (Figure 2–83).

Q&A

Why did the Slide Show gadget show up at the top of the Sidebar?

When you attach a gadget to the Sidebar, Windows Vista automatically places it at the top of the Sidebar.

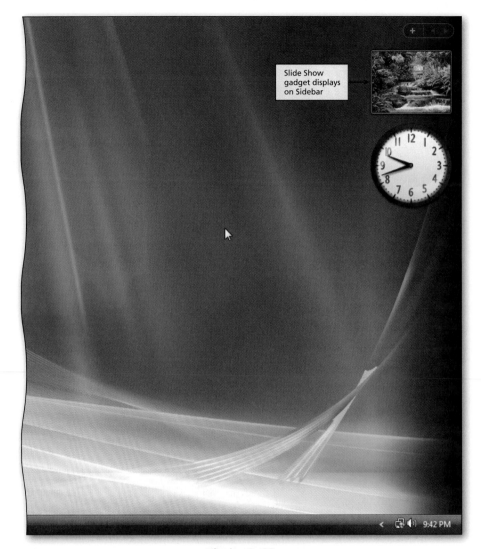

Slide Show gadget displays on Sidebar

Figure 2–83

To Move the Slide Show Gadget

Now you move the Slide Show gadget back to its original location.

1 Click and drag the Slide Show gadget below the Clock gadget to put it back into its original position.

To Close and Show the Sidebar

You may want to hide the Sidebar to maximize and unclutter your screen while you are working with other application programs. The following steps close and then show the Sidebar.

1
- Right-click an open area of the Sidebar to display the shortcut menu (Figure 2–84).

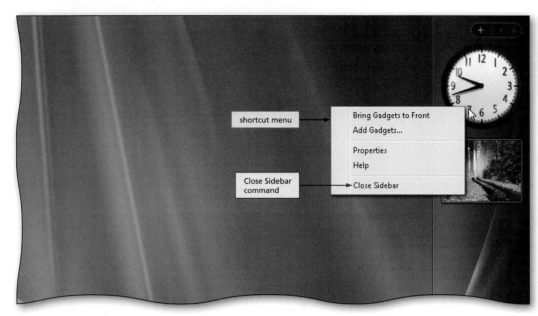

Figure 2–84

2
- Click the Close Sidebar command to close the Sidebar (Figure 2–85).

Figure 2–85

- Display the Start menu, click All Programs, and then click the Accessories folder to expand the Accessories list (Figure 2–86).

- Click the Windows Sidebar command to show the Sidebar.

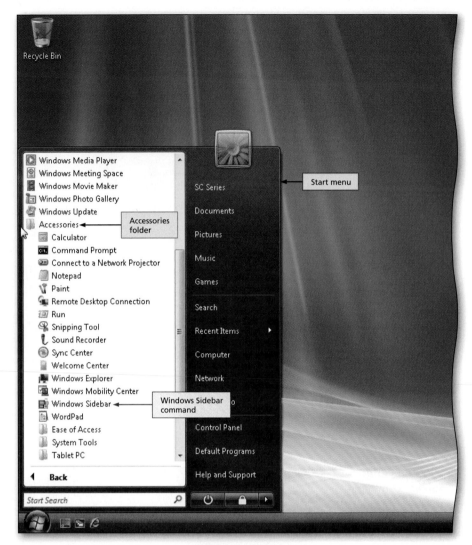

Figure 2–86

To Log Off from the Computer

After restoring the Windows Sidebar, you decide to log off from the computer, because you are done working with it. The following steps log off your account from the computer.

1. Display the Start menu.

2. Point to the arrow to the right of the Lock this computer button to display the Shut Down options menu.

3. Click the Log Off command, and then wait for Windows Vista to prompt you to save any unsaved data, if any, and log off.

To Turn Off the Computer

The following step turns off the computer. If you are not sure whether you should turn off the computer, read the following step without actually performing it.

 Click the Shut Down button to turn off the computer.

Chapter Summary

In this chapter, you learned to create text documents using both the application-centric approach and document-centric approach. You moved these documents to the Documents folder and modified and printed them. You created a new folder in the Documents folder, placed documents in the folder, and copied the new folder onto a USB drive. You worked with multiple documents open at the same time. You placed a document shortcut on both the Start menu and on the desktop. Using various methods, you deleted shortcuts, documents, and a folder. Finally, you learned how to customize a gadget, rearrange gadgets on the Sidebar, search for new gadgets online, place a gadget on the desktop, and hide and show the Sidebar. The items listed below include all the new Windows Vista skills you have learned in this chapter.

1. Launch a Program and Create a Document (WIN 76)
2. Save a Document to the Documents Folder (WIN 78)
3. Open the Print Dialog Box from an Application Program (WIN 81)
4. Print a Document (WIN 82)
5. Edit a Document (WIN 83)
6. Close and Save a Document (WIN 83)
7. Open the Documents Folder (WIN 85)
8. Create a Blank Document in the Documents Folder (WIN 86)
9. Name a Document in the Documents Folder (WIN 87)
10. Open a Document with WordPad (WIN 88)
11. Enter Data into a Blank Document (WIN 89)
12. Save a Text Document in Rich Text Format (RTF) (WIN 90)
13. Change the View to Small Icons (WIN 92)
14. Arrange the Items in a Folder in Groups by Type (WIN 93)
15. Create and Name a Folder in the Documents Folder (WIN 94)
16. Move a Document into a Folder (WIN 97)
17. Change Location Using the Address Bar (WIN 99)
18. Display and Use the Preview Pane (WIN 100)
19. Close the Preview Pane (WIN 102)
20. Change Location Using the Back Button on the Address Bar (WIN 103)
21. Add a Shortcut on the Start Menu (WIN 104)
22. Open a Folder Using a Shortcut on the Start Menu (WIN 107)
23. Remove a Shortcut from the Start Menu (WIN 108)
24. Create a Shortcut on the Desktop (WIN 109)
25. Delete the Pearson Daily Reminders (Thursday) Text File (WIN 110)
26. Open and Modify a Document in a Folder (WIN 111)
27. Open and Modify Multiple Documents (WIN 111)
28. Open an Inactive Window (WIN 113)
29. Close Multiple Open Windows and Save Changes from the Taskbar (WIN 114)
30. Print Multiple Documents from within a Folder (WIN 115)
31. Copy a Folder onto a USB Drive (WIN 117)
32. Open a Folder Stored on a USB Drive (WIN 119)
33. Safely Remove a USB Drive (WIN 120)
34. Restore an Item from the Recycle Bin (WIN 122)
35. Delete Multiple Files from a Folder (WIN 123)
36. Customize the Clock Gadget (WIN 125)
37. Undo the Changes to the Clock Gadget (WIN 128)
38. Rearrange Gadgets on the Sidebar (WIN 129)
39. Search for Gadgets Online (WIN 130)
40. Place a Gadget on the Desktop (WIN 132)
41. Remove a Gadget from the Desktop (WIN 133)
42. Close and Show the Sidebar (WIN 135)

Learn It Online

Test your knowledge of chapter content and key terms.

Instructions: To complete the Learn It Online exercises, start your browser, click the Address bar, and then enter the Web address scsite.com/winvista/learn. When the Windows Vista Learn It Online page is displayed, click the link for the exercise you want to complete and then read the instructions.

Chapter Reinforcement TF, MC, and SA
A series of true/false, multiple-choice, and short-answer questions that tests your knowledge of the chapter content.

Flash Cards
An interactive learning environment where you identify chapter key terms associated with displayed definitions.

Practice Test
A series of multiple-choice questions that tests your knowledge of chapter content and key terms.

Who Wants To Be a Computer Genius?
An interactive game that challenges your knowledge of chapter content in the style of a television quiz show.

Wheel of Terms
An interactive game that challenges your knowledge of chapter key terms in the style of the television show *Wheel of Fortune*.

Crossword Puzzle Challenge
A crossword puzzle that challenges your knowledge of key terms presented in the chapter.

Apply Your Knowledge

Reinforce the skills and apply the concepts you learned in this chapter.

Creating a Document with WordPad
Instructions: Use the WordPad application to create the homework list shown in Figure 2–87.

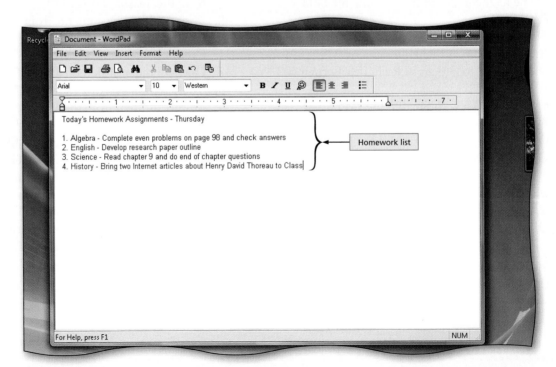

Figure 2–87

Perform the following tasks:

Part 1:   Launching the WordPad Application
1. Click the Start button.
2. Launch WordPad. The Document - WordPad window displays an insertion point (flashing vertical line) in the blank area below the menu bar.

Part 2:   Creating a Document Using WordPad
1. Type Today's Homework Assignments - Thursday and then press the ENTER key twice.
2. Type 1. Algebra - Complete even problems on page 98 and check answers and then press the ENTER key.
3. Type 2. English - Develop research paper outline and then press the ENTER key.
4. Type 3. Science - Read chapter 9 and do end of chapter questions and then press the ENTER key.
5. Type 4. History - Bring two Internet articles about Henry David Thoreau to Class and then press the ENTER key.

Part 3:   Printing the Today's Homework Document
1. Click File on the menu bar, and then click Print to print the document.

Part 4:   Save and Close the WordPad Window
1. Insert a USB drive.
2. Save your document as Homework Assignment to the USB drive.
3. Close WordPad.

Extend Your Knowledge

Extend the skills you learned in this chapter and experiment with new skills. You may need to use Help to complete the assignment.

Finding File and Folder Help

Instructions: Use Windows Help and Support to learn about files and folders.

Perform the following tasks:

Part 1:   Creating a Document in the Documents Folder
1. Create a WordPad document in the Documents folder. Save the document as Working with Files and Folders.
2. Maximize the Working with Files and Folders - WordPad window.

Part 2:   Launching Windows Help and Support
1. Click the Start button on the taskbar.
2. Click Help and Support on the Start menu.
3. Click Windows basics in the Find an Answer area.
4. Scroll down to Programs, files, and folders area.
5. Click Working with files and folders. The Working with files and folders page displays in the topic pane (Figure 2–88 on the next page).

Continued >

Extend Your Knowledge *continued*

Part 3:   Copying a Set of Steps to the WordPad Window

1. Scroll down to the Creating and deleting files area.

2. Drag through the heading steps below the heading to highlight them.

3. Right-click the highlighted text to display a shortcut menu.

4. Click Copy on the shortcut menu.

5. Click the Working with Files and Folders button in the taskbar button area to display the Working with Files and Folders - WordPad window.

6. Right-click the text area of the WordPad window to display a shortcut menu.

7. Click Paste. The heading and steps display in the window.

8. Click File on the menu bar and then click Save to save the document.

9. Click the Windows Help and Support button in the taskbar button area to display the Windows Help and Support window.

10. Click the Back button on the navigation toolbar.

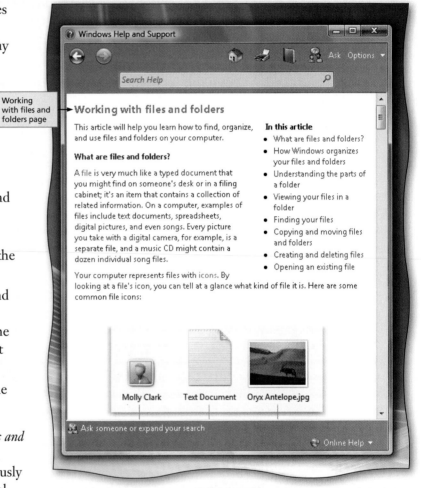

Figure 2–88

Part 4:   Copying Other Headings and Steps to the WordPad Window

1. Using the procedure previously shown in Part 3, copy the following headings and steps to the WordPad window: Copying and moving files and folders, Finding your files, and Opening an existing file.

2. Click File on the menu bar and then click Save to save the document.

3. Click File on the menu bar, click Print on the File menu, and then click the Print button to print the document.

4. Close the Working with Files and Folders - WordPad window.

5. Close the Windows Help and Support window.

6. Insert a USB drive and copy the Working with Files and Folders document in the Documents folder to the USB drive.

7. Delete the Working with Files and Folders document from the Documents folder and empty the Recycle Bin.

In the Lab

Use the guidelines, concepts and skills presented in this chapter to increase your knowledge of Windows Vista. Labs are listed in order of increasing difficulty.

Lab 1: Windows Vista Seminar Announcement and Schedule

Instructions: A two-day Windows Vista seminar will be offered to all teachers at your school. You have been put in charge of developing two text documents for the seminar. One document announces the seminar and will be sent to all teachers. The other document contains the schedule for the seminar. You prepare the documents shown in Figures 2-89 and 2-90 using WordPad.

Perform the following tasks:

Part 1: Creating the Windows Vista Seminar Announcement Document

1. Open a new WordPad document. Save the document as Windows Vista Seminar Announcement on the desktop.

2. Enter the text shown in Figure 2–89.

3. Save the document.

4. Print the document.

5. Close the document.

6. Move the document to the Documents folder.

7. Create a folder in the Documents folder called Windows Vista Seminar Documents.

8. Place the Windows Vista Seminar Announcement document in the Windows Vista Seminar Documents folder.

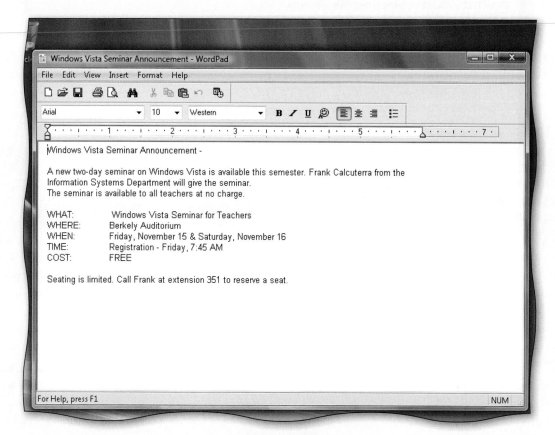

Figure 2–89

Continued >

In the Lab *continued*

Part 2: Creating the Windows Vista Seminar Schedule Document

1. Open a new WordPad document. Save the document as Windows Vista Seminar Schedule on the desktop.

2. Enter the text shown in Figure 2-90.

3. Save the document.

4. Print the document.

5. Close the document.

6. Move the Windows Vista Seminar Schedule document to the Documents folder.

7. Place the Windows Vista Seminar Schedule document in the Windows Vista Seminar Documents folder.

8. Move the Windows Vista Seminar Documents folder to your USB drive.

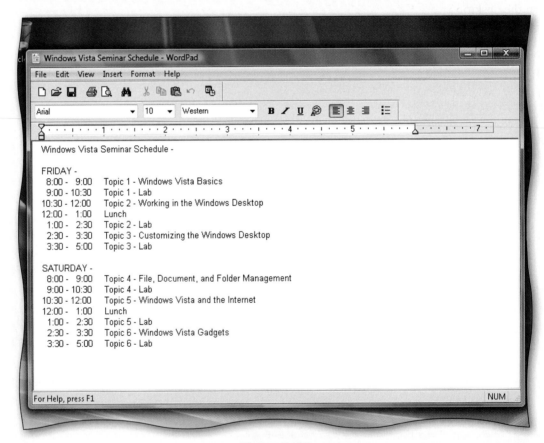

Figure 2–90

In the Lab

Lab 2: Researching Online Gadgets

Instructions: You are asked to create a list of gadgets that your company might find useful. Using the Windows Vista Sidebar Web site, you will create a gadget list that lists the gadgets and the categories in which they are located. Your boss is interested in four main categories. Create the headings shown in Figure 2–91 using the application-centric approach and WordPad. Then follow the steps to find some potentially useful gadgets online.

Perform the following tasks:

1. Start WordPad.

2. Enter the text shown in Figure 2–91.

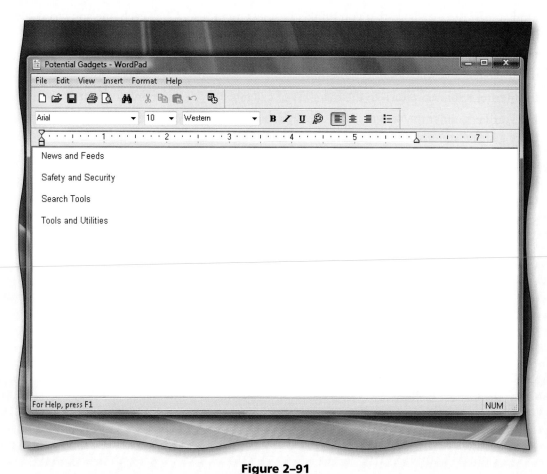

Figure 2–91

Continued >

In the Lab *continued*

3. Use Save As to save the document in the Documents folder with the file name `Potential Gadgets`.

4. Click the Add Gadgets button on the Windows Sidebar.

5. Click, Get more gadgets online, to open the Windows Vista Sidebar Web site.

6. Click on the link for News and feeds.

7. Find at least three gadgets that you think a business might use. Click each one and write down the name of the gadget and who developed it.

8. In WordPad, under the News and feeds heading, enter a numbered list stating the names of the three gadgets and who developed them.

9. In Internet Explorer, return to the main list of gadgets. Click on the link for Safety and security.

10. Find at least three gadgets that you think a business might use. Click each one and write down the name of the gadget, who developed it, and why it might be of use to a business.

11. In WordPad, under the Safety and Security heading, enter a numbered list stating the names of the three gadgets and who developed them.

12. In Internet Explorer, return to the main list of gadgets. Click on the link for Search tools.

13. In WordPad, under the Search Tools heading, enter a numbered list stating the names of the three gadgets and who developed them.

14. In Internet Explorer, return to the main list of gadgets. Click on the link for Tools and utilities.

15. In WordPad, under the Tools and Utilities heading, enter a numbered list stating the names of the three gadgets and who developed them.

16. Save the document.

17. Print the document from WordPad.

18. Close WordPad.

19. Insert a USB drive in an open USB port.

20. Right-click the Potential Gadgets icon in the Documents folder and then click Send To.

21. Click USB DISK.

22. Close the Documents folder.

23. Safely Remove the USB drive.

24. Close the Gadget Gallery.

25. Close Internet Explorer.

In the Lab

Lab 3: Creating, Saving, and Printing Automobile Information Documents

Instruction: For eight months, you have accumulated data about your 2006 Dodge Viper automobile. Some of the information is written on pieces of paper, while the rest is in the form of receipts. You have decided to organize this information using your computer. You create the documents shown in Figures 2-92 and 2-93 using the application-centric approach and WordPad.

Perform the following tasks:

Part 1:   Creating the Automobile Information Document
1. Create a new WordPad document. Save the document on the desktop with the file name, Automobile Information.
2. Type the text shown in Figure 2–92.

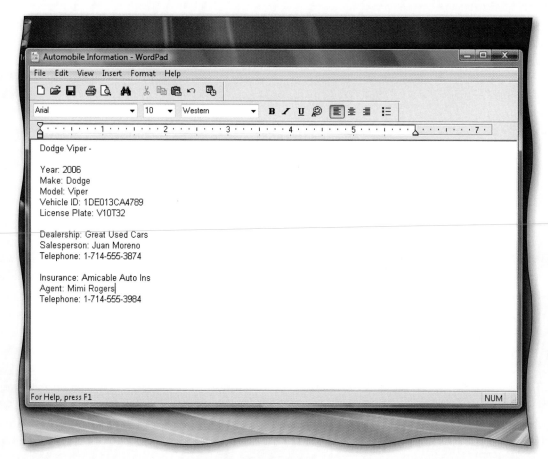

Figure 2–92

3. Save the document.
4. Print the document.
5. Create a folder in the Documents folder called Automobile Documents.
6. Place the Automobile Information document in the Automobile Documents folder.

Continued >

In the Lab *continued*

Part 2: Other Automobile Documents

1. Create the Phone Numbers document (Figure 2–93a), the Automobile Gas Mileage document (Figure 2–93b), and the Automobile Maintenance document on the desktop (Figure 2–93c).

2. Move each document into the Documents folder.

3. Print each document.

4. Place each document in the Automobile Documents folder.

5. Move the Automobile Documents folder to a USB drive.

(a)

(b)

(c)

Figure 2–93

Cases and Places

Apply your creative thinking and problem solving skills to design and implement a solution.

• EASIER   ••MORE DIFFICULT

• 1 Creating Employer Request List

Your employer is concerned that some people in the company are not thoroughly researching purchases of office supplies. She has prepared a list of steps she would like everyone to follow when purchasing office supplies: (1) Determine your department's need for office supplies; (2) Identify at least two Internet sites that sell the office supplies you need; and (3) Obtain prices for the office supplies from their Web sites.

Your employer wants you to use WordPad to prepare a copy of this list to post in every department. Save and print the document. After you have printed one copy of the document, try experimenting with different WordPad features to make the list more eye-catching. If you like your changes, save and print a revised copy of the document.

• 2 Locating Gadgets Online

As you have learned, the Windows Sidebar provides a place for useful gadgets. You would like to find out more about gadgets and install one for yourself. Visit the Windows Vista Sidebar Web site and find out how to get gadgets that will provide up-to-date news. Download one and try it out. Write a brief report about what you found online and what you think about news gadgets. Include the name and developer of the gadget you installed.

•• 3 Researching Retraining Costs

Retraining employees can be an expensive task for a business of any size. Many Windows Vista users believe the Windows Vista operating system is an intuitive, easy-to-learn operating system which can reduce retraining costs. Using the Internet, current computer magazines, or other resources, research this topic and write a brief report summarizing your findings. Explain those features that you think make the Windows Vista operating system an easy-to-use operating system.

•• 4 Research Gadgets for Personal Use

Make it Personal

Just like for business, there are lots of useful gadgets for you to find and use. Look online for a Multimedia gadget that will let you play a radio station or watch a TV show. Pick a few that you find interesting. Download and install them. Write a brief report comparing and contrasting them. Which one is the easiest to use? Which one is the worst? If you decide you do not like any of the ones you downloaded, try a couple of more until you find one you like. Include in your report how likely you will or will not download more gadgets to use in the future.

•• 5 Researching Course Registration Procedures

Working Together

Registering for classes can be a daunting task for incoming college freshmen. As someone who has gone through the process, prepare a guide for students who are about to register for the first time next semester. Working with classmates, research and create your guide. Your guide should be two or more documents, include a schedule of key dates and times, a description of the registration procedure, and suggestions for how students can make registration easier. Give the documents suitable names and save them in a folder in the Windows Vista Documents folder. Print each document.

3 File and Folder Management

Objectives

You will have mastered the material in this chapter when you can:

- View the contents of a drive and folder using the Computer folder window

- View the properties of files and folders

- Find files and folders from a folder window

- Find files and folders using Search

- Cascade, stack, and view windows side by side on the desktop

- View the contents of the Pictures folder window

- Open and use the Windows Photo Gallery

- View pictures as a slide show

- E-mail a picture

- View the contents of the Music folder window

- View information about an audio file

- Play an audio file using Windows Media Player

- Create a backup on a USB drive and a CD

- Restore a folder from a backup on a USB drive

3 | File and Folder Management

Introduction

In Chapter 2, you used Windows Vista to create documents on the desktop and work with documents and folders in the Documents folder. Windows Vista also allows you to examine the files and folders on the computer in a variety of other ways, enabling you to choose the easiest and most accessible manner when working with the computer. The Computer folder window and the Documents folder window provide two ways for you to work with files and folders. In addition, the Pictures folder window allows you to organize and share picture files, and the Music folder window allows you to organize and share your music files. This chapter will illustrate how to work with files in the Computer, Documents, Pictures, and Music folder windows.

Overview

As you read this chapter, you will learn how to work with the Computer, Pictures and Music folders by performing these general tasks:

- Opening and using the Computer folder window
- Searching for files and folders
- Managing open windows
- Opening and using the Pictures folder window
- Using the Windows Photo Gallery
- Opening and using the Music folder window
- Playing a music file in Windows Media Player
- Backing up and restoring a folder using a USB drive

Plan
Ahead

Working with the Windows Vista Desktop
Working with the Windows Vista desktop requires a basic knowledge of how to use the Windows Vista desktop, insert a USB drive, access the Internet, and use a printer.

1. **Determine the permissions you have on the computer you will be using.** Each user account can have different rights and permissions. Depending on which rights and permissions have been set for your account, you may or may not be able to perform certain operations.

2. **Identify how to add a USB drive to your computer.** Depending upon the setup of your computer, there may be several ways to add a USB drive to your computer. You should know which USB ports you can use to add a USB drive to your computer.

3. **Determine if your computer has speakers.** Some computer labs do not provide speakers with their computers. If you are going to be using a computer in a lab, you need to know if the computer has speakers or if you will need to bring a set of headphones.

4. **Find out if you have access to the sample files installed with Windows Vista.** To complete the steps in this chapter, you will need access to the sample pictures, videos and sounds installed with Windows Vista.

(continued)

(continued)

Plan
Ahead

5. **Determine if your computer has a CD or DVD burner.** Some labs do not provide CD or DVD burners. If you are going to be using a computer in a lab, you need to know if you have access to a CD or DVD burner to back up your files.

6. **Check to see if e-mail is configured.** To complete the e-mail portion of this chapter, you will need to have access to an e-mail program. You need to make sure that the e-mail program has been configured before you use it.

7. **Understand copyright issues.** When working with multimedia files, you should be aware that most pictures, movies, and music files are copyrighted. Before you use them, you should make sure that you are aware of any copyrights. Just because you can download a picture or music file from the Internet does not mean that it belongs to you.

The Computer Folder Window

As noted in previous chapters, the Start menu displays the Computer command. Selecting the **Computer command** displays a window that contains the storage devices that are installed on the computer. The Computer folder window looks very similar to the Documents folder window that you worked with in the previous chapter. This is due to Windows Vista relying on folder windows to display the contents on the computer. A **folder window** consists of an Address bar at the top, a toolbar containing variable options, a navigation pane on the left below the toolbar, a headings bar and list area on the right below the toolbar, and a Details pane at the bottom of the window. Depending upon which folder you are viewing, Computer, Documents, Pictures, etc., the folder window will display the toolbar options that are most appropriate for working with the folder contents. The toolbar of the Computer folder window shows the Organize, Views, Systems properties, Uninstall or change a program, and Map network drive buttons, but these options will change as the objects displayed change. Although the list area of the Computer window shows groupings based upon the different types of devices connected to your computer, it will display files and folders depending upon your selections.

To Open and Maximize the Computer Folder Window

The following steps open and maximize the Computer folder window so that you can view its contents.

1 Display the Start menu.

2 Click the Computer command to open the Computer folder window. If necessary, maximize the Computer folder window.

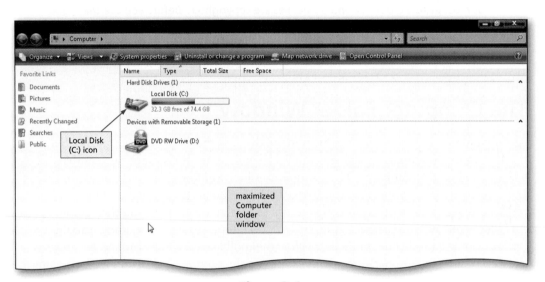

Figure 3–1

The list area of the Computer folder window is organized to group objects based upon the different types of devices connected to your computer. The Hard Disk Drives group contains the **Local Disk (C:) icon** that represents the hard disk on the computer. The **hard disk** is where you can store files, documents, and folders. Storing data on a hard disk is more convenient than storing data on a USB drive because the hard disk is faster, and generally has more storage room available. A computer always will have at least one hard disk drive, normally designated as drive C. On the computer represented by the Computer folder window in Figure 3–1, the icon consists of an image of a hard disk and a **disk label**, or title, Local Disk, and a drive letter (C:). The label is not required and may differ depending upon the name assigned to the hard disk. For example, some people label their drives based upon usage; therefore, it could be called PRIMARY (C:) where PRIMARY is the label given to the hard disk as it is the drive that houses the operating system and main programs.

The Devices with Removable Storage group contains the DVD RW Drive (D:) icon, indicating that there is a DVD burner attached to your computer. The CD RW Drive (D:) icon would indicate that your computer has a CD burner instead of a DVD burner. If your computer has a CD or DVD drive that only reads CD and DVDs, and cannot burn to the discs, you would not see the RW. **RW** is an abbreviation of rewritable, which means that the drive can write data onto read/writable CDs or DVDs. The DVD RW Drive (D:) icon represents the DVD rewritable drive attached to the computer, also known as a DVD burner. The label for the drive is DVD RW Drive, and the drive letter assigned to this drive is (D:). The icon consists of an image of a DVD disc on top of an image of a DVD drive because the drive does not currently contain a DVD. If you were to insert a CD or a DVD in the drive, such as an audio CD containing music, Windows Vista would change the icon to reflect a music CD and change the label to display the artist's name.

To Display Properties for the Local Disk (C:) Drive in the Details Pane

The Details pane of a folder window displays the properties of devices, files, or folders. Every drive, folder, file, and program in Windows Vista is considered an object. Every object in Windows Vista has properties that describe the object. A **property** is a characteristic of an object such as the amount of storage space on a storage device or the number of items in a folder. The properties of each object will differ, and in some cases, you can change the properties of an object. For example, in the Local Disk (C:) properties, you would check the Space free property to determine how much space is available on the C drive. To determine the drive's capacity, you would view the Total size property. The following step displays the properties for the Local Disk (C:) in the Details pane of the Computer folder window.

1

- Click the Local Disk (C:) icon to select the drive and display the properties in the Details pane (Figure 3–2).

Experiment

- See what properties display for the other drives and devices shown. Click each one and note what properties display in the Details pane. Return to the Local Disk (C:) when you are done.

Q&A

Why do the properties of my Local Disk differ from those in the figure?

Because the size of the drive and contents of your drive will be different than the one in the figure, the properties of the drive also will be different. Depending upon what has been installed on the drive and how it is formatted, the space used, file system, space free, and total size properties will vary.

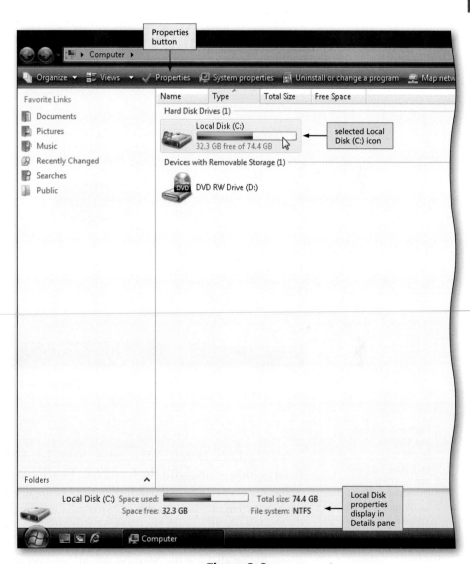

Figure 3–2

To Display the Local Disk (C:) Properties Dialog Box

The properties shown in the Details pane are just a few of the properties of the C: drive. In fact, the Details pane is used to highlight the common properties of a hard disk that most people want to know: the size of the drive, how much space is free, how much space is used, and how the drive is formatted. However, you can display much more detailed information about the hard disk. The Properties dialog box will allow you to view all of the properties of the C: drive. The following step displays the Properties dialog box for the Local Disk (C:) drive.

- Click the Properties button on the toolbar to display the Local Disk (C:) Properties dialog box (Figure 3–3).

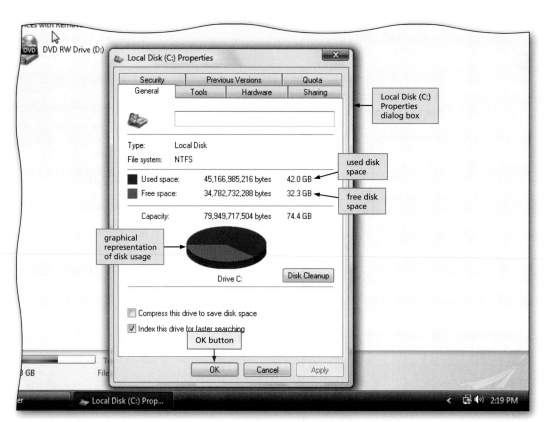

Figure 3–3

Other Ways

1. Right click the Local Disk (C:) icon, click Properties
2. Click drive icon, press ALT, on File menu click Properties
3. Select drive icon, press ALT+ENTER

The Local Disk (C:) Properties dialog box includes tabs that contain advanced features for working with the hard disk. The Tools sheet in the Local Disk (C:) Properties dialog box, accessible by clicking the Tools tab, allows you to check errors, defragment the hard drive, or back up the hard drive. The Hardware sheet, accessible by clicking the Hardware tab, allows you to view a list of all disk drives, troubleshoot disk drives that are not working properly, and display the properties for each disk drive. The Sharing sheet, accessible by clicking the Sharing tab, allows you to share the contents of a hard disk with other computer users. However, to protect a computer from unauthorized access, sharing the hard disk is not recommended. Other tabs may display in the Local Disk (C:) Properties dialog box on your computer. The Security sheet displays the security settings for the drive, such as user permissions. The Previous Versions sheet allows you to work with copies of your hard disk that are created when using backup utilities or from automatic saves. Finally, the Quota sheet can be used to see how much space is being used by various user accounts.

To Close the Local Disk (C:) Properties Dialog Box

Now that you have reviewed the Local Disk (C:) Properties dialog box, you should close it.

1

• Click the OK button to close the Local Disk (C:) Properties dialog box (Figure 3–4).

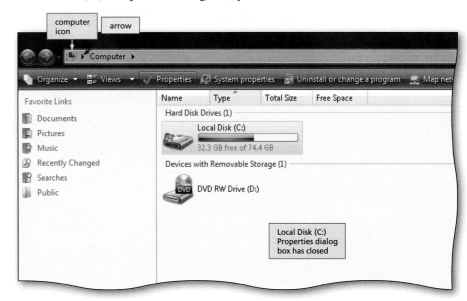

Figure 3–4

Other Ways

1. Click the Cancel button
2. Click the Close button
3. Press ESC

To Switch Folders Using the Address Bar

Found on all folder windows, the Address bar lets you know which folder you are viewing. A useful feature of the Address bar is its capability to allow you to switch to different folder windows by clicking on the arrow directly after the first item listed on the Address bar. Clicking the arrow displays a command menu, containing options for showing the desktop on a folder window, or switching to the Computer folder, the Recycle Bin, the Control Panel, the Public folder, your personal folder, and the Network folder. The following steps change the folder window from showing the Computer folder to showing the desktop, and then returning to the Computer folder.

1

• Click the arrow to the right of the computer icon on the Address bar to display a menu that contains folder switching commands (Figure 3–5).

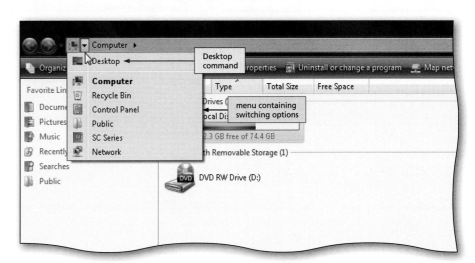

Figure 3–5

2

- Click the Desktop command to switch to viewing the contents of the desktop in a folder window (Figure 3–6).

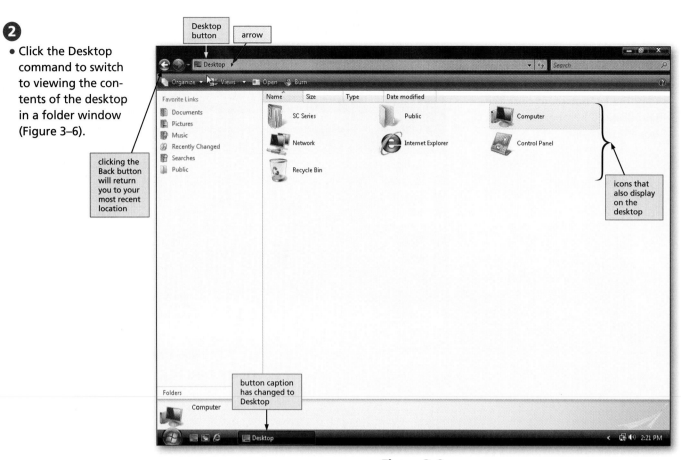

Figure 3–6

3

- Click the arrow to the right of the Desktop button on the Address bar to display a menu containing switching options (Figure 3–7).

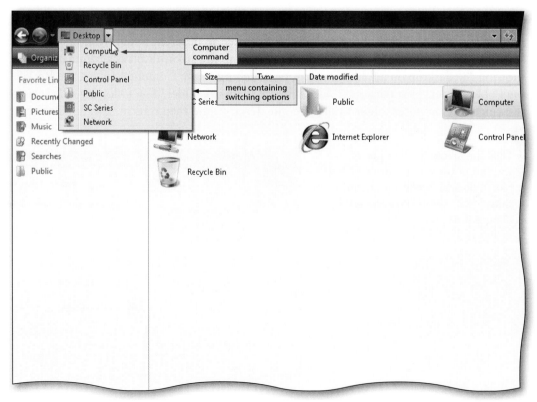

Figure 3–7

4

• Click the Computer command to switch to the Computer folder (Figure 3–8).

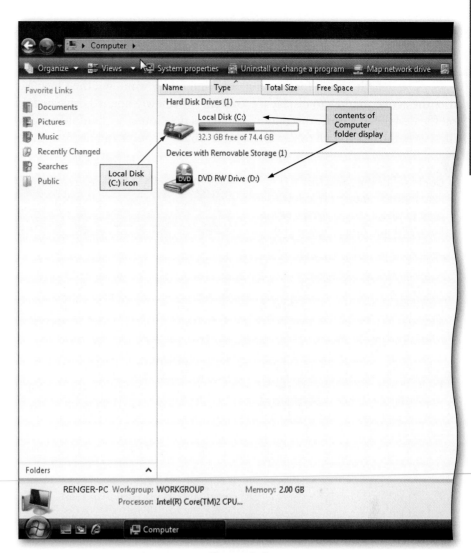

Figure 3–8

To View the Contents of a Drive

In addition to viewing the contents of the Computer folder, you can view the contents of drives and folders. In previous chapters, you have viewed windows for folders and windows for drives. In fact, the contents of any folder or drive on a computer can display in a folder window.

The default option for opening drive and folder windows, the Open each folder in the same window option, uses the active window to display the contents of a newly opened drive or folder. Because only one window displays on the desktop at a time, this option eliminates the clutter of multiple windows on the desktop. The following step illustrates the Open each folder in the same window option and displays the contents of the C: drive.

1

- Double-click the Local Disk (C:) icon in the Computer folder window to display the contents of the Local Disk (C:) drive (Figure 3–9).

Q&A ◄ Why do I see different folders?

The contents of the Local Disk (C:) window you display on your computer can differ from the contents shown in Figure 3–9 because each computer has its own folders, application programs, and documents. The manner in which you interact with and control the programs and documents in Windows Vista is the same, regardless of the actual programs or documents.

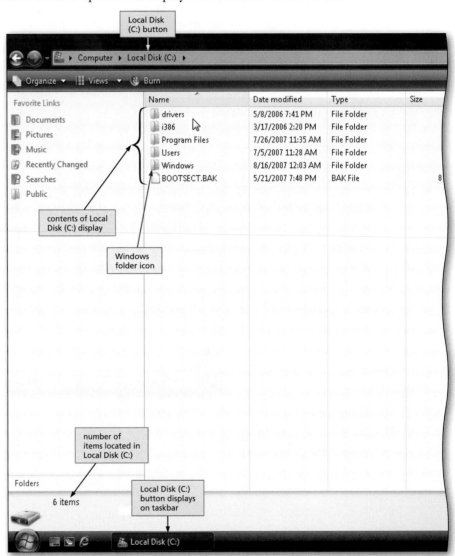

Figure 3–9

Other Ways

1. Right-click Local Disk (C:), click Open
2. Click Local Disk (C:), press ENTER

To Preview the Properties for a Folder

When you move your mouse over a folder icon, a preview of the folder properties will display in a tooltip format. A **tooltip** is a brief description that appears when you hold the mouse over an object on the screen. Not every item will cause a tooltip to display, but many times they will appear and provide useful information. The properties typically consist of the date and time created, the folder size, and the name of the folder. One folder in the Local Disk (C:) window, the **Windows folder**, contains programs and files necessary for the operation of the Windows Vista operating system. As such, you should exercise caution when working with the contents of the Windows folder because changing the contents of the folder may cause the programs to stop working correctly. The following step shows a preview of the properties for the Windows folder.

1

• Point to the Windows folder icon to display a preview of the properties for the Windows folder (Figure 3–10).

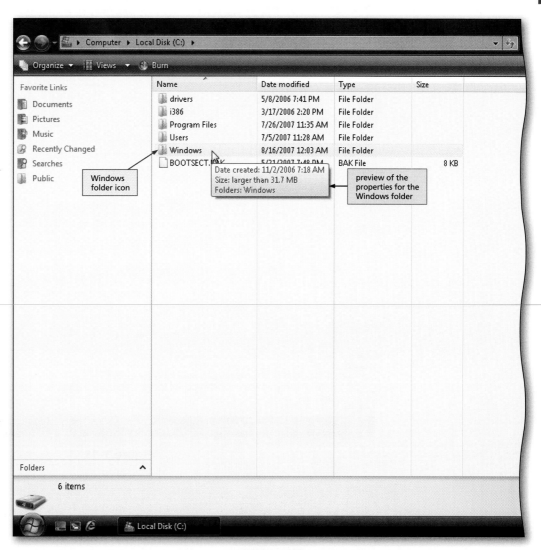

Figure 3–10

To Display Properties for the Windows Folder in the Details Pane

Just like with drives, properties of folders can be displayed in the Details pane. The following step displays the properties for the Windows folder in the Details pane of the Computer folder window.

- Click the Windows folder icon to display the properties in the Details pane (Figure 3–11).

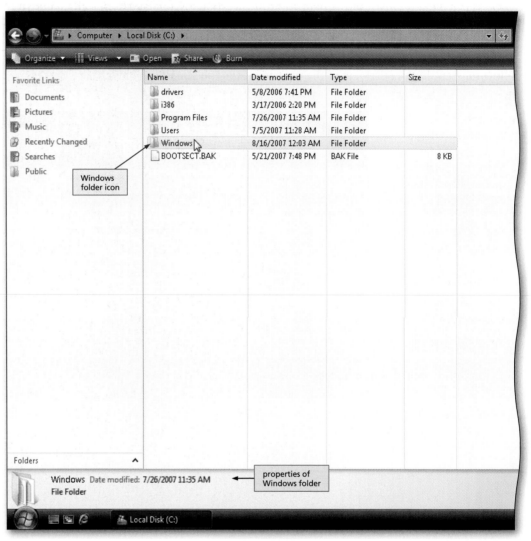

Figure 3–11

To Display All of the Properties for the Windows Folder

If you want to see all of the properties for the Windows folder, you will need to open up the Properties dialog box. The following steps display the Properties dialog box for the Windows folder.

1

• Right-click the Windows folder icon to display a shortcut menu (Figure 3–12). (The commands on your shortcut menu may differ.)

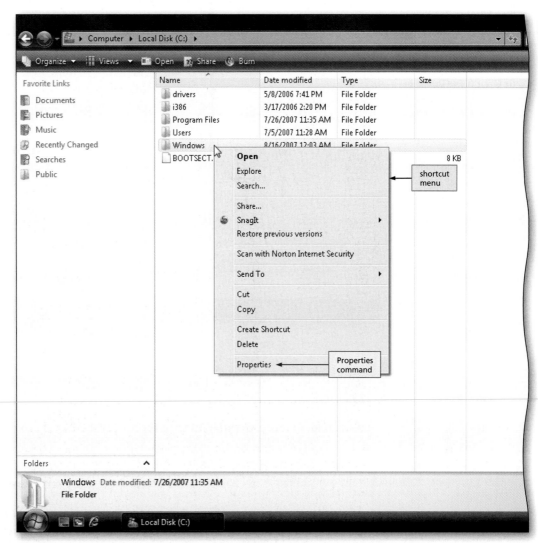

Figure 3–12

2

- Click the Properties command to display the Windows Properties dialog box (Figure 3–13).

Experiment

- Click the various tabs in the Properties dialog box to see the different properties available for a folder.

Q&A Why might you want to look at the properties of a folder?

When you are working with folders, you might need to look at folders' properties in order to make changes, such as configuring a folder for sharing over a network or hiding folders from users who do not need access to them. You even can customize the appearance of a folder to be different than the default Windows folder view.

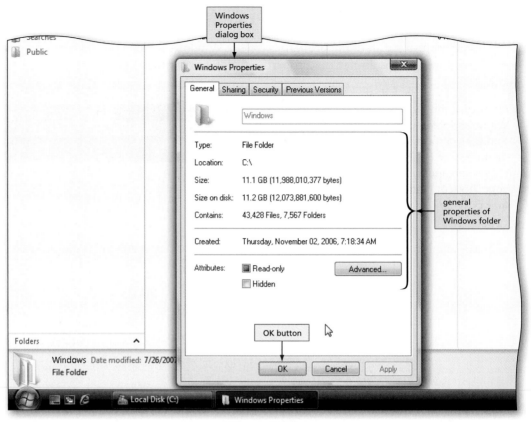

Figure 3–13

Q&A Why are the tabs of the Windows folder properties different than for the Local Disk (C:) properties?

Drives, folders and files have different properties, and therefore need different tabs. A folder's Properties dialog box typically shows the General, Sharing, Security, and Previous Versions tabs; however, depending upon your Windows Vista version and installed applications, the tabs may differ. The Properties dialog box always will have the General tab, although what it displays may differ.

To Close the Properties Dialog Box

Now that you have seen all of the properties, you should close the Properties dialog box.

1 Click the OK button to close the Windows Properties dialog box.

To View the Contents of a Folder

The following step opens the Windows folder so that you can view its contents.

1

- Double-click the Windows folder icon to display the contents of the Windows folder. If necessary, switch to Design view (Figure 3–14).

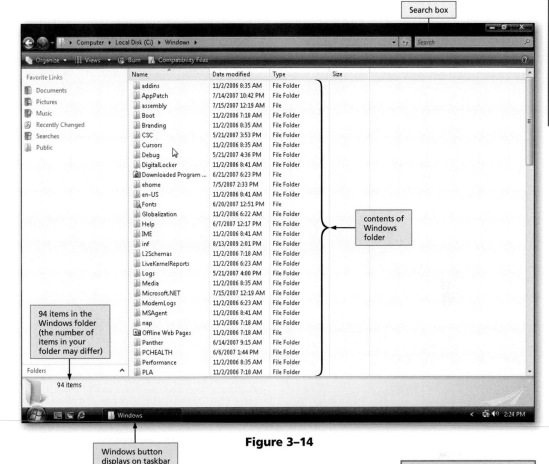

Figure 3–14

Other Ways

1. Right-click the Windows icon, click Open
2. Click the Windows icon, press ENTER

Searching for Files and Folders

The majority of objects displayed in the Windows folder, as shown in Figure 3–14, are folder icons. Folder icons always display in alphabetical order at the top of the list of objects in a folder window, before the icons for applications or files.

A folder such as the Windows folder contains many folders and files. When you want to find a particular file or folder but have no idea where it is located, you can use the Search box to find the file or folder quickly. Similar to the Search box on the Start menu, as soon as you start typing, the window will update to show search results that match what you typed. As Windows Vista is searching for files or folders that match what you entered, you will see a searching message displayed in the list area, an animated circle will attach to the pointer, and an animated progress bar will appear on the Address bar to provide live feedback as to how much of the search has been completed. When searching is complete, you will see a list of all items that matched your search criteria.

If you know only a portion of a file's name and can specify where the known portion of the name should appear, you can use an asterisk in the name to represent the unknown characters. For example, if you know a file starts with the letters MSP, you can type `msp*` in the Search box. All files that begin with the letters msp, regardless of what letters follow, will display. However, with Windows Vista's powerful search capabilities, you would get the same results if you did not include the asterisk. If you wanted all files with a particular extension, you can use the asterisk to stand in for the name of the files. For example, to find all the text files with the extension rtf, you would type `*.rtf` in the Search box. Windows Vista would find all the files with the rtf extension.

To Search for a File and Folder in a Folder Window

The following step uses the Search box to search the Windows folder for all the objects that contain 'aero'.

1

• Type `aero` in the Search box to search for all files and folders that match the search criteria (Figure 3–15).

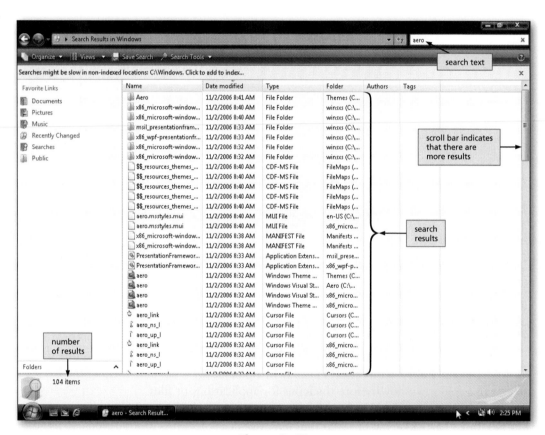

Figure 3–15

To Return to the Computer Folder Window

As you have learned, you can return to the Windows folder by clicking the Back button at the top of the folder window; however, you also can return to where you were prior to searching by clearing the Search Box. The following steps will return you to the Computer folder window.

- Double-click the search text, aero, to select it.

- Press the DELETE key to remove the search text from the Search box and redisplay all files and folders in the Windows folder (Figure 3–16).

- Click the Computer button on the Address bar to return to the Computer folder window.

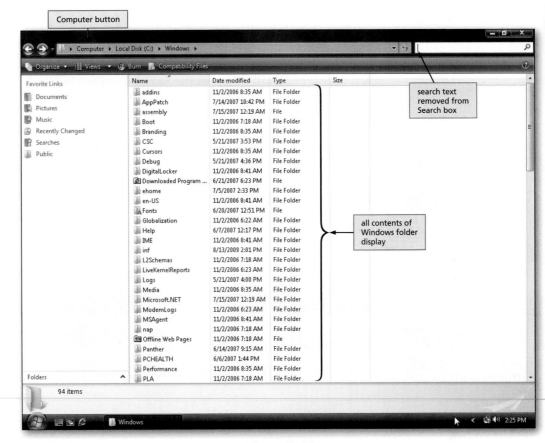

Figure 3–16

Using the Search Window to Find Files

Another way to search is to use the Search window. The Search window is accessible via the Start menu. It contains a Search box similar to the one found in the folder window, but also includes a Search toolbar. Using the Search toolbar, you can limit your search to specific types of files, including e-mail, documents, pictures, and music. The Search window also includes a link to Advanced Search options.

Using Advanced Search allows you to select a specific location to search, such as other computers on a network. Normal search only goes through the locations that have been indexed by Windows Vista. An **indexed location** is a location that has been added to the Search Index for Windows. The Search Index allows Search to find files and folders faster than without an index. Windows Vista builds this automatically as you create files and folders. Locations on Network computers are not automatically added to your computer's Search Index.

BTW

Hidden Files and Folders
Hidden files and folders usually are placed on your hard disk by software vendors such as Microsoft and often are critical to the operation of the software. Rarely will you need to designate a file as hidden. You should not delete a hidden file as doing so may interrupt how or whether an application program works. By default, hidden files and folders are not displayed in a file listing.

Advanced Search also allows you to search for files and folders by location, date, size, name, tags, and authors. You can search for a file based on when you last worked with the file, or search for files containing specific text. You also can choose to search non-indexed, hidden, and system files as well. Additionally, if you have edited the properties of a file or folder and added tags, you will then be able to find them using the Tags text box in Advanced Search.

If the search results were not satisfactory, you can refine the search by changing the file name or keywords, looking in more locations, or changing whether hidden and system files are included in the search. If no files were found in the search, a message (No items match your search) will appear in the Search Results window. In this case, you may want to double-check the information you entered or select different parameters to continue the search. For now, you will work with a basic search using the Search window, but in later chapters, you will experiment with all the features of an advanced search.

To Search for Files Using Advanced Search

The following steps search for all files with the name, forest, using Advanced Search.

1

- Display the Start menu.

- Click the Search command to display the Search Results window (Figure 3–17).

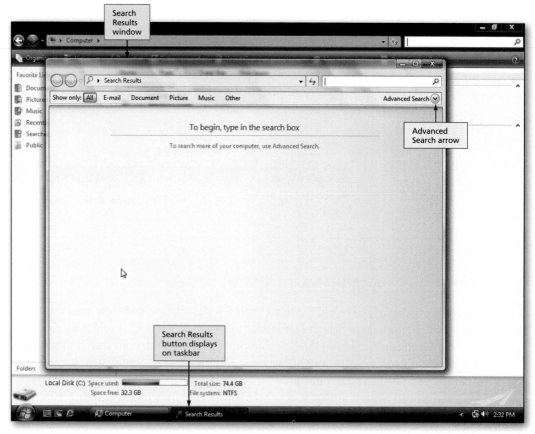

Figure 3–17

2

- Click the Advanced Search arrow to display the Advanced Search pane (Figure 3–18).

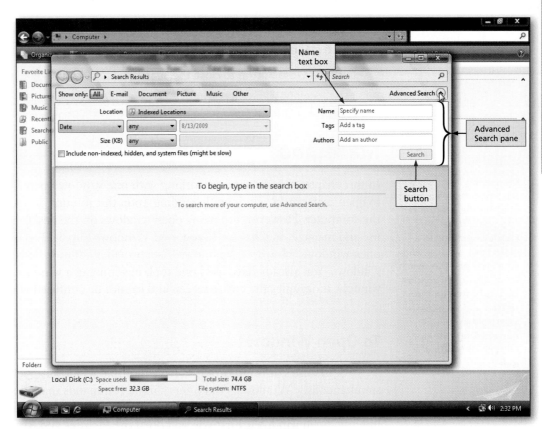

Figure 3–18

3

- Type `forest` in the Name text box.

- Click the Search button to search for all files and folders that match the search criteria, forest (Figure 3–19).

 Experiment

- Click the different results to view them. Consider how they match the search criteria.

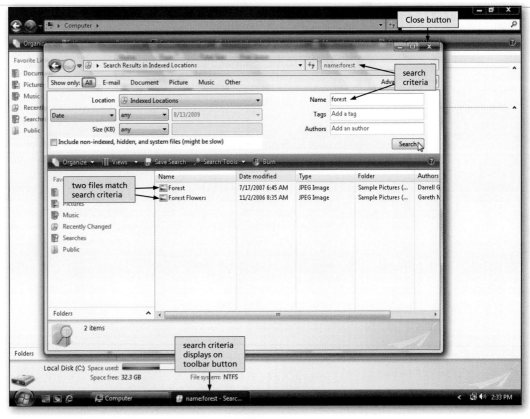

Figure 3–19

To Close the Search Window

You will be conducting more advanced searches in a later chapter; however, now that you have finished searching, you should close the Search window.

1 Click the Close button to close the Search Results window.

Managing Open Windows

BTW

Managing Windows
Having multiple windows open on the desktop can intimidate some users. Consider working in a maximized window, and when you want to switch to another open window, click its button on the taskbar and then maximize it. Many people find working with one maximized window is easier.

In this chapter, you have been working with one window open. Windows Vista allows you to open many more windows depending upon the amount of RAM you have installed on the computer. However, too many open windows on the desktop can become difficult to use and manage. In Chapter 1, you used Windows Flip 3-D to navigate through multiple open windows. However, Windows Vista provides additional tools for managing open windows. You already have used one tool, maximizing a window. When you maximize a window, it occupies the entire screen and cannot be confused with other open windows.

To Open Windows

Sometimes, it is important to have multiple windows appear on the desktop simultaneously. Windows Vista offers simple commands that allow you to arrange multiple windows in specific ways. The following sections describe the ways that you can manage mulitple open windows. First you will open the Pictures and Music folder windows.

1 Display the Start menu.

2 Click the Pictures command to open the Pictures folder window.

3 Display the Start menu.

4 Click the Music command to open the Music folder window.

To Cascade Open Windows

One way to organize windows on the desktop is to display them in a cascade format, where they overlap one another in an organized manner. Windows Vista only cascades open windows. Windows that are minimized or closed will not be cascaded on the desktop. When you cascade open windows, the windows are resized to be the same size to produce the layered cascading effect. The following steps cascade the open windows on the desktop.

1
- Right-click an open area on the taskbar to display a shortcut menu (Figure 3–20).

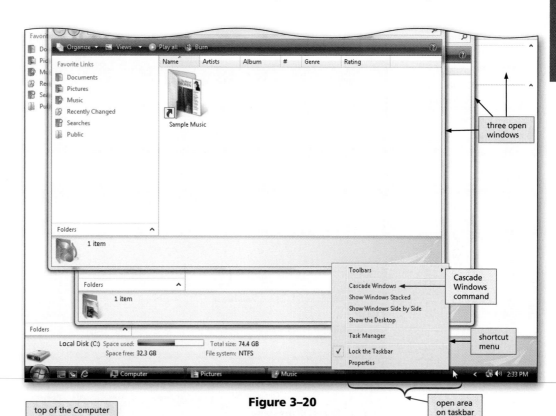

Figure 3–20

2
- Click the Cascade Windows command on the shortcut menu to cascade the open windows (Figure 3–21).

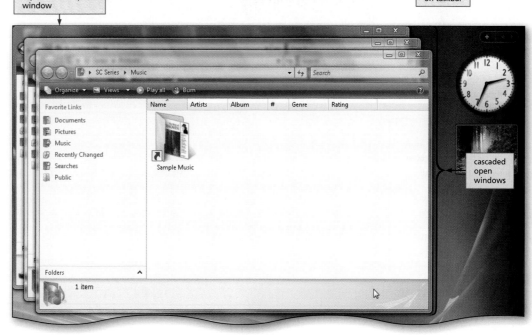

Figure 3–21

Other Ways
1. Right-click an open area on the taskbar, press D

To Make a Window the Active Window

When windows are cascaded, as shown in Figure 3–21 on the previous page, they are arranged so that you can see them easily. In order to work in one of the windows, you first must make it the active window. When you make the Computer folder window the active window, it will remain the same size and remain in the same relative position as placed by the Cascade Windows command. The following step makes the Computer folder window the active window.

- Click the top of the Computer folder window to make it the active window (Figure 3–22).

Q&A

What happens if I click the wrong window?

Click the remaining windows until the Computer folder window displays in the foreground.

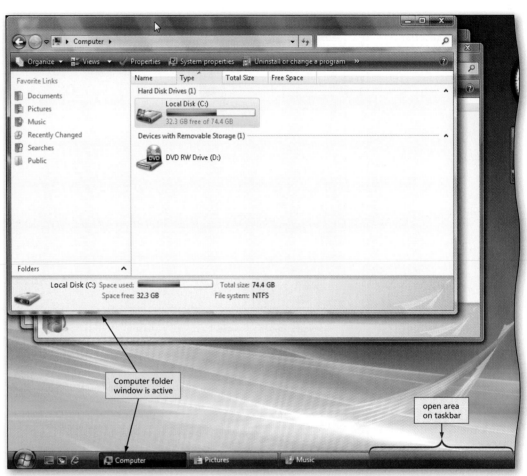

Figure 3–22

Other Ways

1. Click Computer button in taskbar button area
2. Press ALT+TAB until Computer folder window is selected, release ALT key
3. Click anywhere in window to make it active

To Undo Cascading

Now that you have seen the effect of the Cascade Windows command, you will undo the cascade operation and return the windows to the size and location they were before cascading. Depending upon the task at hand, cascading the windows may not allow you to view the contents of the windows the way you would like. The following steps undo the previous cascading of the windows.

- Right-click an open area on the taskbar to display the shortcut menu (Figure 3–23).

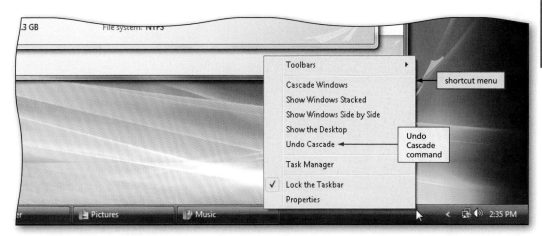

Figure 3–23

- Click the Undo Cascade command to return the windows to their original sizes and locations (Figure 3–24).

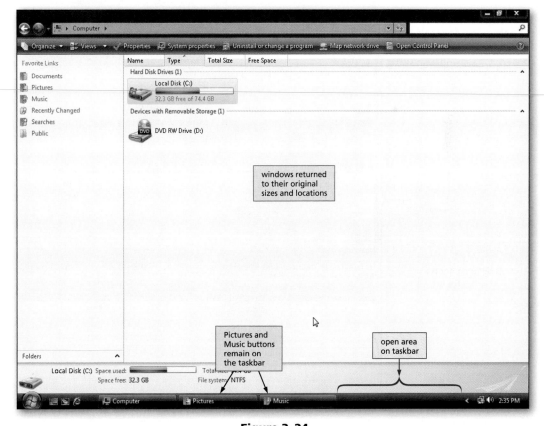

Figure 3–24

Other Ways

1. Right-click an open area on taskbar, press U
2. Press CTRL+Z

To Stack Open Windows

While cascading arranges the windows on the desktop so that each of the each of the window's title bars is visible, it is impossible to see the contents of each window. Windows Vista also can stack the open windows, which allows you to see partial contents of each window. The windows will be resized to the full width of the screen and arranged on top of each other vertically, like a stack of books. Each window will be the same size, and you will be able to see a portion of each window. The following steps stack the open windows.

- Right-click an open area on the taskbar to display the shortcut menu (Figure 3-25).

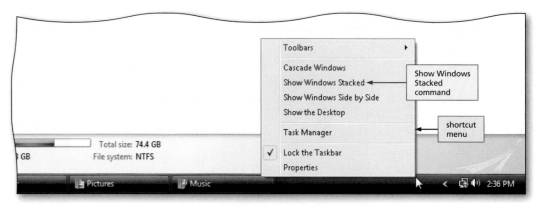

Figure 3–25

- Click the Show Windows Stacked command to stack the open windows (Figure 3–26).

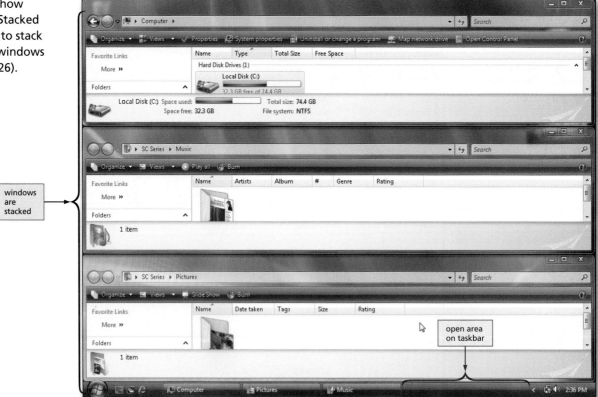

Figure 3–26

Other Ways

1. Right-click an open area on taskbar, press T until Show Windows Stacked is selected, press ENTER

To Undo Show Windows Stacked

While the stacked windows are arranged so that you can view all of them, it is likely that the reduced size of an individual window makes working in the window difficult. You will undo the stacking operation to return the windows to the size and position they occupied before stacking. If you want to work in a particular window, you should maximize the window. The following steps return the windows to their original sizes and position.

- Right-click an open area on the taskbar to display the shortcut menu (Figure 3–27).

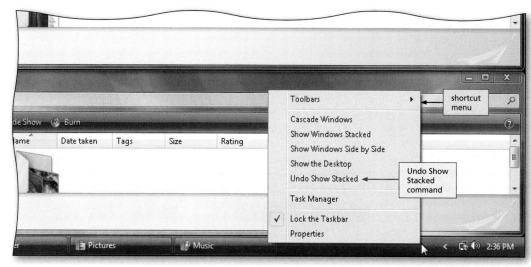

Figure 3–27

- Click the Undo Show Stacked command to return the windows to their original sizes and locations (Figure 3–28).

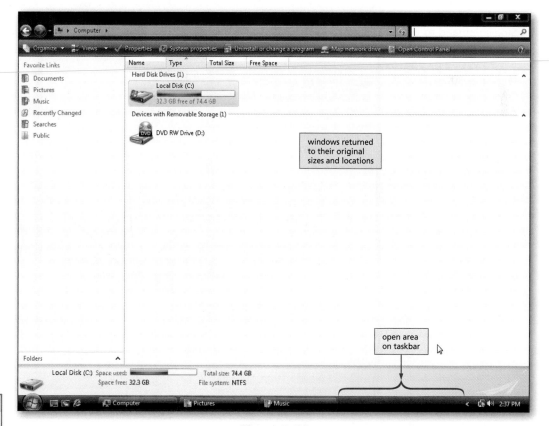

Figure 3–28

Other Ways
1. Right-click an open area on taskbar, press U
2. Press CTRL+Z

To Show Windows Side by Side

While stacking arranges the windows vertically above each other on the desktop, it also is possible to arrange them horizontally from left to right, or side by side. The Show Windows Side by Side command allows you to see partial contents of each window horizontally. The following steps show the open windows side by side.

- Right-click an open area on the taskbar to display the shortcut menu (Figure 3-29).

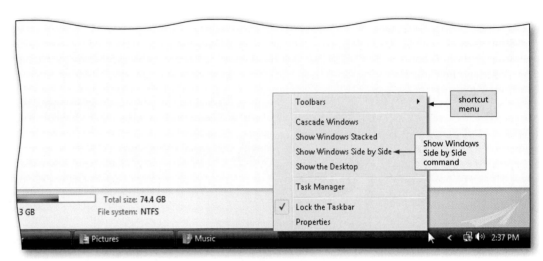

Figure 3–29

- Click the Show Windows Side by Side command to display the open windows side by side (Figure 3–30).

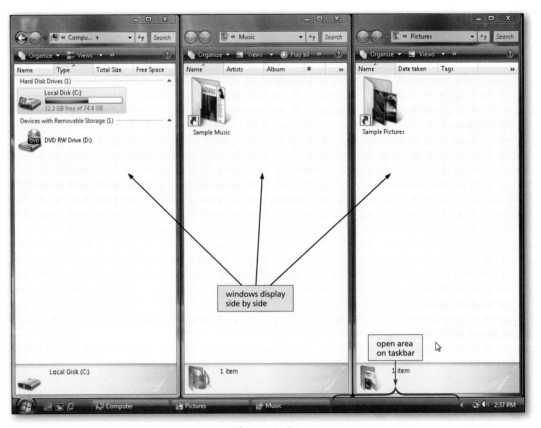

Figure 3–30

Other Ways

1. Right-click an open area on taskbar, press I

To Undo Show Windows Side by Side

The following steps undo the side by side operation and return the windows to the arrangement shown in Figure 3–28 on page WIN 173.

- Right-click an open area on the taskbar to display the shortcut menu (Figure 3–31).

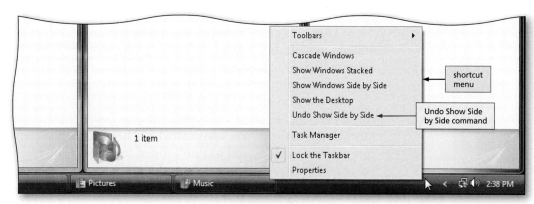

Figure 3–31

- Click the Undo Show Side by Side command to return the windows to their original sizes and locations (Figure 3–32).

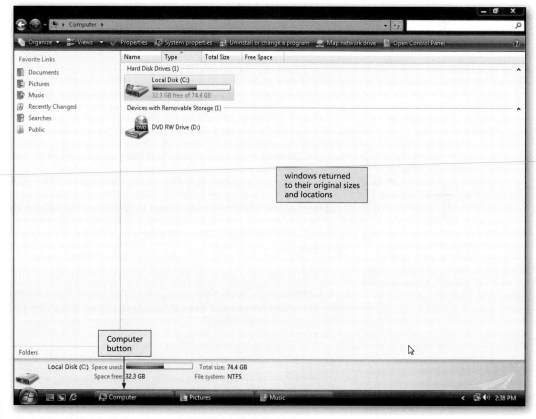

Figure 3–32

Other Ways

1. Right-click an open area on taskbar, press U
2. Press CTRL+Z

The Pictures Folder

You can organize your pictures and share them with others using the Pictures folder. The Pictures folder was created to encourage users to organize their pictures in one location. By putting all your pictures in the Pictures folder, you always know where to find your pictures. When you save pictures from a digital camera, scanner, or hard drive, by default,

Windows Vista stores the pictures in the Pictures folder. Applications that you install to work with pictures also can be saved to this folder.

Using this folder will allow you to view the pictures as a slide show, share pictures with others, e-mail pictures to friends, print pictures, publish pictures to the Internet, and order prints of a picture from the Internet. You will work with a few of the options now, and the rest will be covered in a later chapter where multimedia files will be covered in greater depth.

There are many different formats for picture files. Some pictures have an extension of .bmp to indicate a bitmap file. Other pictures might have the extension .gif extension to indicate that they are of the Graphics Interchange Format. There are too many file types to mention; however, some common ones are .bmp, .jpg, .gif, and .tif.

When working with pictures, you should be aware that most images that you did not create yourself, like other multimedia files, are copyrighted. A **copyright** means that a picture belongs to the person who created it. The pictures that come with Windows Vista are part of Windows Vista and you are allowed to use them; however, they are not yours. You only can use them according to the rights given to you by Microsoft. Pictures that you take using your digital camera are yours, because you created them. Before using pictures and other multimedia files, you should be aware of any copyrights associated with them, and you should know whether you are allowed to use them for your intended purpose.

To Search for Pictures

You want to copy three files, Monet, Psychedelic, and Pine_Lumber, from the Windows folder to the Pictures folder; but first, you have to find these files. Because the three files all have the .jpg extension, you can search for them using an asterisk (*) in place of the file name, as discussed earlier in this chapter. The following steps open the Windows folder window and display the icons for the files you wish to copy.

1 Click the Computer button on the taskbar to switch to the Computer folder window.

2 Double-click the Local Disk (C:) icon in the Computer folder window.

3 Double-click the Windows folder icon in the Local Disk (C:) window.

4 Type *.jpg in the Search box and then press the ENTER key to search for all files with a jpg file extension.

5 Scroll down the right pane of the Windows folder window until the icons for the Monet, Pine_Lumber, and Psychedelic files are visible in the right pane (Figure 3–33). If one or more of these files are not available, select any of the other picture files.

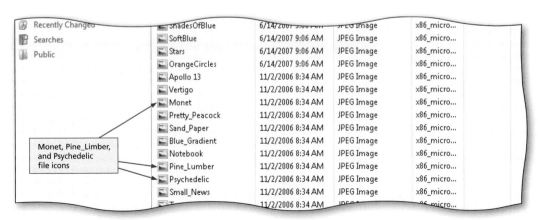

Figure 3–33

To Copy Files to the Pictures Folder

In Chapter 2, you learned how to move and copy document files on the desktop to a folder, how to copy a folder onto a USB drive, and how to delete files. Another method you can use to copy a file or folder is the **copy and paste method**. When you **copy** a file, you place a copy of the file in a temporary storage area of the computer called the **Clipboard**. When you **paste** the file, Windows Vista copies it from the Clipboard to the location you specify. You now have two copies of the same file.

Because the search results include the pictures you were looking for, you now can select the files and then copy them to the Pictures folder. Once the three files have been copied into the Pictures folder, the files will be stored in both the Pictures folder and Windows folder on drive C. Copying and moving files are common tasks when working with Windows Vista. If you want to move a file instead of copying a file, you would use the Cut command on the shortcut menu to move the file to the Clipboard, and the Paste command to copy the file from the Clipboard to the new location. When the move is complete, the files are moved into the new folder and no longer are stored in the original folder.

The following steps copy the Monet, Pine_Lumber, and Psychedelic files from the Windows folder to the Pictures folder.

1

- Hold down the CTRL key and then click the Monet, Pine_Lumber, and Psychedelic icons.

- Release the CTRL key.

- Right-click any highlighted icon to display a shortcut menu (Figure 3–34).

Q&A

Are copying and moving the same?

No! When you copy a file, it is located in both the place to which it was copied and in the place from which it was copied. When you move a file, it is located only in the location to which it was moved.

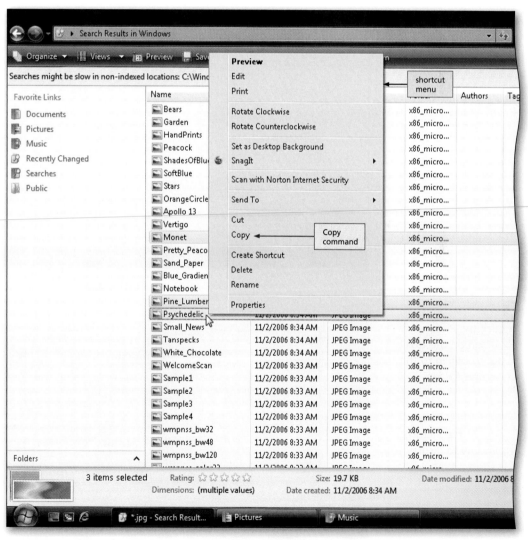

Figure 3–34

• Click the Copy command on the shortcut menu to copy the files to the Clipboard (Figure 3–35).

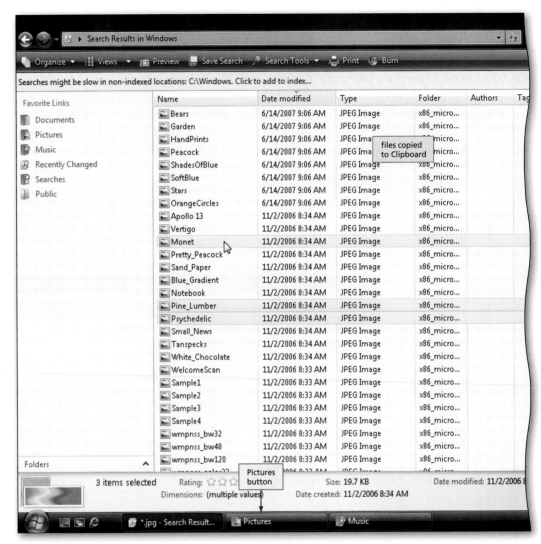

Figure 3–35

• Click the Pictures button on the task-bar to switch to the Pictures folder window.

• Right-click an open area of the Pictures window to display a shortcut menu (Figure 3–36).

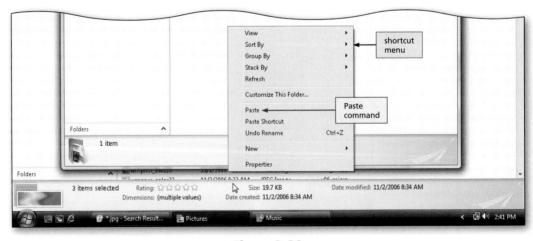

Figure 3–36

4

• Click the Paste command on the shortcut menu to paste the files in the Pictures folder (Figure 3–37).

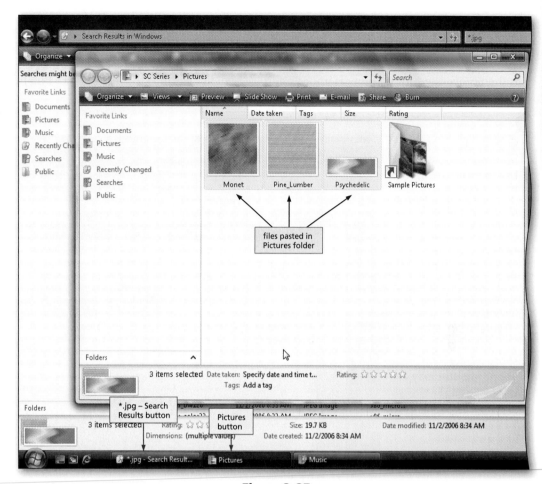

Figure 3–37

To Close the Search Results Window

You no longer need the Search Results window open, so you can close it. Whenever you are not using a window, it is a good idea to close it so as not to clutter your desktop. The following steps close the Search Results window.

1 Click the *.jpg - Search Results button on the taskbar to display the Search Results window.

2 Close the Search Results window.

Other Ways

1. Select file icons, press ALT, on Edit menu click Copy, display window where you want to store file, press ALT, on Edit menu click Paste

2. Select file icons, press ALT, on Edit menu click Copy To Folder, click arrow next to your user name, click Pictures, click Copy button

3. Select file icons, press CTRL+C, display the window where you want to store file, press CTRL+V

To Create a Folder in the Pictures Folder

When you have several related files stored in a folder with with a number of unrelated files, you may wish to create a folder to contain the related files so that you can find and reference them easily. To reduce clutter and improve the organization of files in the Pictures folder, you will create a new folder in the Pictures folder window and then move the Monet, Pine_Lumber, and Psychedelic files into the new folder. The following steps create the Backgrounds folder in the Pictures folder.

- Click the Pictures button on the task-bar to make the Pictures folder window the active window.

- Right-click any open part of the list area of the Pictures folder window to display a shortcut menu (Figure 3–38). (The commands on the shortcut menu on your computer may differ slightly.)

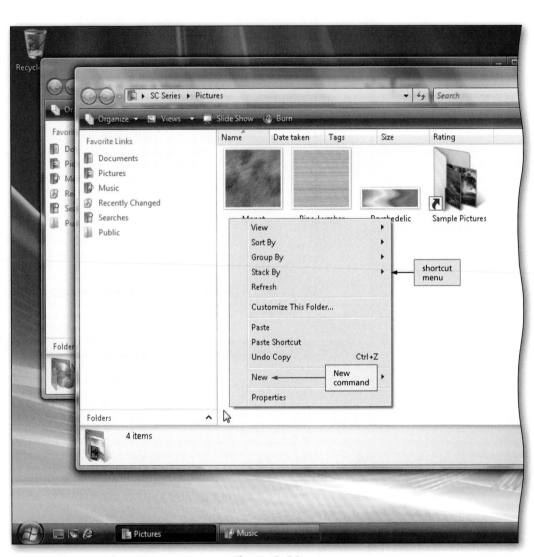

Figure 3–38

2

- Point to the New command on the shortcut menu to display the New sub-menu (Figure 3–39). (The commands on the New submenu on your computer may differ slightly.)

Figure 3–39

3

- Click the Folder command on the New submenu to create a new folder in the Pictures folder.

- Type Backgrounds in the icon title text box, and then press the ENTER key to assign the name to the new folder (Figure 3–40).

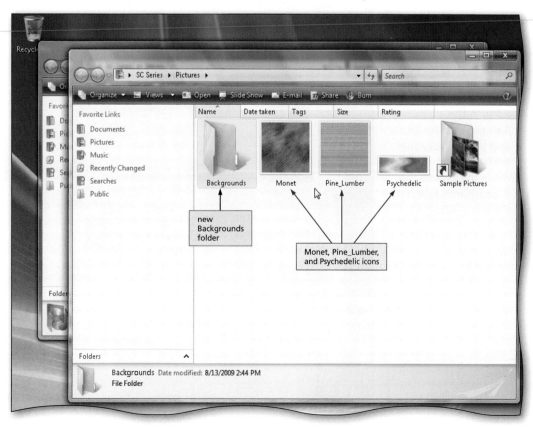

Figure 3–40

Other Ways

1. Press ALT, click File menu, point to New, click Folder, type file name, press ENTER

2. Press ALT+F, press W twice, press RIGHT ARROW, press F, type file name, press ENTER

To Move Multiple Files into a Folder

After you create the Backgrounds folder in the Pictures folder, the next step is to move the three picture files into the folder. The following steps move the Monet, Psychedelic, and Pine_Lumber files into the Backgrounds folder.

1

- Click the Monet icon, hold down the CTRL key, and then click Pine_Lumber and Psychedelic icons to select all three icons (Figure 3–41).

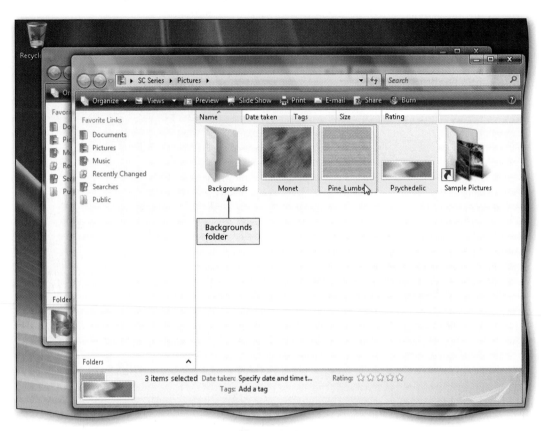

Figure 3–41

2

- Drag the selected icons to the Backgrounds folder, and then release the mouse button to move the files to the Backgrounds folder (Figure 3–42).

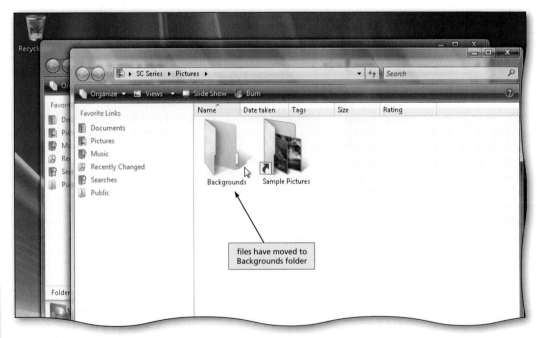

Other Ways

1. Drag icons individually to folder icon
2. Right-click icon, click Cut, right-click folder icon, click Paste

Figure 3–42

To Refresh the Image on a Folder

After moving the three files into the Backgrounds folder, it still appears as an empty open folder icon. To replace the empty folder icon with a Live Preview of the three files stored in the Backgrounds folder (Monet, Pine_ Lumber, Psychedelic), the Pictures folder window must be refreshed. The following steps refresh the Pictures folder window to display the Live Preview for the Backgrounds folder.

- Right-click any open part of the list area to display a shortcut menu (Figure 3–43).

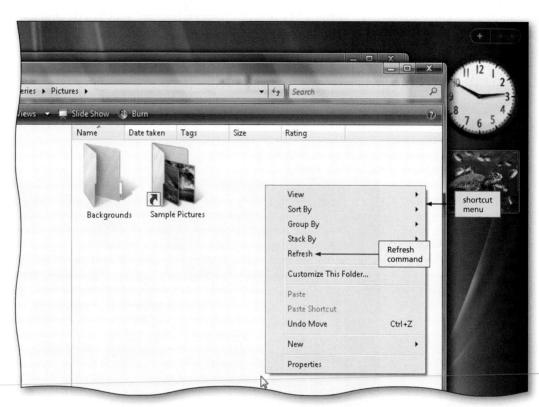

Figure 3–43

- Click the Refresh command to refresh the list area (Figure 3–44).

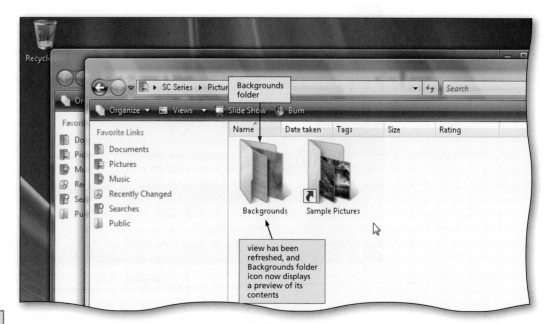

Figure 3–44

To View and Change the Properties of a Picture

As mentioned earlier in the chapter, in Windows Vista, all objects have properties. You already have explored the properties of a drive, now you will review the properties of a picture. Picture properties include the Date taken, Tags, Rating, Dimensions, and Size. Date taken refers to the date the person created the picture. Tags are keywords you associate with a Picture file to aid in its classification. For example you could tag a family photo with the names of the people in the photo. When you create a tag, it should be meaningful. For example, if you have pictures from a family vacation at the beach and you add a title of vacation; later on, you will be able to find the file using the tag, 'vacation', in a search. Be aware that you only can search for tags that you already have created. If your family vacation photo was saved as "photo1.jpg" and tagged with the tag "vacation", you will not find it by searching for "beach" as it is not part of the name or tag. Rating refers to the ranking, in stars, that you assign to a picture. You can rate a picture from zero to five stars. Date taken, Tags, and Rating all can be changed using the Details pane. Because you do not know when the Background pictures were created, you only will change the Tags and Rating properties. The following steps display and change the Tags and Rating properties of the Monet image in the Backgrounds folder.

- Display the contents of the Backgrounds folder.

- Click the Monet icon to select it (Figure 3–45).

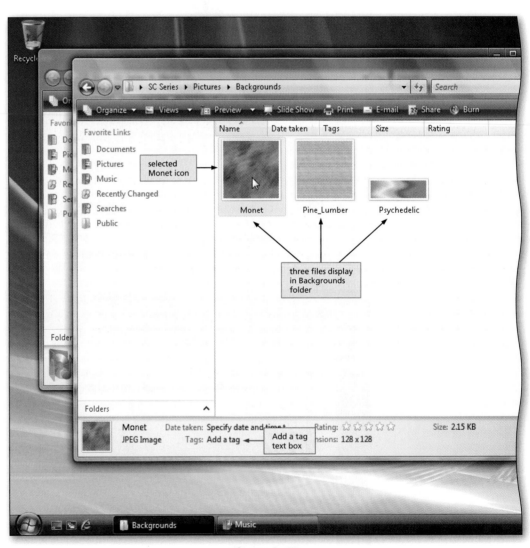

Figure 3–45

2

- Click the Add a tag text box in the Details pane to activate it (Figure 3–46).

Figure 3–46

3

- Type A Work of Art in the text box to create a tag for the picture (Figure 3–47).

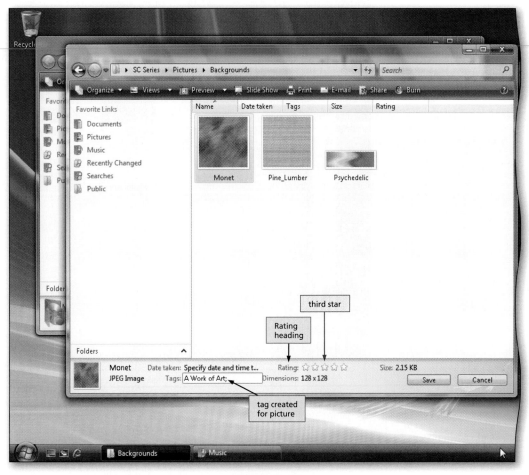

Figure 3–47

4

- Click the third star next to the Rating heading in the Details pane to assign a 3-star rating to the picture (Figure 3–48).

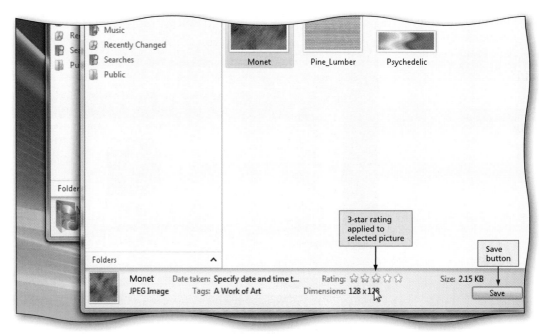

Figure 3–48

5

- Click the Save button in the Details pane to save the changes to the Tags and Rating (Figure 3–49).

Figure 3–49

Other Ways

1. Right-click icon, click Properties, click Details tab, enter text next to Tags, click third star next to Rating, click OK

To Open a Picture in the Windows Photo Gallery

You can view the images in a folder in the Windows Photo Gallery or as a slide show. The **Windows Photo Gallery** is a program that allows you to view each image separately, and work with the pictures in your Pictures folder. It can be used to view pictures individually or as part of a slide show. A later chapter will cover the Windows Photo Gallery in more detail. For now, you will look at the basics of Windows Photo Gallery.

The buttons on the toolbar at the bottom of the Windows Photo Gallery allow you to move through the images and rotate an image clockwise or counterclockwise. The following steps display the Monet image in the Backgrounds folder in the Windows Photo Gallery.

- If necessary, select the Monet icon.

- Click the Preview button on the toolbar to open the Monet picture in the Windows Photo Gallery (Figure 3–50).

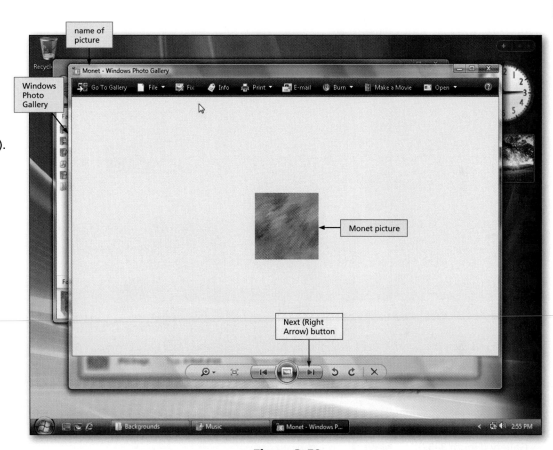

Figure 3–50

Other Ways
1. Right-click icon, click Preview

To Navigate through Your Pictures

To navigate through your pictures, you use the buttons at the bottom of the Windows Photo Gallery window. The Next (Right Arrow) button allows you to move forward to the next photo, and the Previous (Left Arrow) button allows you to move backward to the photo you already have seen. The following steps navigate through the pictures in the Backgrounds folder using the Windows Photo Gallery.

- Click the Next (Right Arrow) button to view the Pine_Lumber image in the Windows Photo Gallery (Figure 3–51).

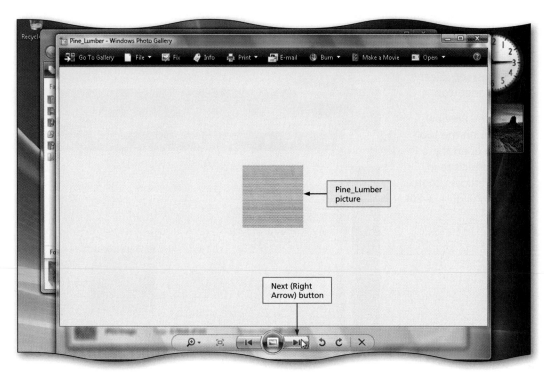

Figure 3–51

2

- Click the Next (Right Arrow) button to view the Psychedelic image in the Windows Photo Gallery (Figure 3–52).

Figure 3–52

To Close the Windows Photo Gallery

Now that you have seen all of the pictures, the next step is to close the Windows Photo Gallery.

1 Click the Close button to close the Windows Photo Gallery.

To View Your Pictures as a Slide Show

The **Slide Show** displays each image in the folder in a presentation format on your computer screen. Each picture will be shown one at a time while everything else on the desktop is hidden from sight. Slide Show allows you to view pictures by automatically moving through the pictures or by using the navigation buttons to view the next or previous picture. You also can rotate a picture clockwise or counterclockwise, pause the slide show, and exit the slide show. The following step opens the images in the Backgrounds folder as a slide show.

1

• Click the Slide Show button on the Pictures folder window toolbar to view the selected files as a slide show (Figure 3–53).

• Watch the show for a few seconds to see the pictures change.

Q&A

Can I change the Slide Show speed?

Yes, you can use the Slide Show options button to select speeds of slow, medium and fast. The Slide Show options button is next to the Exit button.

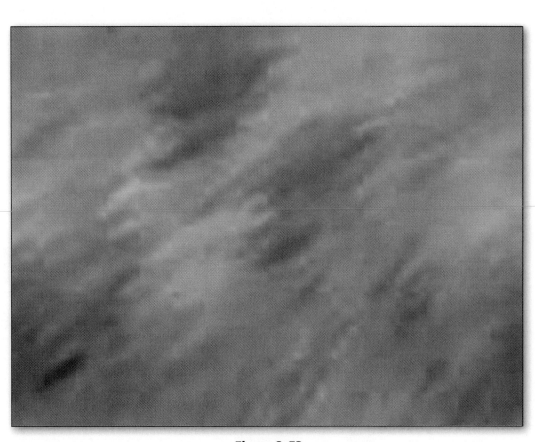

Figure 3–53

To End a Slide Show

When you are done viewing the slide show, the next step is to end it. The following steps exit the slide show.

1
- Move the mouse and then click the Exit button on the toolbar (Figure 3-54).

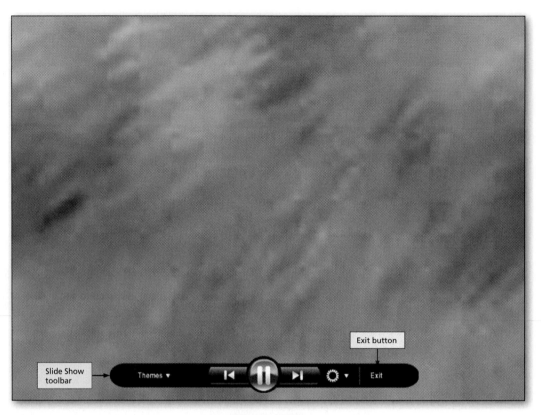

Figure 3–54

2
- Click the Exit button on the Slide Show toolbar to exit the slide show (Figure 3–55).

Figure 3–55

To E-Mail a Picture

Electronic mail (e-mail) is an important method of exchanging messages and files between business associates and friends. Windows Vista provides options to send files using the e-mail program that you have installed on your computer. Windows Vista includes the Windows Mail e-mail program, which can be configured to work with most e-mail accounts, even Web-based e-mail such as Windows Live Hotmail and Gmail.

E-mailing large images can be time-consuming and often results in the file not reaching its destination. As a result, Windows Vista makes it easy to reduce the size of an image at the time you send it. If you do not have Windows Mail configured, read but do not complete the following steps. The following steps e-mail an image to a friend.

1

- If necessary, click the Monet icon to select it.

- Click E-mail button on the toolbar to display the Attach Files dialog box (Figure 3–56).

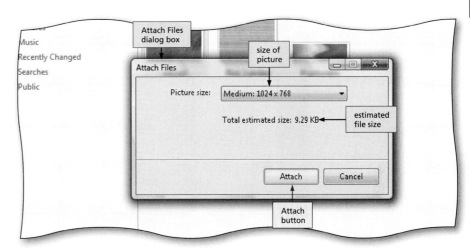

Figure 3–56

2

- Click the Attach button to compose a new e-mail message and attach the picture to the e-mail message (Figure 3–57).

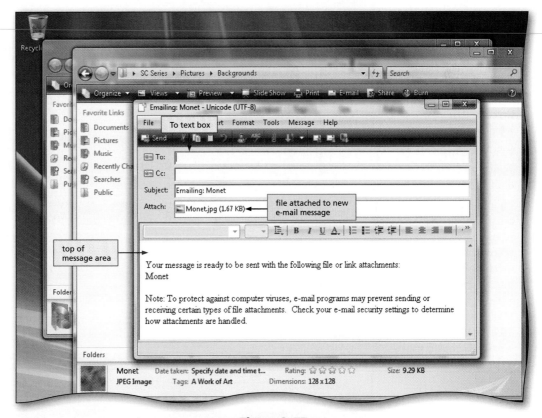

Figure 3–57

3

- Type `rayenger@ yahoo.com` in the To text box.

- Click at the top of the message area.

- Type `I thought you might like this picture for your collection.` in the message area (Figure 3–58).

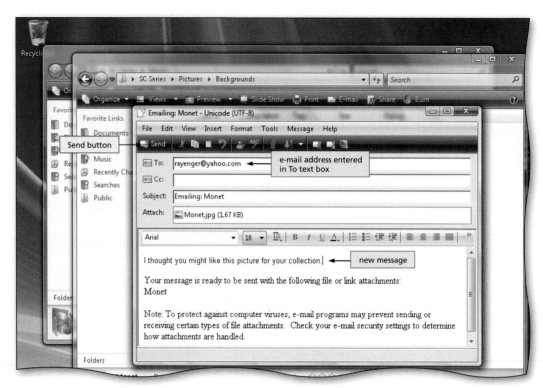

Figure 3–58

4

- Click the Send button to display the Windows Mail dialog box while the message is sending, and to close the Emailing Monet - Unicode (UTF-8) window (Figure 3–59).

Q&A Why does my Windows Mail show a different account?

Your computer has been configured to use an e-mail account for that machine. For example, at home you may set up Windows Mail to use a Hotmail account while at work you would use a company e-mail account.

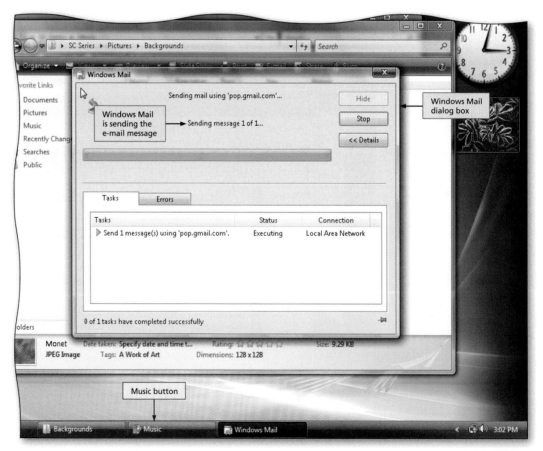

Figure 3–59

The Music Folder

The **Music** folder can be used to store your music files. If you have any digital music players installed, they will use this location by default when you download, play, rip, and burn music. When you **rip** a file, you extract the audio data from a CD and transfer it to your hard disk. After the file has been ripped, it will be in a format that is compatible with your computer as opposed to a CD player. When you **burn** music, you take files that are compatible with your computer and copy them onto a CD in the format that can be played in CD players. Some CD players can play music files in the same format as your computer; therefore, the burn process does not always result in a file format change.

You can arrange your music files into organized collections. The Sample Music folder, installed by Windows Vista, contains samples of music for you to experiment with so that you can make sure that your sound card and speakers are working properly. If you use a music program such as iTunes or Windows Media Player, you will be able to add additional music files to your collection. Music files come in a variety of formats, similar to how picture files have different formats. Common music file formats include are .wav, .wma, .mp3, .mp4, and .mid. For example, audio podcasts often are saved in the .mp3 format. You can use the Music folder window to view, organize, and play your music.

Just like other media files, you should be aware of copyrights. If you download music from the Internet, make sure that you have the right copyright to do so. It is illegal to download and share music that you do not have the rights to download and share.

To Switch to the Music Folder

You want to view the contents of the Music folder in order to understand how music is stored and arranged. To see this, you will switch to the Music window. The following step makes the Music folder the active window.

1 Click the Music button on the taskbar to display the Music folder window (Figure 3–60).

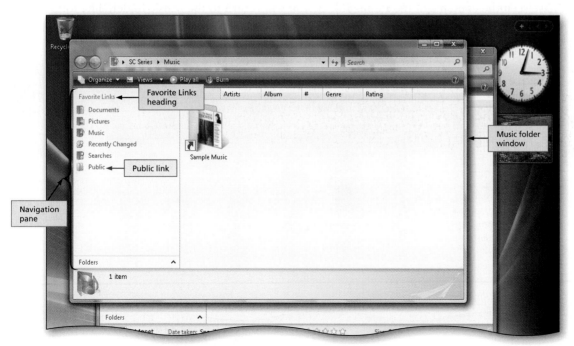

Figure 3–60

To Open the Public Folder

To see the sample music files, you will need to open the Sample Music folder. The Sample Music folder is located in the Public Music folder, although a shortcut to the Sample Music folder appears in the Music folder window. When you view the contents of the Sample Music folder, notice that the Address bar reflects the fact that you are in the Public folder. The **Public folder** contains a collection of folders that are shared amongst all of the user accounts. Anything that you want to share with other users should be placed in one of the Public folders. The following step opens the Public folder.

- Click the Public link under the Favorite Links heading of the Navigation pane to display the Public folder (Figure 3–61).

Q&A

What are Favorite Links?

The Favorite Links area contains a list of locations that you commonly use. By using Favorite Links, you quickly can go to those locations without having to search for or navigate to them. Windows Vista automatically builds this list during installation.

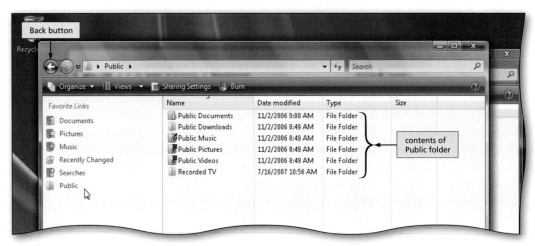

Figure 3–61

To Return to the Music Folder

Now that you have seen the contents of the Public folder, you will return to the Music folder. The following step switches back to the Music folder.

- Click the Back button on the Address bar to return to the Music folder (Figure 3–62).

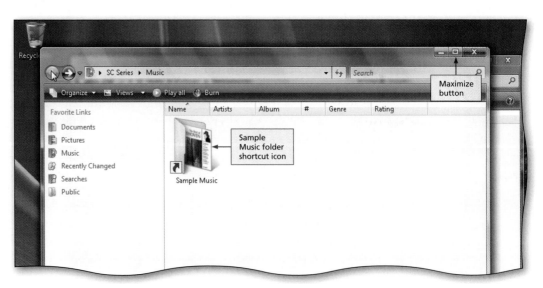

Figure 3–62

To Open the Sample Music Folder

In Figure 3–62, the Live Preview shows an album cover image. In order for an album cover to be displayed by Live Preview, your music files must include the album cover image. An album cover image usually is included when the music files are created. If you download music files, they often will have the album art included, but not every music file will have album art. You want to review the music files already installed on the computer, so you open the Sample Music folder. The following steps open the Sample Music folder.

1

- Double-click the Sample Music folder icon to open the Sample Music folder.

- If necessary, click the Maximize button to maximize the Sample Music window (Figure 3–63).

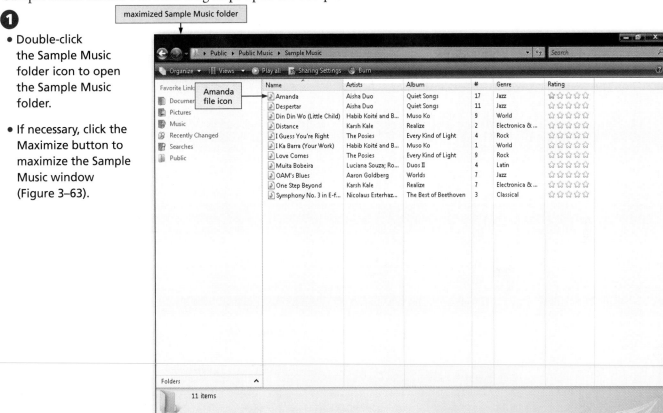

Figure 3–63

To View Information about a Music File

Similar to the Pictures folder, when you view a folder that contains music files, the folder structure and options will be specific to music files. In the Music folder, after the column titled Name, all of the remaining columns, Artists, Album, #, Genre, and Rating, are properties of the music files. The Artists column contains the name of the recording artist, while the Album column contains the name of the album that includes the song. The number symbol (**#**) indicates the track number of the song on the album, while Genre provides the classification of the music file. Finally, Rating is similar to the picture Ratings; you can rate the music files from zero to five stars.

Once you select a file, its properties display in the Details pane. As with picture files, you can use the Details pane to change the properties. The steps on the following pages display the properties of the Amanda music file in the Details pane and change the rating to four stars.

1

- Click the Amanda file icon to select the music file (Figure 3–64).

Figure 3–64

2

- Click the fourth star next to the Rating heading in the Details pane to rate the music file (Figure 3–65).

Figure 3–65

❸

• Click the Save button to save the changes to the Amanda music file properties (Figure 3–66).

Figure 3–66

To Reset the Rating for a Music File

Because the Amanda file is in the Sample Music folder that is shared by everyone who uses this computer, you should clear your rating. However, if you are working on your own computer and you agree with the rating, you could leave the rating at four stars. The following steps will reset the rating of the Amanda file back to its original value.

- Position the mouse pointer at the left edge of the first star so that all stars appear clear, and then click the mouse.

- Click the Save button to save the changes to the Amanda music file properties (Figure 3–67).

Figure 3–67

To Play a Music File in Windows Media Player

There are several ways to play a music file. The easiest way is to use the toolbar of the Music folder window. If you click the Play button, you will play the current song. Clicking the Play all button will play all of the music files in the folder. **Windows Media Player** is the default Windows Vista program for playing and working with digital media files such as music or video files.

In addition to playing music files, Windows Media Player can rip and burn music, maintain a music library, sync with portable audio players, and even download music. Windows Media Player also works with other multimedia files, including movies. The features of Windows Media Player will be discussed in a later chapter.

In Windows Media Player, there are buttons for controlling the playback of the music file. The following steps play the Amanda music file in Windows Media Player.

1

- If necessary, select the Amanda file.

- Click the Play button on the toolbar to open and play the Amanda music file in Windows Media Player (Figure 3–68).

Q&A

Why am I unable to hear any music?

Check the speakers attached to your computer. Your speakers may not be turned on, or the volume may not be turned up on the speakers or computer. If you are in a lab using a computer without speakers. you will need a pair of headphones to listen to the music file.

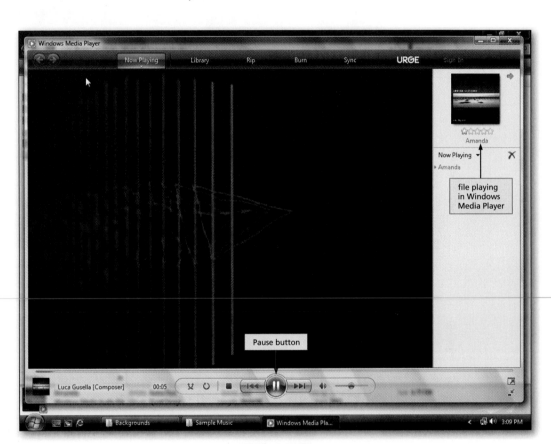

Figure 3–68

To Pause a Music File

After you have listened to the Amanda music file, you can stop playing the recording. The following step pauses the Amanda music file that is playing in Windows Media Player.

1

• Click the Pause button on the toolbar at the bottom of the window to pause the song in Windows Media Player (Figure 3–69).

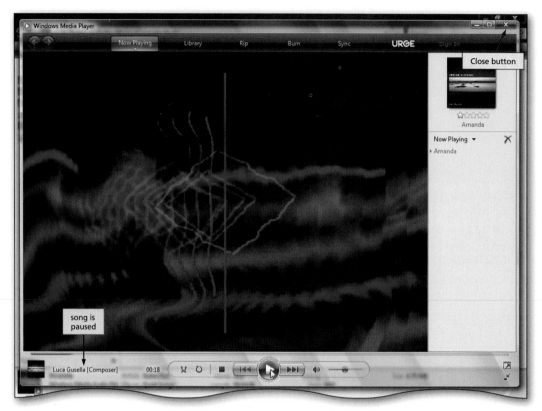

Figure 3–69

To Close Windows Media Player

Now that you are done using the Windows Media Player and the Sample Music folder window, you should close them.

1 Click the Close button on the Windows Media Player window to close the window.

2 Click the Close button on the Sample Music folder window to close the window.

Backing Up Files and Folders

It is very important that you make backups of your important files and folders. A **backup** is a copy of files and folders that are stored at a different location than the originals. While you can back up files and folders on the same drive where they were created, it is not considered as secure as backing them up to a separate drive. For example, you would not back up your C: drive files and folders on the C: drive. If something goes wrong with the C: drive, it would affect any backups stored there as well. Typically, you would store the backups on other hard drives, USB drives, CDs, DVDs, or even tape drives.

Backing up files and folders is a security aid; if something happens to your primary copy of a file or folder, you can restore it from the backup. Depending upon the size of the files and folders you are backing up, you might use a USB drive, a CD, a DVD, an external hard drive, or any other available storage device to back up your files. You might even consider creating a scheduled backup. A **scheduled backup** is a backup that is made according to dates and times that you predetermine. It always occurs on those dates and times.

After you have created a backup, you should store your backup away from the computer. Many people store their backups right by their computer, which is not a good practice, for security reasons. If a mishap occurs where the computer area is damaged, or someone steals the computer, or any other number of events occur, the backup still will be safe if it is stored in a different location. Most corporations make regular backups of their data and store the backups off site.

When you **restore** files or folders from a backup, you copy the files or folders from the backup location to the original location. If your hard disk crashes, a virus infects your computer, or an electrical surge damages your computer, you can restore the files and folders that you have stored on the backup. Before restoring files or folders, make sure that the location to where you are restoring the files is now secure. For example, before restoring files on a drive that has been infected by a virus, first make sure the virus is gone.

First, you will back up your files and folders using a USB drive. A USB drive is handy for backing up files and folders created on a computer in a classroom, computer lab, or Internet café, where you have to remove your files before you leave.

To Insert a USB Drive and Open It in a Folder Window

First you need to insert the USB drive so that you can back up your data to your USB drive. The following step inserts a USB drive and open it in a folder window.

 Insert a USB drive into any open USB port on your computer to display the Auto Play window. Under the General Options heading, click the Open folder to view files command to open a folder window.

To Create a Backup on a USB Drive

With the USB drive connected, you are ready to make a backup. You decide to back up your Backgrounds folder. By copying this folder to the USB drive, you will be adding a measure of security to your data. The following steps copy the Backgrounds folder from the Pictures folder to the USB drive.

• Click the Backgrounds button on the taskbar to make the Backgrounds window the active window (Figure 3–70).

Figure 3–70

2

- Click the Pictures button on the Address bar to change the location to the Pictures folder (Figure 3–71).

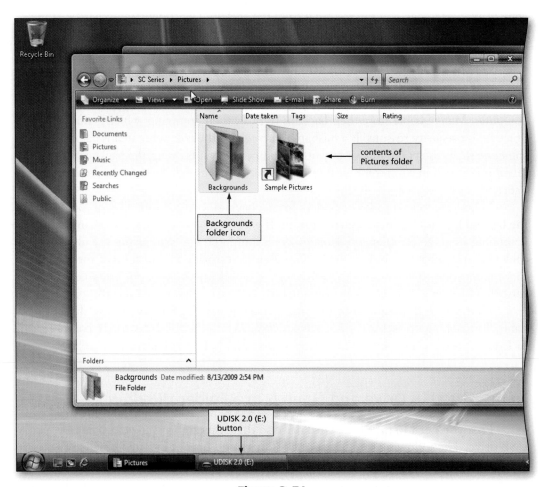

Figure 3–71

3

- If necessary, click the Backgrounds folder icon to select the Backgrounds folder.

- Right-click the Backgrounds folder to display a shortcut menu (Figure 3–72).

- Click the Copy command on the shortcut menu to copy the folder to the Clipboard.

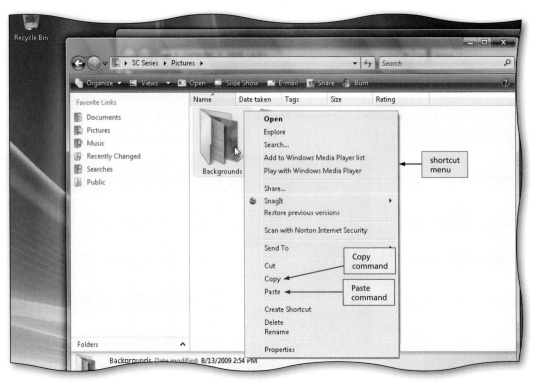

Figure 3–72

- Click UDISK 2.0 (E:) button on the taskbar to make the UDISK 2.0 (E:) window the active window.

- Right-click an open area in the list area to display a shortcut menu.

- Click the Paste command on the shortcut menu to paste a copy of the Backgrounds folder onto the USB drive (Figure 3–73).

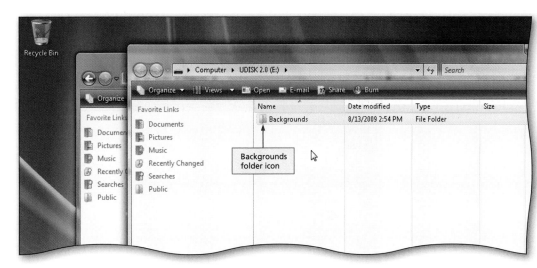

Figure 3–73

To Rename a Folder

Because the folder on the USB drive is a backup copy of the original folder, it is a good idea to change its name to reflect that it is a backup. The following steps rename the folder on the USB drive to indicate that it is a backup folder.

1

- If necessary, click the Backgrounds folder icon to select the Backgrounds folder.

- Right-click the Backgrounds icon to display a shortcut menu (Figure 3–74).

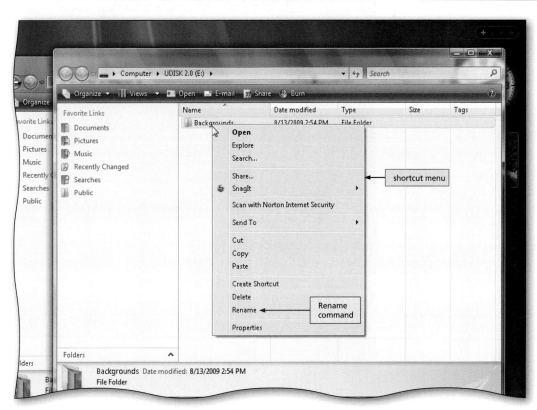

Figure 3–74

2

- Click the Rename command to open the name of the folder in a text box (Figure 3–75).

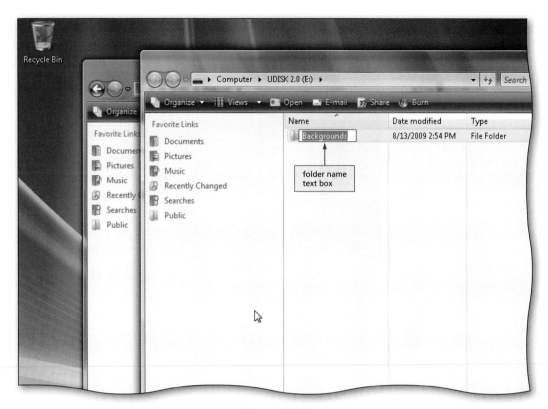

Figure 3–75

3

- Type Backgrounds - Backup as the new name for the folder (Figure 3–76).

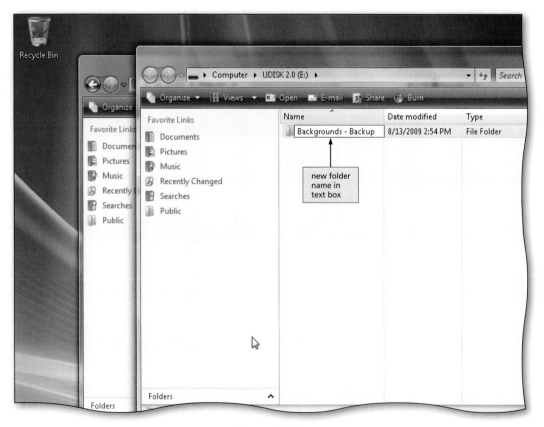

Figure 3–76

4

• Press the ENTER key to apply the new name to the folder (Figure 3–77).

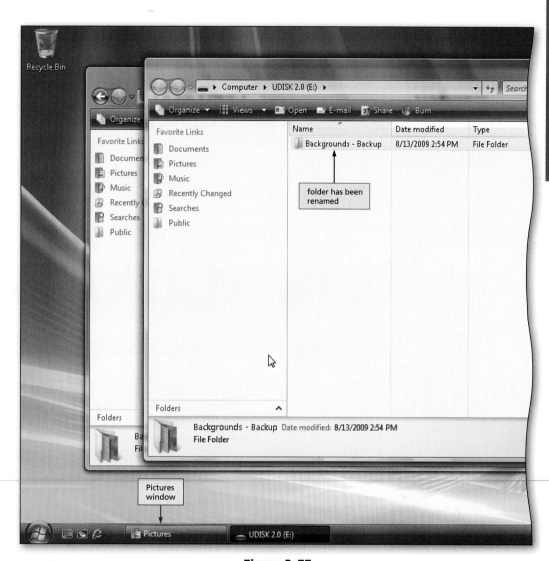

folder has been renamed

Pictures window

Figure 3–77

To Create a Backup on a CD

Copying a folder to a USB drive is one method of creating a backup. Another way to make a backup is to burn the files to a CD. The process of backing up files to CD requires that you have a CD or DVD drive that can write data onto CDs or DVDs. You also need a blank writable CD or DVD.

In this backup process, the CD or DVD will be formatted with the Live File System. The **Live File System** is a file storage system that allows you to add files continually to the CD or DVD until you are ready to write the data to the CD or DVD (similar to how you can add files to a USB drive). The files are not actually burned onto the CD or DVD until you eject the CD or DVD. When you eject the CD or DVD, Windows Vista finalizes the CD by burning the files onto the CD. Finalizing a CD means that the CD is prepared for later use in your computer or another computer. Because the CD is formatted with the Live File System, you only will be able to use it in computers that are formatted with the Windows XP or Windows Vista operating systems.

The following steps back up the Backgrounds folder from the Pictures folder to a blank CD. If you do not have access to a CD or DVD burner or do not have a blank CD or DVD read the following steps without performing them.

- Click the Pictures button on the taskbar to make the Pictures folder window the active window.

- If necessary, select the Backgrounds folder (Figure 3–78).

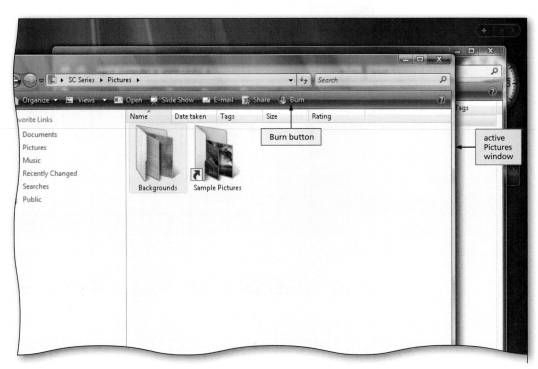

Figure 3–78

- Click the Burn button on the toolbar to begin the burn process and display the Burn to Disc dialog box (Figure 3–79).

Figure 3–79

3

• Insert a blank CD into the drive to continue the burn process (Figure 3–80). If the AutoPlay dialog box displays, click the Close button to close the AutoPlay dialog box.

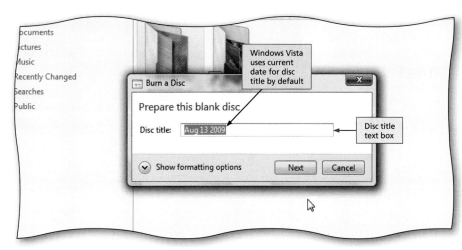

Figure 3–80

4

• Type Backup – Aug in the Disc title text box to provide a name for the disc (Figure 3–81).

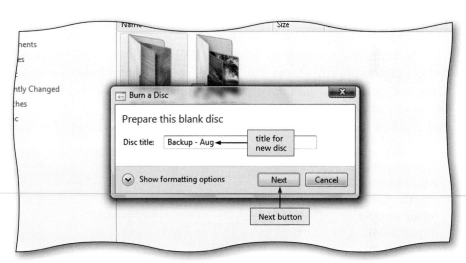

Figure 3–81

5

• Click the Next button to continue the burn process and display the Calculating time remaining dialog box that shows the progress of the burning process (Figure 3–82).

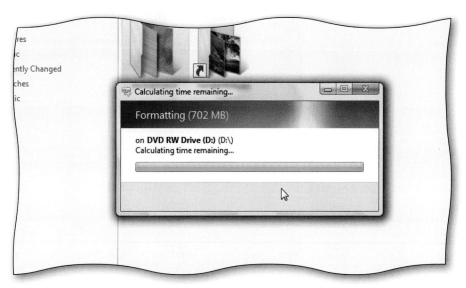

Figure 3–82

● Once the burning process has completed, the contents of the Backup – Aug disc appear in a new folder window (Figure 3–83).

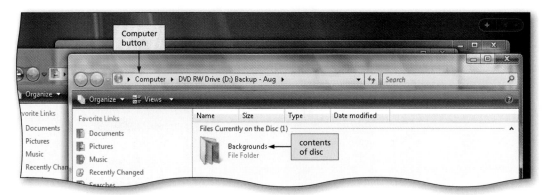

Figure 3–83

To Eject a CD

Now that the process is complete, the Backup - Aug folder is shown in a new folder window (Figure 3–83). You can continue to add files to this disc until you run out of storage space on the CD or DVD. Once you are ready to remove the disc, you eject it. Before the computer ejects the disc, the CD will be finalized. The following steps eject and finalize the CD.

● Click the Computer button on the Address bar to display the Computer folder window (Figure 3–84).

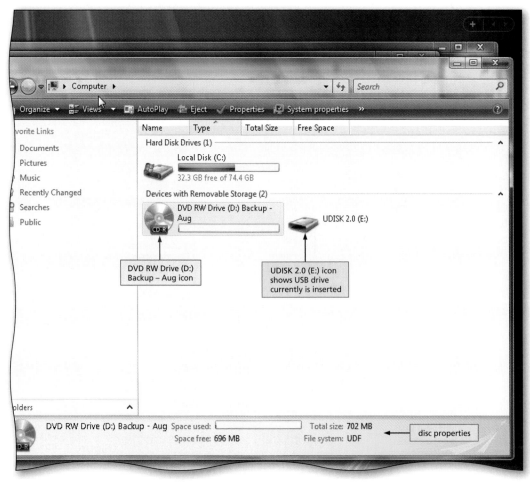

Figure 3–84

2

- Right-click the DVD RW Drive (D:) : Backup - Aug icon to display a shortcut menu (Figure 3–85). The drive name and letter may be different on your computer.

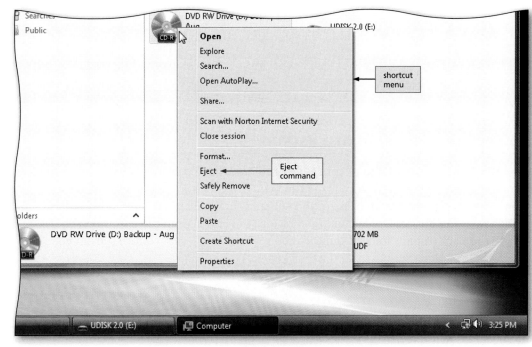

Figure 3–85

3

- Click the Eject command on the shortcut menu to have Windows Vista finalize and eject the CD (Figure 3–86).

- Remove the CD from the computer's CD drive.

Figure 3–86

To Close the Computer Folder Window

Now that you have ejected the CD, you should close the Computer folder window. The following step closes the Computer folder window.

1 Click the Close button on the Computer folder window to close the window.

To Restore a Folder from a Backup

Whenever you need to restore a file or folder from a backup copy, you need to insert the removable media where the backup copy was stored, and then you can copy the backup to the destination drives or folders. To learn how to restore a folder from backup, you will first simulate an accidental loss of data by deleting the Background folder from the Pictures folder, and then restore the folder from the backup on your USB drive. The following steps delete the Backgrounds folder from the Pictures folder and then restore it from your backup copy.

- Click the Pictures button on the task-bar to make the Pictures folder window the active window (Figure 3–87).

Figure 3–87

2

- Delete the Backgrounds folder to simulate an accidental loss of data.

- Empty the Recycle Bin (Figure 3–88).

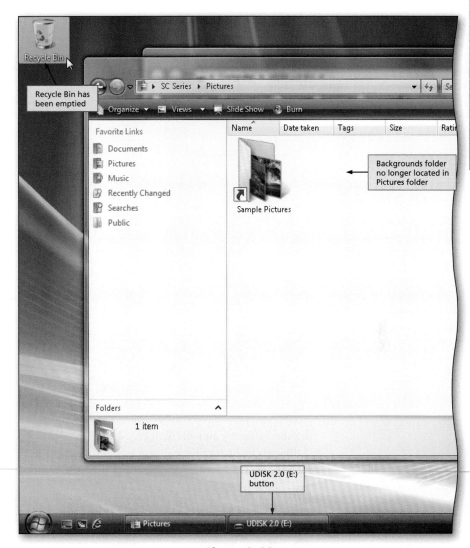

Figure 3–88

3

- Click the UDISK 2.0 (E:) button on the taskbar to make the UDISK 2.0 (E:) window the active window.

- Copy the Backgrounds - Backup folder to place a copy on the Clipboard.

- Click the Pictures button on the taskbar to make the Pictures window the active window.

- Paste the Backgrounds - Backup folder to place a copy in the Pictures folder (Figure 3–89).

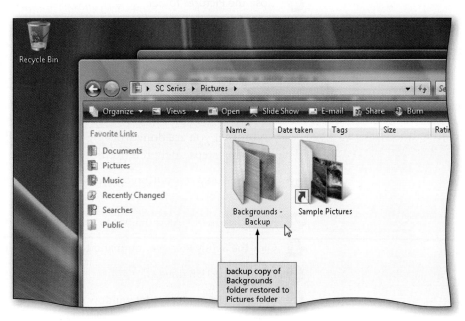

Figure 3–89

- Rename the folder Backgrounds to finish the restoration process (Figure 3–90).

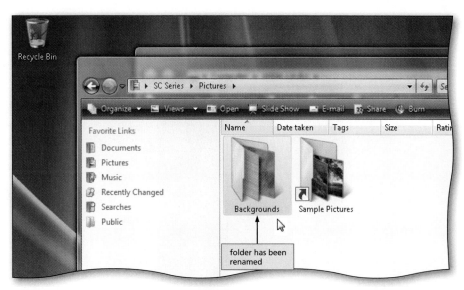

Figure 3–90

To Delete a Folder from the Pictures Folder

You now have restored the Backgrounds folder after a mishap. This process would be the same if you were working from a CD or DVD backup. To return the Pictures folder to its original state, you will delete the Backgrounds folder. The following steps delete the Backgrounds folder.

1. Right-click the Backgrounds folder to display a shortcut menu.

2. Click the Delete command on the shortcut menu.

3. Click the Yes button in the Delete Folder dialog box.

4. Close the Pictures folder.

5. Empty the Recycle Bin.

To Remove the USB Drive

Now that you are done working with the USB drive, you should safely remove it. The following steps safely remove the USB drive.

1. Click the Computer button on the Address bar of the UDISK 2.0 (E:) window to display the Computer folder window.

2. Right click the UDISK 2.0 (E:) icon to display a shortcut menu.

3. Click the Safely Remove command to prepare the drive to be removed.

4. Remove the USB drive.

5. Close the Computer folder window.

To Log Off from and Turn Off the Computer

After completing your work with Windows Vista, you should close your user account by logging off of the computer, and then turn off the computer.

1 Display the Start menu.

2 Click the Shutdown options button.

3 Click the Log Off command to Log Off of the computer.

4 Click the Shut Down button to turn off the computer.

Chapter Summary

In this chapter, you learned about the Computer folder window. You learned how to view the properties of drives and folders, as well as how to view their content. You worked with files and folders in the Pictures folder window, reviewed and changed their properties, viewed images in Windows Photo Gallery and as a slide show, and e-mailed a picture to a friend. As part of this process, you also learned how to copy and move files as well as how to create folders. Next, you saw how to work with files and folders in the Music folder window. You changed the rating of a music file and learned how to listen to a music file using the Windows Media Player. Finally, you gained knowledge of how to make a backup of files and restore the files, including how to copy, rename, and delete files and folders. The items listed below include all of the new Windows Vista skills you have learned in this chapter.

1. Open and Maximize the Computer Folder Window (WIN 152)
2. Display Properties for the Local Disk (C:) Drive in the Details Pane (WIN 153)
3. Display the Local Disk(C:) Properties Dialog Box (WIN 154)
4. Close the Local Disk (C:) Properties Dialog Box (WIN 155)
5. Switch Folders Using the Address Bar (WIN 155)
6. View the Contents of a Drive (WIN 158)
7. Preview the Properties for a Folder (WIN 159)
8. Display Properties for the Windows Folder in the Details Pane (WIN 160)
9. Display All of the Properties for the Windows Folder (WIN 161)
10. View the Contents of a Folder (WIN 163)
11. Search for a File and Folder in a Folder Window (WIN 164)
12. Return to the Computer Folder Window (WIN 165)
13. Search for Files Using Advanced Search (WIN 166)
14. Cascade Open Windows (WIN 169)
15. Make a Window the Active Window (WIN 170)
16. Undo Cascading (WIN 171)
17. Stack Open Windows (WIN 172)
18. Undo Show Windows Stacked (WIN 173)
19. Show Windows Side by Side (WIN 174)
20. Undo Show Windows Side by Side (WIN 175)
21. Copy Files to the Pictures Folder (WIN 177)
22. Create a Folder in the Pictures Folder (WIN 180)
23. Move Multiple Files into a Folder (WIN 182)
24. Refresh the Image on a Folder (WIN 183)
25. View and Change the Properties of a Picture (WIN 184)
26. Open a Picture in the Windows Photo Gallery (WIN 187)
27. Navigate through Your Pictures (WIN 188)
28. View Your Pictures as a Slide Show (WIN 189)
29. End a Slide Show (WIN 190)
30. E-Mail a Picture (WIN 191)
31. Open the Public Folder (WIN 194)
32. Return to the Music Folder (WIN 194)
33. Open the Sample Music Folder (WIN 195)
34. View Information about a Music File (WIN 195)
35. Reset the Rating for a Music File (WIN 198)
36. Play a Music File in Windows Media Player (WIN 199)
37. Pause a Music File (WIN 200)
38. Create a Backup on a USB Drive (WIN 201)
39. Rename a Folder (WIN 203)
40. Create a Backup on a CD (WIN 206)
41. Eject a CD (WIN 208)
42. Restore a Folder from a Backup (WIN 210)

Learn It Online

Test your knowledge of chapter content and key terms.

Instructions: To complete the Learn It Online exercises, start your browser, click the Address bar, and then enter the Web address scsite.com/winvista/learn. When the Windows Vista Learn It Online page is displayed, click the link for the exercise you want to complete and then read the instructions.

Chapter Reinforcement TF, MC, and SA
A series of true/false, multiple-choice, and short-answer questions that test your knowledge of the chapter content.

Flash Cards
An interactive learning environment where you identify chapter key terms associated with displayed definitions.

Practice Test
A series of multiple-choice questions that test your knowledge of chapter content and key terms.

Who Wants To Be a Computer Genius?
An interactive game that challenges your knowledge of chapter content in the style of a television quiz show.

Wheel of Terms
An interactive game that challenges your knowledge of chapter key terms in the style of the television show *Wheel of Fortune*.

Crossword Puzzle Challenge
A crossword puzzle that challenges your knowledge of key terms presented in the chapter.

Apply Your Knowledge

Reinforce the skills and apply the concepts you learned in this chapter.

File and Program Properties
Instructions: You want to demonstrate to a friend how to display the properties of a bitmap image, display the image using the Paint program instead of the Windows Photo Gallery program, and print the image. The **Paint program** is an application program included with Windows Vista to display and create images. You also want to demonstrate how to display the properties of an application program.

Perform the following tasks and answer the questions:

Part 1: Displaying File Properties
1. Click the Start button and then click Computer on the Start menu.
2. Double-click the Local Disk (C:) icon. If necessary, click Show the contents of this folder.
3. Double-click the Windows icon. If necessary, click the Show the contents of this folder link.
4. Search for the White_Chocolate picture file. If the White_Chocolate icon is not available on your computer, find the icon of another image file.
5. Right-click the White_Chocolate icon. Click Properties on the shortcut menu. Answer the following questions about the White_Chocolate file.
    a. What type of file is White_Chocolate? _____
    b. What program is used to open the White_Chocolate image? _____
    c. What is the path for the location of the White_Chocolate file? _____
    d. What is the size (in bytes) of the White_Chocolate file? _____
    e. When was the file created? _____

f. When was the file last modified? _____

g. When was the file last accessed? _____

Part 2:   Using the Paint Program to Display an Image

1. Click the Change button in the White_Chocolate Properties dialog box. Answer the following questions.

 a. What is the name of the dialog box that displays? _____

 b. Which program is used to open the White_Chocolate file? _____

 c. Which other program(s) is recommended to open the file? _____

 d. List the other programs you can use to open the file? _____

2. Click the Paint icon in the Open With dialog box.

3. Click the OK button in the Open With dialog box.

4. Click the OK button in the White_Chocolate Properties dialog box.

5. Double-click the White_Chocolate icon to launch the Paint program and display the White_Chocolate image in the White_Chocolate – Paint window (Figure 3–91).

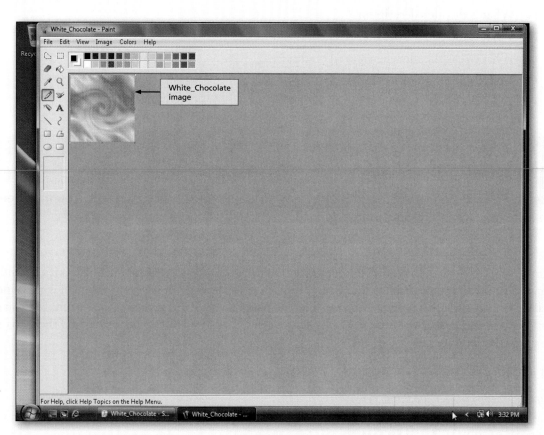

Figure 3–91

6. Print the White_Chocolate image by clicking File on the menu bar, clicking Print on the File menu, and then clicking the Print button in the Print dialog box.

7. Click the Close button in the White_Chocolate – Paint window.

Continued >

Apply Your Knowledge *continued*

Part 3:   Resetting the Program Selection in the Open With Dialog Box

1. Right-click the White_Chocolate icon. Click Properties on the shortcut menu. Answer the following question.

   a.   What program is used to open the White_Chocolate image? _____

2. Click the Change button in the White_Chocolate Properties dialog box.

3. If necessary, click the Windows Photo Gallery icon in the Open With dialog box to select the icon.

4. Click the OK button in the Open With dialog box.

5. Click the OK button in the White_Chocolate Properties dialog box.

Part 4:   Displaying Program Properties

1. Return to the Windows folder and scroll the right pane of the Windows folder window until the HelpPane icon displays. If the HelpPane icon does not appear, scroll to display another file.

2. Right-click the icon. Click Properties on the shortcut menu. Answer the following questions.

   a.   What type of file is selected? _____

   b.   What is the file's description? _____

   c.   What is the path of the file? _____

   d.   What size is the file when stored on disk? _____

3. Click the Cancel button in the Properties dialog box.

4. Close the Windows window.

Extend Your Knowledge

Extend the skills you learned in this chapter and experiment with new skills. You may need to use Help to complete the assignment.

Creating a Picture

Instructions: You want to use the Paint program to design a happy birthday image for a friend and then e-mail the message to the friend. The Paint program is an application program supplied with Windows Vista to display and create bitmap images. The file name of the Paint program is mspaint, but you do not know the location of the program on the hard drive. You first will use Search to find the mspaint file on the hard drive.

Perform the following tasks and answer the questions:

Part 1:   Searching for the Paint Program

1. Click the Start button and then click Computer on the Start menu.

2. Double-click the Local Disk (C:) icon.

3. Double-click the Windows folder icon.

4. Type mspaint in the Search box.

Part 2:   Creating a Bitmap Image

1. Double-click the mspaint icon in the Search Results window to launch Paint and display the Untitled – Paint window. *Hint*: The file type of the Paint program is Application (Figure 3–92).

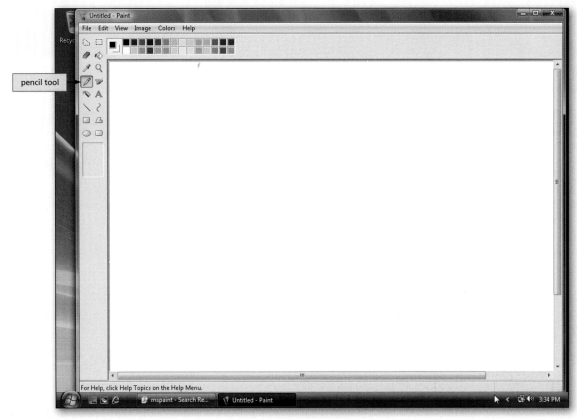

Figure 3–92

2. Use the Pencil tool shown in Figure 3–92 to write the message Happy Birthday Stephen in the Untitled – Paint window. *Hint:* Hold the left mouse button down to write and release the left mouse button to stop writing. If you make a mistake and want to start over, click Image on the menu bar and then click Clear Image to remove the image.

3. Click File on the menu bar and then click Save As. When the Save As dialog box displays, type Happy Birthday in the File name text box, and then click the Save button in the Save As dialog box to save the file in the Pictures folder.

4. Print the image.

5. Click the Close button in the Happy Birthday - Paint window.

6. Click the Close button in the Search Results window.

Part 3: E-mail the Happy Birthday Image

1. Click the Happy Birthday icon in the Pictures window to select the icon.

2. Click E-mail on the toolbar.

3. Click the Attach button in the Attach Files dialog box.

4. Type your instructors e-mail address in the To text box. Type Have a happy birthday! in the message area.

5. Click the Send button on the toolbar.

Part 4: Deleting the Happy Birthday Image

1. Click the Happy Birthday icon to select the file.

2. Click Organize on the toolbar, and then click Delete.

3. Click the Yes button in the Delete File dialog box.

4. Click the Close button in the Pictures window.

In the Lab

Using the guidelines, concepts and skills presented in this chapter to increase your knowledge of Windows Vista. Labs are listed in order of increasing difficulty.

Lab 1 Using Search to Find Picture Files

Instructions: You know that searching is an important feature of Windows Vista. You decide to use Search to find the images on the hard drive. You will store the files in a folder in the Pictures folder, print the images, and e-mail them to a friend.

Perform the following tasks and answer the questions:

Part 1:   Searching for Files in the Search Results Window

1. If necessary, launch Microsoft Windows Vista and log on to the computer.
2. Click the Start button on the taskbar and then click Search on the Start menu. Maximize the Search Results window.
3. In the Search box, type Garden.jpg as the entry.
4. Copy the image to the Pictures folder.
5. Click the Close button in the Search Results window.

Part 2:   Searching for Files from Another Window

1. Click the Start button on the taskbar and then click Computer on the Start menu.
2. Click the Search box.
3. Type Forest.jpg as the entry.
4. Copy the image to the Pictures folder.
5. Click the Close button in the Search Results window.

Part 3:   Searching for Groups of Files

1. Click the Start button on the taskbar, click Search on the Start menu, and then click the arrow to the right of Advanced Search to expand the Advanced Search options. Maximize the Search Results window.
2. In the Name text box, type cr* as the entry. Click Search (Figure 3–93).
3. Answer the following question.
    a.   How many files were found? _____
4. Click the Creek icon to select the icon. If the Creek icon does not display, select another icon.
5. Copy the image to the Pictures folder.

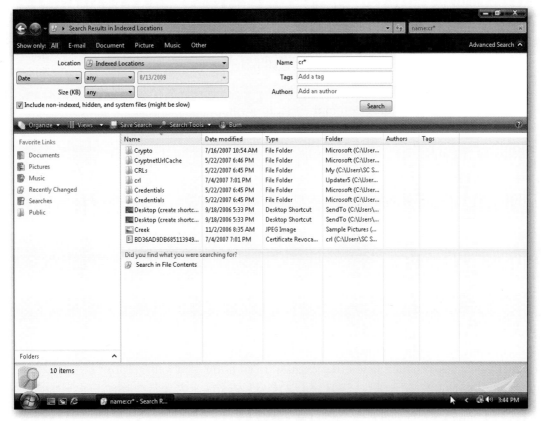

Figure 3–93

Part 4:   Creating the More Backgrounds Folder in the Pictures Folder
1. If necessary, open the Pictures folder window and make it the active window.
2. Make a new folder, type More Backgrounds in the icon title text box, and then press the ENTER key.
3. Select the icons of the images you copied to the Pictures folder.
4. Move the images to the More Backgrounds folder.
5. Refresh the thumbnail image on the More Backgrounds folder.

Part 5:   Printing the Images
1. Open the More Backgrounds folder.
2. Select the pictures.
3. Click Print on the toolbar to display the Print Pictures dialog box.
4. Use the scroll bar to select the Wallet option.
5. Click the Print button to print the pictures.

Part 6:   E-mail the Files in the More Backgrounds Folder
1. If necessary, click the More Backgrounds icon to select the icon.
2. Click E-mail on the toolbar.
3. Click the Attach button in the Attach Files dialog box.
4. Type rayenger@yahoo.com in the To text box. Type I searched the computer to find these background images. I thought you might like to see them. in the message area.
5. Click the Send button on the toolbar.

Continued >

In the Lab *continued*

Part 7: Moving the More Backgrounds Folder to a USB Drive
1. Insert a formatted USB drive into an open USB port.
2. Click the Pictures button on the Address bar.
3. Select the More Backgrounds icon in the Pictures window.
4. Right-click the More Backgrounds icon.
5. Click Send To and then click USB drive.
6. Click the Close button in the Pictures window.
7. Safely remove the USB drive from the computer.

In the Lab

Lab 2 Finding Pictures Online

Instructions: A classmate informs you that the Internet is a great source of photos, pictures, and images. You decide to launch the Internet Explorer program, search for well-known candy and drink logos on the Internet, and then save them in a folder. A **logo** is an image that identifies businesses, government agencies, products, and other entities. In addition, you want to print the logos and e-mail them to your instructor.

Perform the following tasks and answer the questions:

Part 1: Launching the Internet Explorer Program
1. Click the Start button and then click Computer on the Start menu.
2. Click the Folders button.
3. Expand the Local Disk (C:) folder.
4. Expand the Program Files folder.
5. Display the contents of the Internet Explorer folder.
6. Double-click the iexplore icon to launch Internet Explorer and display the Microsoft Internet Explorer window.

Part 2: Finding and Saving Logo Images
1. Type www.jellybelly.com on the Address bar in the Windows Internet Explorer window and then click the Go button.
2. Find the jelly belly bean man. Right-click the jelly belly bean man, click Save Picture As on the shortcut menu, type jelly belly logo in the File name text box in the Save Picture dialog box, and then click the Save button to save the logo in the Pictures folder.
3. Type www.jollyrancherfruitchews.com on the Address bar in the Windows Internet Explorer window and then click the Go button. Locate the Jolly Rancher picture that matches the one in Figure 3-94 and use the file name, Jolly Rancher logo, to save the Jolly Rancher logo in the Pictures folder.
4. Close the Internet Explorer window.
5. Click the Start button and then click Pictures. The Jelly Belly logo and Jolly Rancher image, display in the Pictures window (Figure 3–94). The logos in the Pictures window on your computer may be different from the logos shown in Figure 3–94 if the businesses have changed their logos.

Figure 3–94

Part 3:   Displaying File Properties

1. Right-click each logo file in the Pictures folder window, click Properties, answer the question about the logo below, and then close the Properties dialog box.

   a.   What type of file is the Jelly Belly logo file? _____

   b.   What type of file is the Jolly Rancher logo file? _____

2. Click an open area of the Pictures folder window to deselect the Jolly Rancher logo file.

Part 4:   Creating the Candy Logos Folder in the Pictures Folder Window

1. Make a new folder in the Pictures folder window, type Candy Logos in the icon title text box, and then press the ENTER key.

2. Click the Jelly Belly logo, hold down the CTRL key, and then click the Jolly Rancher logo.

3. Right-drag the icons to the Candy Logos icon and then click Move Here on the shortcut menu.

4. Refresh the image on the Candy Logos folder.

Part 5:   Printing the Logo Images

1. Open the Candy Logos folder.

2. Select both of the logos.

3. Click Print on the toolbar to display the Print Pictures dialog box.

4. Click the Print button to print the pictures.

Continued >

In the Lab *continued*

Part 6: E-mail the Files in the Candy Logos Folder
1. Click the Back button on the toolbar to display the Pictures folder window.

2. E-mail the pictures to your instructor with a brief message describing the pictures.

3. Click the Send button on the toolbar.

Part 7: Moving the Candy Logos Folder to a USB Drive
1. Insert a formatted USB drive into an open USB port.

2. Copy the Candy Logos folders to the USB drive.

3. Safely remove the USB drive from the computer.

4. Delete the Candy Logos folder from the Pictures folder.

In the Lab

Lab 3 Managing Your Music

Instructions: You want to investigate the different ways you can organize the music stored on your computer. Once you determine which method of organizing your music you prefer, you decide that you want to add to your music collection. First you will learn about the copyright laws that pertain to digital music, and then you will research a few Web sites that allow you to download music files.

Perform the following tasks and answer the questions:

Part 1: Organizing Your Music
1. Open the Start menu, and then open the Music folder window. Open the Sample Music folder, and answer the following questions.

   a.   How many files are there? _____

2. Group the files according to Artist.

   a.   How many groupings result? _____

   b.   How many songs are in the largest group? _____

3. Group the files according to Album.

   a.   How many groupings result? _____

   b.   How many songs are in the largest group? _____

   c.   Which method of grouping files do you prefer, and why? _____

Part 2: Researching Copyright Laws Regarding Digital Music Files
1. Click the Internet Explorer icon on the Quick Launch toolbar. Type `www.mpa.org/ copyright_resource_center/` on the Address bar, and then press ENTER.

   a.   What copyrights exist concerning music files? _____

   b.   What should you know before downloading music files? _____

   c.   What are the legal ramifications of downloading and sharing illegal music files? _____

   _____

Part 3:   Finding Music Online

1. Type www.netmusic.com on the Internet Explorer Address bar and press ENTER.

    a.   What types of music can be downloaded from this Web site? _____

    b.   What are the fees? _____

    c.   Are there any free, legal downloads available? _____

    d.   Would you use this service? _____

2. Type music.yahoo.com on the Address bar of Internet Explorer and press ENTER.

    a.   What types of music can be downloaded from this Web site? _____

    b.   What are the fees? _____

    c.   Are there any free, legal downloads available? _____

    d.   Would you use this service? _____

3. Type www.apple.com/itunes on the Address bar of Internet Explorer and press ENTER.

    a.   What types of music can be downloaded from this Web site? _____

    b.   What are the fees? _____

    c.   Are there any free, legal downloads available? _____

    d.   Would you use this service? _____

Cases and Places

Apply your creative thinking and problem solving skills to design and implement a solution.

• Easier   •• More Difficult

• 1 Finding Picture Files

Your seven-year old brother cannot get enough of the graphics that display on computers. Lately, he has been asking about what additional graphics come installed in Windows Vista beyond just the sample pictures. You finally have agreed to show him. Using techniques you learned in this chapter, display the icons for all the graphics image files that are stored on your computer. *Hint*: Graphics files on Windows Vista computers typically use the following file extensions of .bmp, .pcx, .tif, .jpg, or .gif. Once you have found the graphics files, display them and then print the three that you like best.

• 2 Advanced Searching

Your employer suspects that someone has used your computer during off-hours for non-company business. She has asked you to search your computer for all files that have been created or modified during the last ten days. When you find the files, determine if any are WordPad files or Paint files that you did not create or modify. Summarize the number and date they were created or modified in a brief report.

•• 3 Researching Backups

Backing up files is an important way to protect data and ensure that it is not lost or destroyed accidentally. You can use a variety of devices and techniques to back up files from a personal computer. Using Windows Help and Support, research the Backup and Restore Center. Determine the types of devices used to store backed up data, schedules, methods, and techniques for backing up data, and the consequences of not backing up data. Write a brief report of your findings.

•• 4 Researching Photo Printing Sites

Make It Personal

Now that you know how to work with the Pictures folder, you want to find Web sites where you can upload and print your photos. Using the Internet, search for three photo printing Web sites. Find the prices per 4 × 6 photo, the required file formats, and explore any other photo products that you would be interested in purchasing. Write a brief report that compares the three Web sites, and indicate which one you would use.

•• 5 Researching Data Security

Working Together

Data stored on disk is one of a company's most valuable assets. If that data were to be stolen, lost, or compromised so that it could not be accessed, the company could go out of business. Therefore, companies go to great lengths to protect their data. Working with classmates, research how the companies where you each work handle their backups. Find out how each one protects its data against viruses, unauthorized access, and even against such natural disasters such as fire and floods. Prepare a brief report that describes the companies' procedures. In your report, point out any areas where you find a company has not protected its data adequately.

Appendix A

Comparison of the New Features of Windows Vista Editions

The Microsoft Windows Vista operating system is available in a variety of editions. The six editions that you most likely will encounter are Windows Vista Starter, Windows Vista Home Basic, Windows Vista Home Premium, Windows Vista Business, Windows Vista Ultimate, and Windows Vista Enterprise. Because not all computers have the same hardware or are used for the same functions, Microsoft provides these various editions so that each user can have the edition that meets his or her needs. The new features of Windows Vista are listed in Table A–1. Windows Vista Ultimate, the most complete version of Windows Vista, is used as a baseline for clarifying the features of the other editions. Windows Vista Starter is not included in this table as it only contains the core Windows Vista features and only is available in developing countries.

Table A–1 Windows Vista New Features and Comparison of Editions

Ultimate Features	Home Basic	Home Premium	Business	Enterprise
.NET Framework 3.0	✓	✓	✓	✓
64-bit processor support	✓	✓	✓	✓
Ad hoc backup and recovery of user files and folders	✓	✓	✓	✓
Anti-phishing tools	✓	✓	✓	✓
Application Compatibility features	✓	✓	✓	✓
Automatic hard disk defragmentation	✓	✓	✓	✓
Complete PC Backup and Restore			✓	✓
Control over installation of device drivers			✓	✓
Desktop deployment tools for managed networks			✓	✓
Ease of Access Center	✓	✓	✓	✓
Encrypting File System			✓	✓
File tagging	✓	✓	✓	✓

Table A–1 Windows Vista New Features and Comparison of Editions *(continued)*

Ultimate Features	Home Basic	Home Premium	Business	Enterprise
File-based image format (WIM)	✓	✓	✓	✓
Games Explorer	✓	✓	✓	✓
I/O prioritization	✓	✓	✓	✓
Improved file and folder sharing	✓	✓	✓	✓
Improved peer networking	✓	✓	✓	✓
Improved power management	✓	✓	✓	✓
Improved VPN support	✓	✓	✓	✓
Improved wireless networking	✓	✓	✓	✓
Instant Search	✓	✓	✓	✓
Internet Explorer 7	✓	✓	✓	✓
IPv6 and IPv4 support	✓	✓	✓	✓
Maximum RAM (32-bit system)	4 GB	4 GB	4 GB	4 GB
Maximum RAM (64-bit system)	8 GB	16 GB	128+ GB	128+ GB
Multiple user interface languages				✓
Native DVD playback		✓		
Network Access Protection Client Agent			✓	✓
Network and Sharing Center	✓	✓	✓	✓
Network Diagnostics and troubleshooting	✓	✓	✓	✓
New premium games		✓	Optional	Optional
Next-generation TCP/IP stack	✓	✓	✓	✓
Offline Folder support			✓	✓
Parental Controls	✓	✓		
Performance and Hardware Tools	✓	✓	✓	✓
Pluggable logon authentication architecture	✓	✓	✓	✓
Policy-based QOS for networking			✓	✓
Scheduled, networked, incremental and automatic backup		✓	✓	✓
Service Hardening	✓	✓	✓	✓
Shadow Copy			✓	✓
Simultaneous SMB peer network connections	5	10	10	10
Small Business Resources			✓	Optional
Speech Recognition	✓	✓	✓	✓
Stacking and Group By View	✓	✓	✓	✓
Subsystem for UNIX-based applications				✓
Sync Center	✓	✓	✓	✓
System image–based backup and recovery			✓	✓
Themed slide shows		✓		
Two processors support			✓	✓
Universal game controller support	✓	✓	Optional	Optional
Updated games	✓	✓	✓	✓

Table A–1 Windows Vista New Features and Comparison of Editions (continued)

Ultimate Features	Home Basic	Home Premium	Business	Enterprise
User Account Control	✓	✓	✓	✓
Welcome Center	✓	✓	✓	✓
Windows Aero experience		✓	✓	✓
Windows BitLocker Drive Encryption				✓
Windows Calendar	✓	✓	✓	✓
Windows CardSpace	✓	✓	✓	✓
Windows Defender	✓	✓	✓	✓
Windows Display Driver Model (WDDM)	✓	✓	✓	✓
Windows Experience Index	✓	✓	✓	✓
Windows Fax and Scan (optional for Ultimate)			✓	Optional
Windows Firewall	✓	✓	✓	✓
Windows HotStart	✓	✓	✓	✓
Windows Mail	✓	✓	✓	✓
Windows Media Center		✓		
Windows Media Player 11	✓	✓	✓	✓
Windows Meeting Space	View only	✓	✓	✓
Windows Mobility Center	Partial	Partial	✓	✓
Windows Movie Maker	✓	✓	✓	✓
Windows Photo Gallery	✓	✓	✓	✓
Windows ReadyBoost	✓	✓	✓	✓
Windows ReadyDrive	✓	✓	✓	✓
Windows Rights Management Services (RMS) Client			✓	✓
Windows Security Center	✓	✓	✓	✓
Windows Sidebar	✓	✓	✓	✓
Windows SideShow		✓	✓	✓
Windows SuperFetch	✓	✓	✓	✓
Windows Tablet PC		✓	✓	✓
Windows Update	✓	✓	✓	✓
Windows Vista Basic experience	✓	✓	✓	✓
Wireless network provisioning			✓	✓
XPS Document support	✓	✓	✓	✓
Years of product support	5	5	10	10

Appendix B
Windows Vista Security

Windows Vista Security Features

Windows Vista has been engineered to be the most secure version of Windows ever, according to Microsoft. It includes a number of new security features that help you accomplish three important goals: to enjoy a PC free from malware, including viruses, worms, spyware, and other potentially unwanted software, to have a safer online experience, and to understand when a PC is vulnerable, and how to make it more secure from hackers and other intruders.

Malware, short for malicious software, are computer programs designed to do harm to your computer whether just showing inappropriate Web sites to performing identity theft. Examples of malware include viruses, worms, and spyware. A **virus** is a computer program that attaches itself to another computer program or file so that it can spread from computer to computer, infecting programs and files as it spreads. Viruses can damage computer software, computer hardware, and files. A **worm** copies itself from one computer to another by taking advantage of the features that transport files and information between computers. A worm is dangerous because it has the ability to travel without being detected and to replicate itself in great volume. For example, if a worm copies itself to every name in your e-mail address book and then the worm copies itself to the names of all the e-mail addresses of each of your friends' computers, the effect could result in increased Internet traffic that slows down business networks and the Internet. **Spyware** is software that is installed on your computer that monitors the activity that takes place to gather personal information and send it secretly to its creator. Spyware also can be designed to take control of the infected computer.

A **hacker** is an individual who uses his or her expertise to gain unauthorized access to a computer with the intention of learning more about the computer or examining the contents of the computer without the owner's permission.

The Windows Security Center

The **Windows Security Center** can help you to manage your computer's security by monitoring the status of several essential security features on your computer including firewall settings, Windows automatic updating, anti-malware software settings, Internet security settings, and User Account Control settings. Table B–1 contains a list of the four security features and their descriptions.

Table B–1 Security Features and Descriptions

Security Feature	Description
Windows Firewall	Windows Firewall monitors and restricts information coming from the Internet, prevents access without your permission, and protects against hackers.
Automatic Updating	Automatic updating indicates whether Windows Update is turned on. Windows Update checks the Windows Update Web site for high-priority updates that can help protect a computer against attacks. High-priority updates include security updates, critical updates, and service packs.
Malware Protection	Malware protection includes virus, spyware, and other security threat protection. It includes making sure you are using virus protection software.
Other Security Settings	This is where you can view and adjust other security settings including Internet security settings.

To Display the Windows Security Center

The following steps display the Windows Security Center.

1

- Click the Start button on the taskbar to display the Start menu (Figure B–1).

Figure B–1

2

- Click the Control Panel command on the Start menu to open the Control Panel (Figure B–2).

Figure B–2

3

- Click the Security link to display the security features (Figure B–3).

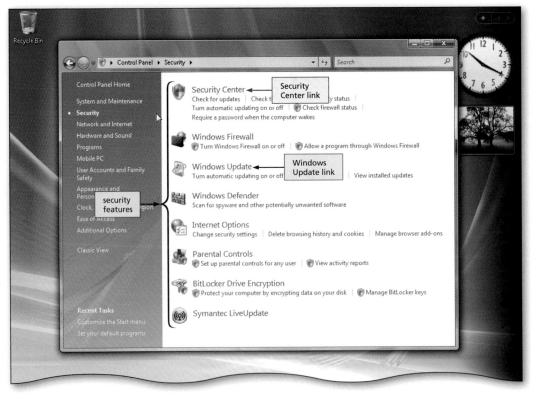

Figure B–3

4

- Click the Security Center link in the right pane of the Control Panel window to display the Windows Security Center.

- If necessary, maximize the Windows Security Center window (Figure B–4).

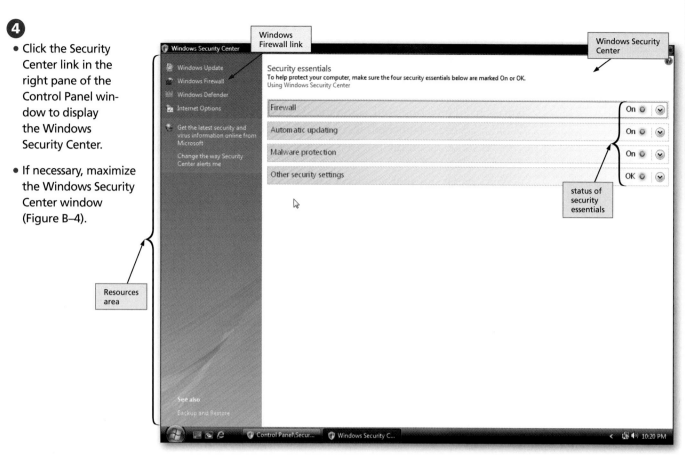

Figure B–4

The right pane provides a snapshot of the four security essentials that Microsoft believes should be turned on and up-to-date. These essential features are Firewall, Automatic updating, Malware protection, and Other security settings. Clicking the down arrow to the right of a security area will expand the area to show additional detail, while clicking the up arrow will collapse the area, hiding the details. User Account Control prompts you for permission to perform many of the operations in this appendix. Status values appear next to the arrow button: "On" and "OK" indicate that the security feature is turned on and working; "Off" means that the security feature is turned off and you should turn it on; and "Check Settings" means that although the feature is turned on, you need to change the settings to what Microsoft recommends for that security feature. It is important to have the On or OK status value showing for each of these features.

On the left pane of the Windows Security Center window is the Resources area containing six links that allow you to open Windows Update to view available updates, open Microsoft Firewall to view and configure firewall features, open Windows Defender to view and configure malware protection options, open Internet Options to view and configure Internet properties, view the latest security and virus information online from Microsoft, and change the way Security Center alerts you to potential issues in the Windows Security Center dialog box.

Managing Windows Firewall

Windows Firewall is a software program that protects your computer from unauthorized users by monitoring and restricting information that travels between your computer and a network or the Internet. Windows Firewall also helps to block computer viruses and worms from infecting your computer. Windows Firewall is automatically turned on when Windows Vista is launched. It is recommended that Windows Firewall remain turned on.

If someone on the Internet or on a network attempts to connect to your computer, Windows Firewall blocks the connection. For example, if you are playing a multiplayer network game and another player asks to join the game, Windows Firewall displays a Windows Security Alert dialog box. The dialog box contains buttons that allow you to block or unblock the connection. If you recognize the player and choose to unblock the connection and allow the player to join the game, Windows Firewall adds an exception for the player to the Windows Firewall Exceptions list. An **exception** is an adjustment made to the firewall settings so that the player can join the game now and in the future.

To Add a Program to the Windows Firewall Exceptions List

You can add a program to the Windows Firewall Exceptions list manually, without waiting for the program to communicate with you. Windows Firewall also limits access by some programs that depend on low security settings. A program that has low security settings requires more access to the operating system than Windows Vista normally allows a program to have. When you run a program with low security settings, you would be prompted many times to allow the program to perform its tasks. You can circumvent the prompts by adding the program to the Exceptions list.

However, with every program you add to the Windows Firewall Exceptions list, the computer becomes easier to access and more vulnerable to attacks by hackers. The more programs you add, the more vulnerable the firewall. To decrease the risk of security problems, only add programs that are necessary and recognizable, and promptly remove any program that is no longer required. The following steps add the Hearts program to the Windows Firewall Exceptions list.

- Click the Windows Firewall link in the Resources Area of the Windows Security Center window to display the Windows Firewall window (Figure B–5).

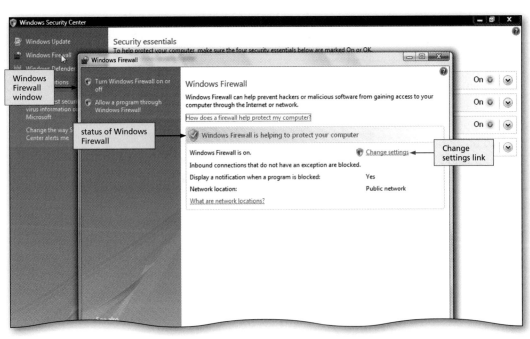

Figure B–5

2

- Click the Change settings link to display the User Account Control dialog box (Figure B–6).

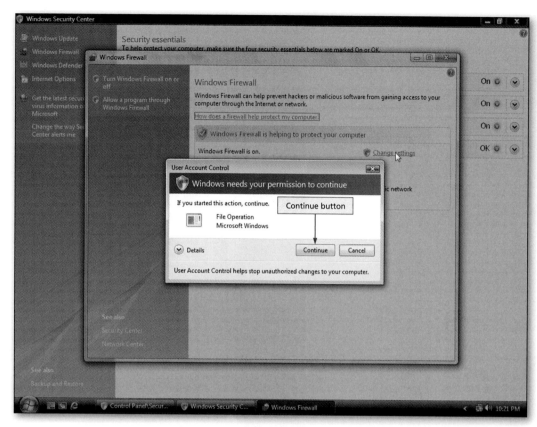

Figure B–6

3

- Click the Continue button to authorize Windows Vista to display the Windows Firewall Settings dialog box (Figure B–7).

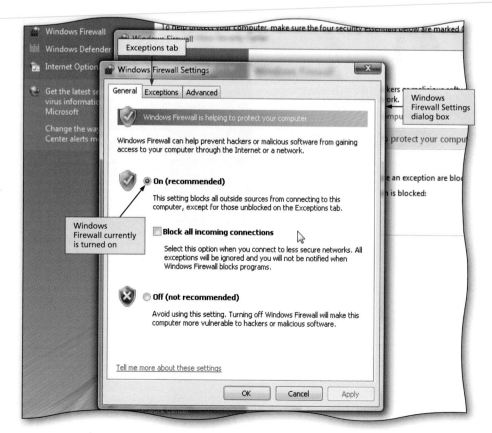

Figure B–7

4

- Click the Exceptions tab to display a list of Windows Firewall exceptions (Figure B–8).

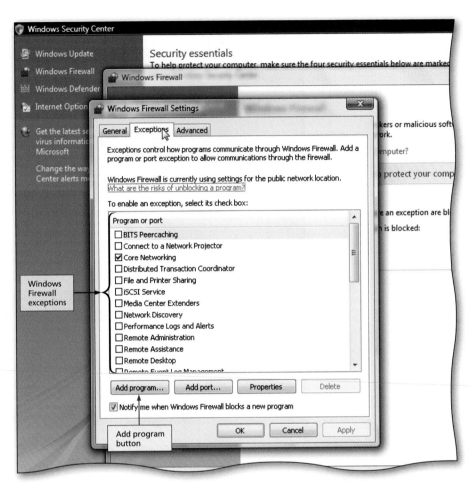

Figure B–8

5

- Click the Add program button to display the Add a Program dialog box. If necessary, scroll the Programs list box to view the Hearts program (Figure B–9).

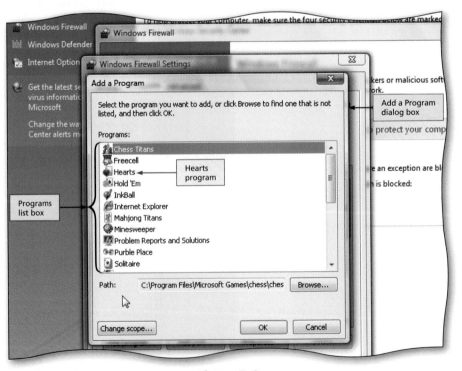

Figure B–9

6

● Click the Hearts program in the Programs list box to select the Hearts program (Figure B–10).

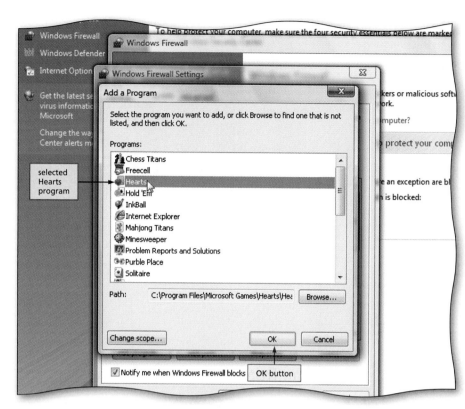

Figure B–10

7

● Click the OK button in the Add a Program dialog box to add the Hearts program to the list of exceptions (Figure B–11).

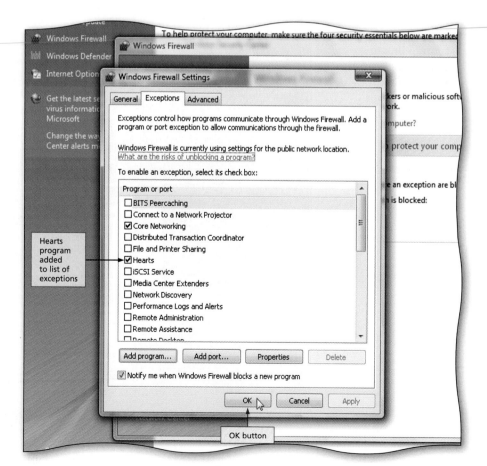

Figure B–11

8

● Click the OK button in the Windows Firewall Settings dialog box to close the dialog box (Figure B–12).

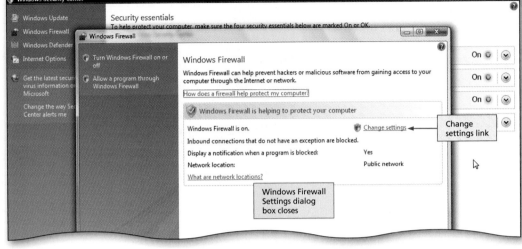

Figure B-12

Other Ways

1. Click Allow a program through Windows Firewall link in the resources area, click Continue, click Exceptions tab, click Add program, click Hearts program, click the OK button, click the OK button.

To Remove a Program from the Exceptions List

After adding the Hearts program to the Windows Firewall Exceptions list, you now will remove the program from the Windows Exceptions list. The following steps remove a program from the Exceptions list.

1

● Click the Change settings link to display the User Account Control dialog box (Figure B–13).

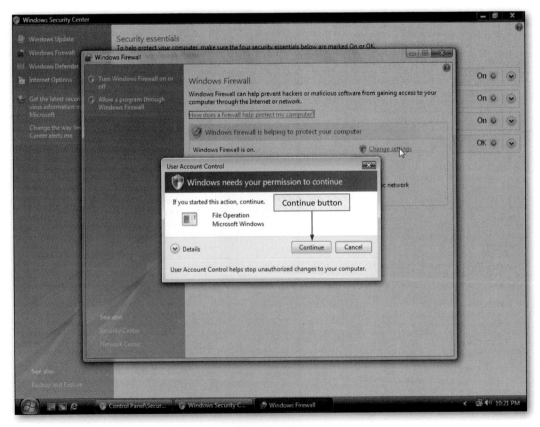

Figure B–13

2

- Click the Continue button to authorize Windows to display the Windows Firewall Settings dialog box (Figure B–14).

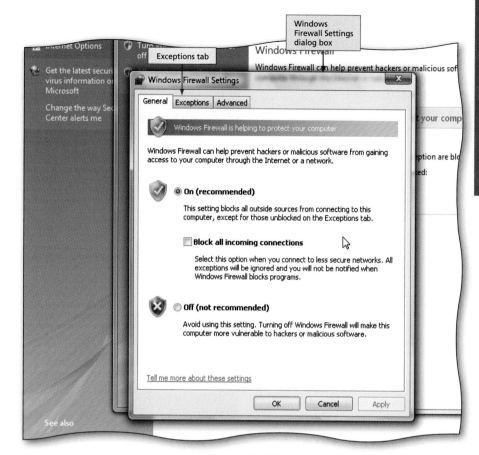

Figure B–14

3

- Click the Exceptions tab to display the list of exceptions.

- If necessary, scroll down to display the Hearts program (Figure B–15).

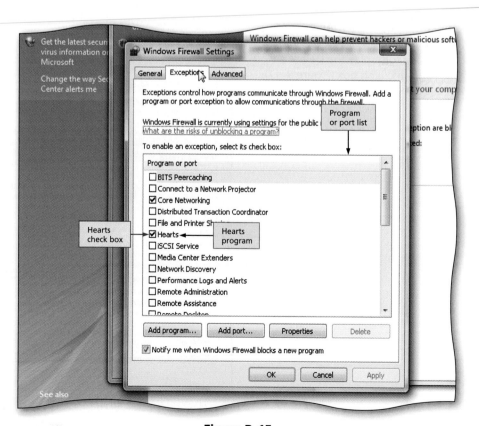

Figure B–15

● Click the Hearts check box in the
Program or port list box to remove
the check mark and to disable the
exception (Figure B–16).

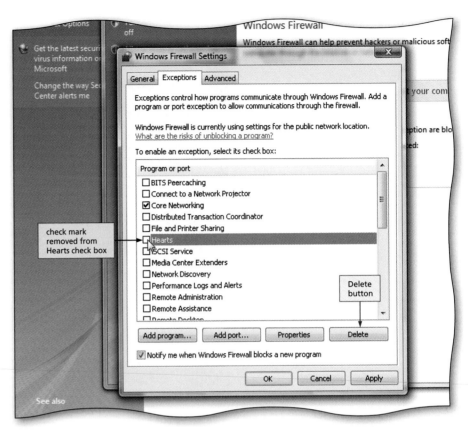

Figure B–16

● Click the Delete button in the
Windows Firewall Settings dia-
log box to display the Delete a
Program dialog box (Figure B–17).

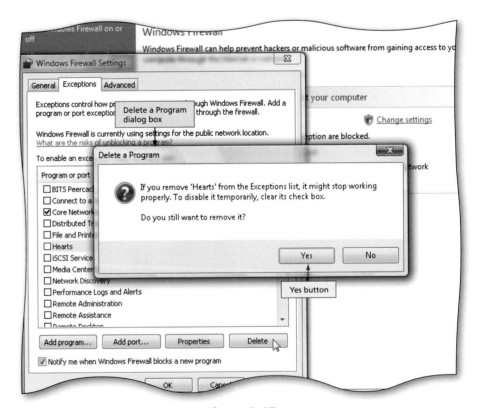

Figure B–17

6

- Click the Yes button in the Delete a Program dialog box to remove the Hearts program from the list of exceptions (Figure B–18).

What does the warning in the dialog box mean?

Some programs that you install cannot function properly unless they are placed in the Program or port list. Hearts is not such a program; therefore, you can ignore the warning and delete it from the list. Normally, before removing a program from the Program or port list, you should know whether this will affect its performance. This information is usually found in the program's documentation or help files.

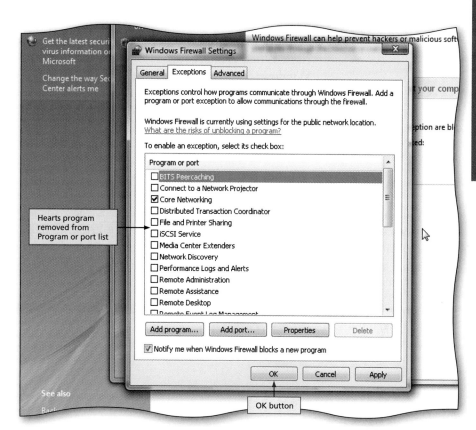

Figure B–18

7

- Click the OK button in the Windows Firewall Settings dialog box (Figure B–19).

8

- Click the Close button to close the Windows Firewall window.

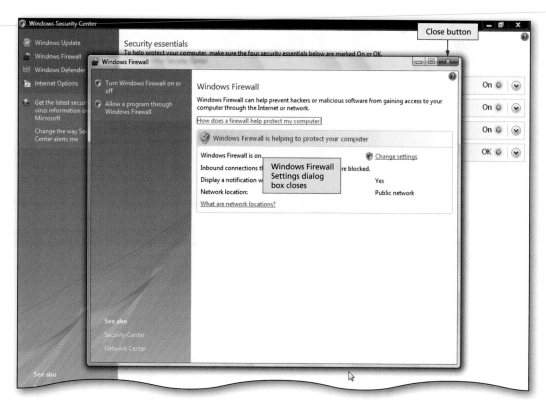

Figure B–19

Windows Update

Windows Update helps to protect your computer from viruses, worms, and other security risks. When Windows Update is turned on and the computer is connected to the Internet, Windows Vista periodically checks with the Microsoft Update Web site to find updates, patches, and service packs, and then automatically downloads them. If the Internet connection is lost while downloading an update, Windows Vista resumes downloading when the Internet connection is available.

To Set an Automatic Update

You want to make sure that Windows Update runs once a week, so you decide to set it to run on a specific day and at a specific time. Once you set the day and time for every Friday at 6:00 AM, Windows Vista will check with the Microsoft Updates Web site to find updates and service packs, and then automatically download any available updates and service packs. The followings steps set an automatic update for a day (Friday) and time (6:00 AM).

1

- Click the Windows Update link in the Windows Security Center window to display the Windows Update window (Figure B–20).

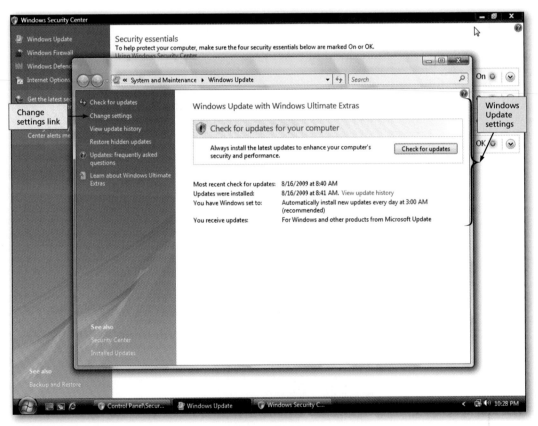

Figure B–20

- Click the Change
settings link to
display the Change
settings window
(Figure B–21).

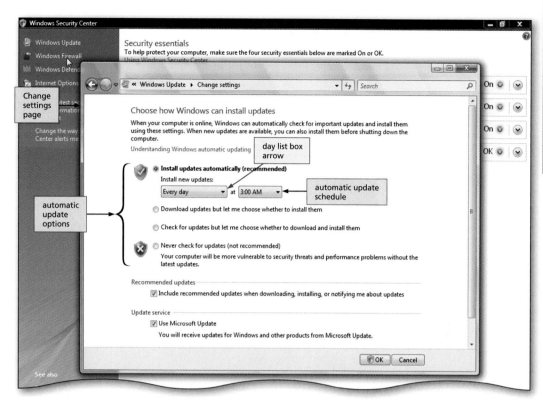

Figure B–21

- Click the day list box
arrow to display a
list of day options
(Figure B–22).

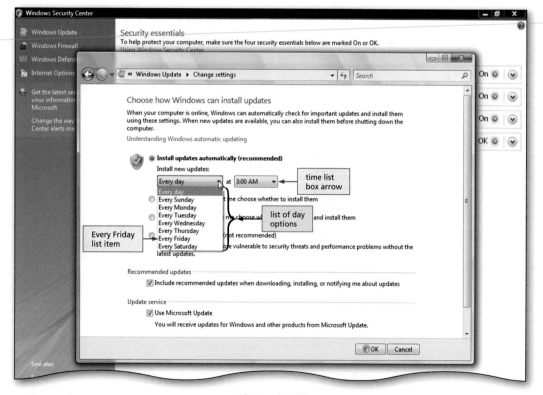

Figure B–22

- Click the Every Friday list item in the list box to set the update day to Every Friday.

- Click the time list box arrow to show the list of time options (Figure B–23).

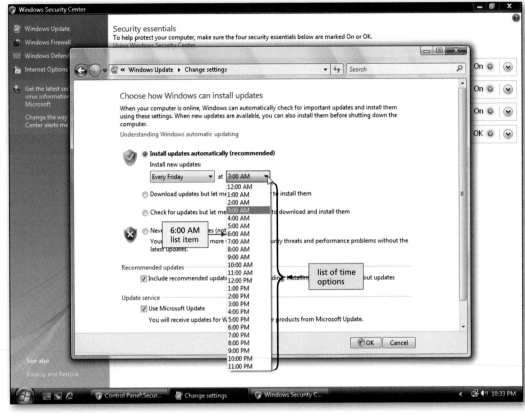

Figure B–23

- Click the 6:00 AM list item in the time list box to set the update time to 6:00 AM (Figure B–24).

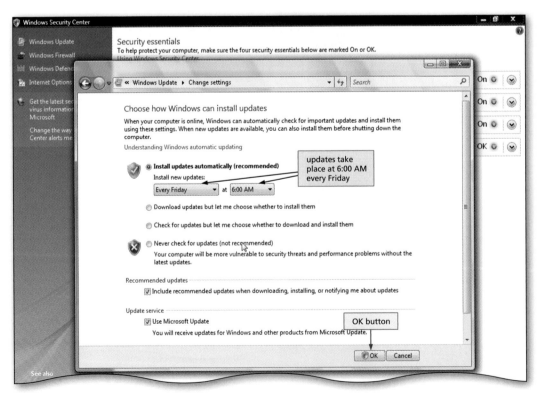

Figure B–24

6

- Click the OK button in the Change Settings window to display the User Account Control dialog box (Figure B–25).

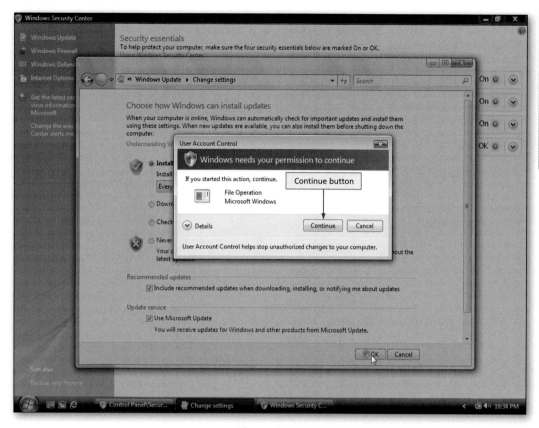

Figure B–25

7

- Click the Continue button in the User Account Control dialog box to authorize the changes (Figure B–26).

Q&A

What does my screen say that Windows is up to date?

If you already have turned on automatic updates, or recently have updated your computer, it is possible that no additional updates are available for download at this time.

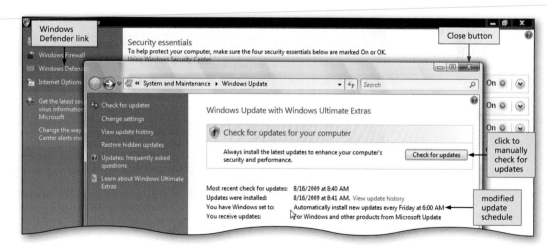

Figure B–26

8

- Verify that your update is scheduled for every Friday at 6:00 AM.

- Click the Close button to close the Windows Update window.

Protecting Against Computer Viruses

Most computer magazines, daily newspapers, and even news broadcasts warn us of computer virus threats. Although these threats sound alarming, a little common sense and a good antivirus program can ward off even the most malicious viruses.

You can protect your computer against viruses by following these suggestions. First, educate yourself about viruses and how they are spread. Downloading a program from the Internet, accessing an online discussion board, or receiving an e-mail message may cause a virus to infect your computer. Second, learn the common signs of a virus. Observe any unusual messages that appear on the computer screen, monitor system performance, and watch for missing files and inaccessible hard disks. Third, recognize that programs on removable media may contain viruses, and scan all removable media before copying or opening files.

Finally, Windows Vista does not include an antivirus program. You should purchase and install the latest version of an antivirus program and use it regularly to check for computer viruses. Many antivirus programs run automatically and display a dialog box on the screen when a problem exists. If you do not have an antivirus program installed on your computer, you can search online for antivirus software vendors to find a program that meets your needs.

To Search for Antivirus Software Vendors

The following steps display an online list of Microsoft approved antivirus software vendors.

❶

- Click the Internet Explorer icon on the Quick Launch toolbar to open the Windows Internet Explorer window (Figure B–27).

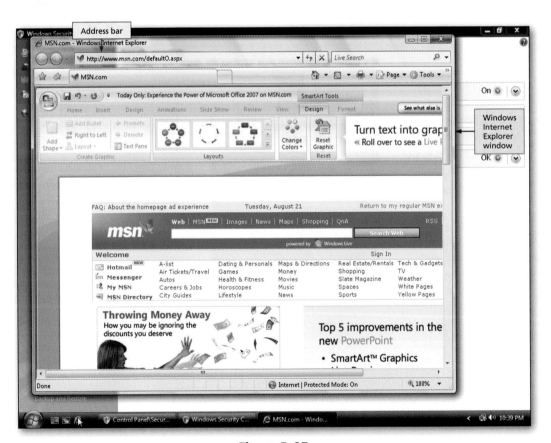

Figure B–27

2

- Type www.
microsoft.com/
protect/viruses/
vista/av.mspx
in the Address bar
and then press the
ENTER key to display
the Windows Vista
Security Software
Providers Web page
(Figure B–28).

- Read the list of
vendors and visit a
few links to learn
more about some
of the vendors and
their products.

Figure B–28

3

- When you have finished, click the Close button on the Windows Internet Explorer window to
close the Windows Internet Explorer window.

Protecting Against Malware

It is important to run anti-malware software whenever you are using your computer. Malware
and other unwanted software can attempt to install itself on your computer any time you
connect to the Internet or when you install some programs using a CD, DVD, or other
removable media. Potentially unwanted or malicious software also can be programmed to run
at unexpected times, not just when it is installed.

Windows Defender is installed with Windows Vista. Windows Defender uses
definitions similar to those used by antivirus programs. A **definition** is a rule for Windows
Defender that identifies what programs are malware and how to deal with them. Windows
Defender scans your computer regularly to find malware and remove it.

To keep up with new malware developments, Windows Defender uses Windows
Update to check regularly for definition updates. This helps you to ensure that your
computer can handle new threats. It is recommended to allow Windows Defender to run
using the default actions.

To View the Windows Defender Settings for Automatic Scanning

The following steps display the automatic scanning settings in Windows Defender.

1

• Click the Windows Defender link in the Windows Security Center to start Windows Defender (Figure B–29).

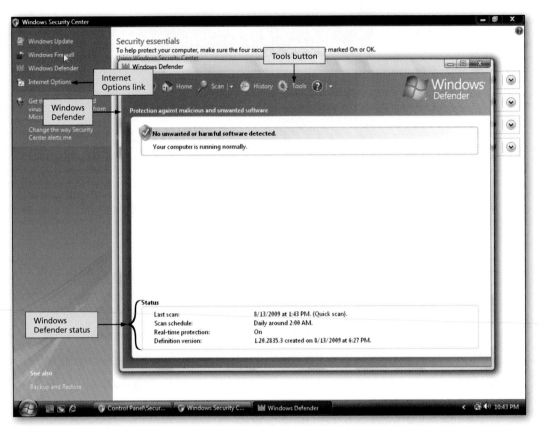

Figure B–29

2

• Click the Tools button on the tool-bar to display the Windows Defender Tools and Settings (Figure B–30).

Figure B–30

- Click the Options link to view the Windows Defender settings for Automatic scanning (Figure B–31).

- Click the Close button to close the Windows Defender window.

Figure B–31

Security Settings in Internet Explorer

In addition to the security features shown earlier in this appendix, Windows Vista also enhances the security features of Windows Internet Explorer. These enhanced security features protect the computer while you browse the Internet or send and receive e-mail. The new Internet Explorer security settings protect the computer, the computer's contents, and the computer's privacy by preventing against viruses and other security threats on the Internet.

To View Pop-up Settings

One new security feature in Internet Explorer is the Pop-up Blocker. **Pop-up Blocker** prevents annoying **pop-up ads**, advertising products or services, from appearing while you view a Web page. Pop-up ads can be difficult to close, often interrupt what you are doing, and can download spyware, which secretly gathers information about you and your computer, and sends the information to advertisers and other individuals.

By default, Pop-up Blocker is turned on by Internet Explorer and set to a Medium setting, which blocks most pop-up ads. Pop-up Blocker also plays a sound and displays an Information Bar in the Internet Explorer window when a pop-up ad is blocked.

If you want to allow certain Web sites to display pop-up ads when you visit the site, you can add the Web site address to the list of allowed sites in the Pop-up Blocker Settings dialog box. The following steps display the Pop-up Blocker Settings dialog box in Internet Explorer.

- Click the Internet Options link in the Windows Security Center window to display the Internet Properties dialog box (Figure B–32).

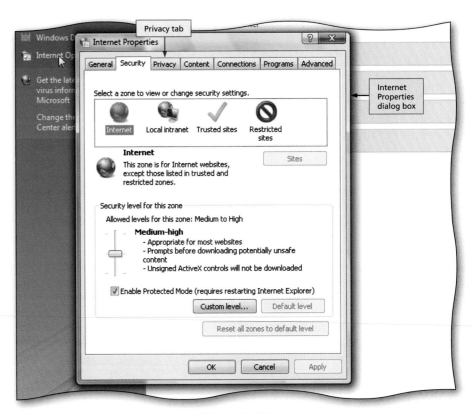

Figure B–32

- Click the Privacy tab in the Internet Properties dialog box to display the Privacy sheet (Figure B–33).

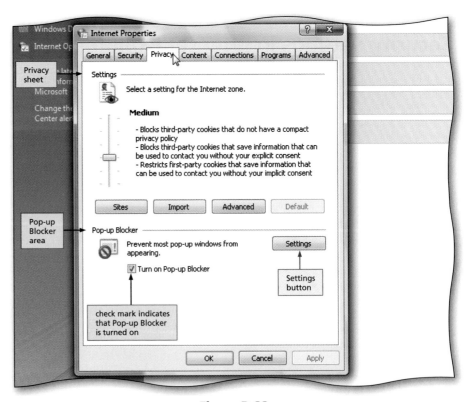

Figure B–33

3

• Click the Settings button in the Pop-up Blocker area to display the Pop-up Blocker Settings dialog box (Figure B–34).

Q&A

How do I block all pop-ups?

If you want to block all pop-ups, click the Filter level list box arrow, and then click High: Block all pop-ups (CTRL+ALT to override) in the Filter level list box. If you want to allow more pop-up ads, click the Filter level list box arrow, and then click Low: Allow pop-ups from secure sites in the Filter level list box.

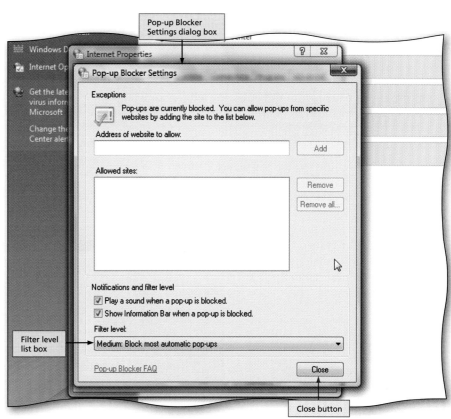

Figure B–34

4

• After viewing the Pop-up Blocker Settings dialog box, click the Close button to close the Pop-up Blocker Settings dialog box (Figure B–35).

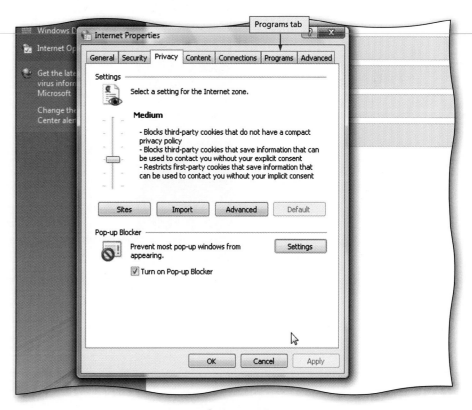

Figure B–35

To View Internet Explorer Add-On Settings

Internet Explorer **add-ons** add functionality to Internet Explorer by allowing different toolbars, animated mouse pointers, and stock tickers. Although some add-ons are included with Windows Vista, thousands are available from Web sites on the Internet. Most Web site add-ons require permission before downloading the add-on, while others are downloaded without your knowledge. Some add-ons do not need permission at all.

Add-ons usually are safe to use, but some may slow down your computer or shut down Internet Explorer unexpectedly. This usually happens when an add-on was poorly built, or created for an earlier version of Internet Explorer. In some cases, spyware is included with an add-on and may track your Web surfing habits. The Manage Add-ons window allows you to display add-ons that have been used by Internet Explorer or that run without permission, enable or disable add-ons, and remove downloaded ActiveX controls.

The following steps display the add-on settings.

- Click the Programs tab in the Internet Properties dialog box to show the Programs sheet (Figure B–36).

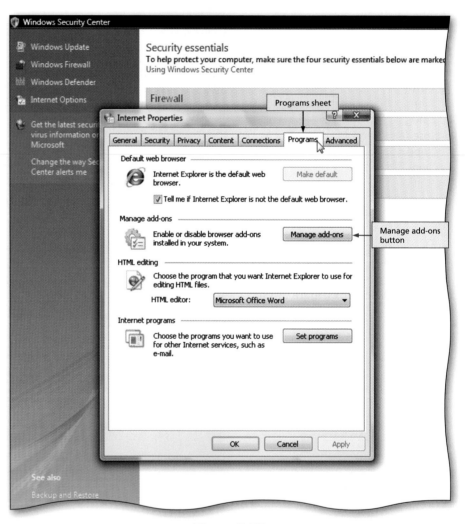

Figure B–36

• Click the Manage add-ons button in the Manage add-ons area to display the Manage Add-ons dialog box (Figure B–37).

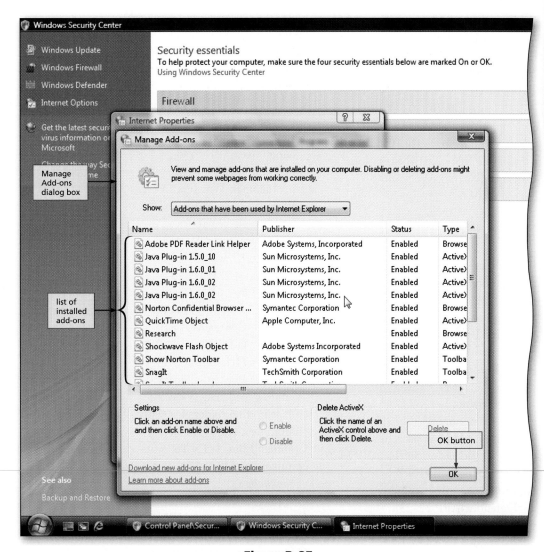

• When finished viewing the add-ons, click the OK button in the Manage Add-ons dialog box to close the Manage Add-ons dialog box.

• Click the OK button in the Internet Properties dialog box to close the Internet Properties dialog box.

Figure B–37

To Close the Windows Security Center and the Control Panel

Now that you have finished reviewing some highlights of the Windows Security Center, you will close the Windows Security Center window and the Control Panel.

1 Click the Close button in the Windows Security Center window to close the Windows Security Center. Click the Close button in the Control Panel window to close the Control Panel.

Summary

Security is an important issue for computer users. You need to be aware of the possible threats to your computer as well as the security features that can be used to protect your computer. The Windows Vista Security Center allows you to view and configure the security features that will help you keep your computer safe.

Index